Rick Steves'
LONDON

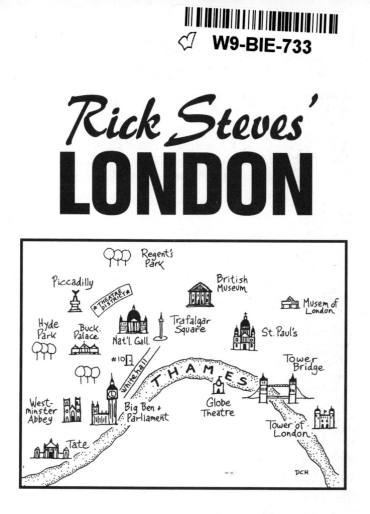

by Rick Steves
and Gene Openshaw

John Muir Publications
Santa Fe, New Mexico

Other JMP travel guidebooks by Rick Steves
Europe 101: History and Art for the Traveler (with Gene Openshaw)
Rick Steves' Europe Through the Back Door
Rick Steves' Mona Winks (with Gene Openshaw)
Rick Steves' Best of Europe
Rick Steves' France, Belgium & the Netherlands (with Steve Smith)
Rick Steves' Germany, Austria & Switzerland
Rick Steves' Great Britain & Ireland
Rick Steves' Italy
Rick Steves' Paris (with Steve Smith and Gene Openshaw)
Rick Steves' Postcards from Europe
Rick Steves' Russia & the Baltics (with Ian Watson)
Rick Steves' Scandinavia
Rick Steves' Spain & Portugal
Asia Through the Back Door (with Bob Effertz)
Rick Steves' Phrase Books: German, Italian, French,
    Spanish/Portuguese, and French/Italian/German

John Muir Publications, P.O. Box 613, Santa Fe, NM 87504
Copyright © 1999 by Europe Through the Back Door, Inc.
Cover copyright © 1999 by John Muir Publications
All rights reserved.

Printed in the United States of America. First printing February 1999.

Portions of this book were originally published in *Rick Steves' Mona Winks*
© 1998, 1996, 1993, 1988 by Rick Steves and Gene Openshaw and in
Rick Steves' France, Belgium & the Netherlands © 1999, 1998, 1997, 1996, 1995
by Rick Steves and Steve Smith.

ISBN 1-56261-467-3
ISSN 1522-3280

For the latest on Rick's lectures, books, tours, and television series, contact Europe
Through the Back Door, Box 2009, Edmonds, WA 98020, tel. 425/771-8303, fax
425/771-0833, Web site: www.ricksteves.com, or e-mail: rick@ricksteves.com.

Europe Through the Back Door Editor: Risa Laib
John Muir Publications Editors: Dianna Delling, Krista Lyons-Gould
Research Assistance in London: Tracy Turner
Production: Janine Lehmann
Cover and Interior Design: Janine Lehmann
Typesetting: Kathleen Sparkes
Maps: David C. Hoerlein
Photography: Rick Steves, unless otherwise noted
Printer: Publishers Press
Cover Photo: Tower Bridge; London, England; Leo de Wys Inc./Steve Vidler

Paris chapter co-authored with Steve Smith, excerpted from *Rick Steves' France,
Belgium & the Netherlands 1999*.

Distributed to the book trade by Publishers Group West, Berkeley, California

CONTENTS
london

INTRODUCTION

Blow through the city on the open deck of a double-decker orientation tour bus, and take a pinch-me-I'm-in-Britain walk through downtown. With a whiff of millennium celebrations already in the air, this is a brilliant time to visit London. And with enough time, you can do the full monty: sip your tea with pinky raised and clotted cream all over your scone.

Ogle the crown jewels at the Tower of London, hear the chimes of Big Ben, and see the Houses of Parliament in action. Hobnob with the tombstones in Westminster Abbey, duck WWII bombs in Churchill's underground Cabinet War Rooms, and brave the earth-shaking Imperial War Museum. Overfeed the pigeons at Trafalgar Square. Cruise the Thames River. Visit with Leonardo, Botticelli, and Rembrandt in the National Gallery. Whisper across the dome of St. Paul's Cathedral and rummage through our civilization's attic at the British Museum.

You'll enjoy some of Europe's best people-watching at Covent Garden and snap to at Buckingham Palace's Changing of the Guard. Just sit in Victoria Station, Piccadilly Circus, or a major tube station, and observe. Spend one evening at a theater and the others catching your breath.

London is much more than its museums and famous landmarks. It's a living, breathing, thriving organism. The city has changed dramatically in recent years, and many visitors are surprised to find how "un-English" it is. Whites are now a minority in major parts of the city that once symbolized white imperialism. Arabs have nearly bought out the area north of Hyde Park. Chinese take-outs outnumber fish-and-chips shops. Many hotels are run by people with foreign accents (who hire English chambermaids), while outlying suburbs are home to huge communities of Indians and Pakistanis. London is learning—sometimes fitfully—

to live as a microcosm of its formerly vast empire. With the English Channel Tunnel complete, many locals see even more holes in their bastian of Britishness.

This Information Is Accurate and Up-to-Date

This book is updated every year. Most publishers of guidebooks that cover a city from top to bottom can afford an update only every two or three years. Since this book is selective, covering only the places I think make the top week or 10 days in and around London, I can update it each summer. Even with an annual update, things change. But if you're traveling with the current edition of this book, I guarantee you're using the most up-to-date information available. This book will help you have an inexpensive, hassle-free trip. Use this year's edition. Saving a few bucks by traveling on old information is not smart. If you're packing an old book, you'll learn the seriousness of your mistake . . . in London. Your trip costs at least $10 per waking hour. Your time is valuable. This guidebook saves you lots of time.

Welcome to My London City Guide

This book is organized in following way:

London Orientation includes tourist information and public transportation. The "Planning Your Time" section offers a suggested schedule with thoughts on how to best use your limited time.

Sights provides a succinct overview of London's most important sights, arranged by neighborhood, with ratings: ▲▲▲—Don't miss; ▲▲—Try hard to see; ▲—Worthwhile if you can make it; No rating—Worth knowing about.

The **Westminster Walk** takes you on a personal tour through downtown London, from Big Ben to Trafalgar Square.

The **Self-Guided Museum Tours** lead you through the British Museum, National Gallery, Tate Gallery, British Library, Westminster Abbey, St. Paul's, and the Tower of London.

Day Trips chapters recommend nearby sights: Greenwich, Cambridge, Bath, and even Paris.

Sleeping is a guide to my favorite budget hotels in three pleasant London neighborhoods.

Eating offers good-value restaurants ranging from inexpensive eateries to splurges, with an emphasis on good value.

London with Children includes my top recommendations to keep your kids (and you) happy in London.

Shopping offers tips on shopping painlessly and enjoyably, without letting it overwhelm your vacation or ruin your budget.

Entertainment is a guide to entertainment and evening fun, music, walks, and theater.

Transportation Connections covers connections by train (including the Eurostar to Paris) and by plane (with detailed information on London's two airports), laying the groundwork for your smooth arrival and departure.

The **Appendix** includes a London timeline, British history, TV tips, handy telephone numbers, a climate chart, and a British/Yankee dictionary.

Throughout this book, when you see a ✪ in a listing, it means that the sight is covered in much more depth in my self-guided walk or one of my museum tours—a page number will tell you just where to look to find more information.

Browse through this book and choose your favorite sights. Then have a great trip! You'll become your own guide with my self-guided walk and museum tours. Traveling like a temporary local, you'll get the absolute most out of every mile, minute, and dollar. You won't waste time on mediocre sights because, unlike other guidebooks, I cover only the best. Since your major financial pitfall is lousy, expensive hotels, I've worked hard to assemble the best accommodations values. And, as you explore the city I know and love, I'm happy you'll be meeting some of my favorite English people.

Trip Costs

Five components make up your trip costs: airfare, surface transportation, room and board, sightseeing/entertainment, and shopping/miscellany.

Airfare: Don't try to sort through the mess. Find and use a good travel agent. A basic, round-trip, U.S.A.-to–London flight costs $500 to $1,000, depending on where you fly from and when.

Surface Transportation: For a typical one-week visit, allow about $30 for tube (subway) tickets. The cost of round-trip trains to day trip destinations ranges from nearly nothing for Greenwich, $20 for Cambridge, $50 for Bath, to a $150 minimum for Paris via Eurostar train. (Save money by taking buses instead of trains.) Add an additional $100 if you take a couple of taxi rides between London's Heathrow airport and your hotel (or save money by taking the tube, train, or airport bus).

Room and Board: You can thrive in London on $70 a day per person for room and board. A $70-a-day budget allows $10 for lunch, $20 for dinner, and $40 for lodging (based on two people splitting the cost of an $80 double room that includes breakfast). That's doable. Students and tightwads do it on $50 a day ($30 per bed-and-breakfast, $20 for meals and snacks). But budget sleeping and eating require the skills and information covered below (and in greater detail in my book, *Rick Steves' Europe Through the Back Door*).

Sightseeing and Entertainment: In London, some of the best sights are free (British Museum, National Gallery, Tate Gallery, British Library, and others). Figure on paying $7 to $15 for the major sights that charge admission (Westminster Abbey–$8, Tower of London–$15), $10 for guided walks, $20 for bus tours, and splurge experiences (plays range from $20 to $60). Given London's free museums, an overall average of $15 a day works for most. Don't skimp here. After all, this category directly powers most of the experiences all the other expenses are designed to make possible.

The British Heritage pass, which gets you into more than 500 British Heritage and National Trust properties, doesn't make sense for a London visit, but is worth considering if you'll be traveling extensively throughout Britain (£28 for seven days, £39 for 15 days, £54 for 30 days; sold at airport information desks and the British Travel Centre on Regent Street in London).

Shopping and Miscellany: Figure $1 per postcard, tea, or ice-cream cone, and $2 per beer. Shopping can vary in cost from nearly nothing to a small fortune. Good budget travelers find that this category has little to do with assembling a trip full of lifelong and wonderful memories.

Exchange Rate
I list prices in pounds (£) throughout this book.

> 1 British pound (£1) = about $1.70

The British pound sterling (£), also called a "quid," is broken into 100 pence (p). Pence means "cents." You'll find coins ranging from 1p to £1 and bills from £5 to £50. To roughly convert pounds to dollars, multiply British prices by 2 and then subtract 10 percent: £6 is about $10.50, £3 is about $5, and 80p is about $1.40.

Prices, Times, and Discounts
The prices in this book, as well as the hours and telephone numbers, are accurate as of late 1998. The economy is flat and inflation is low, so these prices should be pretty accurate in 1999. But Britain is always changing, and I know you'll understand that this, like any other guidebook, starts to yellow even before it's printed.

In Britain you'll be using the 24-hour clock. After 12:00 noon, keep going—13:00, 14:00. . . . For anything over 12, subtract 12 and add p.m. (14:00 is 2:00 p.m.).

This book lists peak-season hours for sightseeing attractions (July and August). Off-season, roughly October through April, expect shorter hours, more lunchtime breaks, and fewer activities. Some places are open only on weekends or closed entirely in the winter. Confirm your sightseeing plans locally, especially when traveling between October and April.

While discounts (called "concessions" in Britain) are not listed in this book, nearly all British sights are discounted for seniors (loosely defined as anyone retired or willing to call themselves a "senior"), youths (ages 8–18), students, groups of 10 or more, and families.

When to Go

July and August are peak season—my favorite time—with very long days, the best weather, and the busiest schedule of tourist fun. Prices and crowds don't go up as dramatically in Britain as they do in much of Europe. Still, travel during "shoulder season" (May, early June, September, and early October) is easier and a bit less expensive. Shoulder-season travelers get minimal crowds, decent weather, the full range of sights and tourist fun spots, and the joy of being able to just grab a room almost whenever and wherever they like—often at a flexible price. Winter travelers find absolutely no crowds and soft room prices, but shorter sightseeing hours. The weather can be cold and dreary, and nightfall draws the shades on sightseeing well before dinnertime. While England's rural charm falls with the leaves, London's sights are fine in the winter.

Plan for rain no matter when you go. Just keep going and take full advantage of "bright spells." Conditions can change several times in a day, but rarely is the weather extreme. Daily averages throughout the year range between 42 and 70 degrees Fahrenheit. Temperatures below 32 or over 80 degrees are cause for headlines (see the climate chart in the Appendix). July and August are not much better than shoulder months. May and June can be lovely. While sunshine may be rare, summer days are very long. The summer sun is up from 6:30 until 22:30 (10:30 p.m.). It's not uncommon to have a grey day, eat dinner, and enjoy hours of sunshine afterwards.

Red Tape and Taxes

You need a passport, but no visa or shots, to travel in Britain.

Sales Tax: Britain's sales tax, the "value added tax" or VAT (17.5%), is built into the price of nearly everything you buy. Tourists can get this VAT refunded on souvenirs they take out of the country. But unless you buy something worth at least $100, your refund won't be worth the trouble. Before you make a substantial purchase of merchandise, ask the store clerk if you will be able to get a VAT refund. You'll likely get a "Tax-Free Shopping Cheque" which is redeemable for cash or credit-card credit at virtually any European airport before you fly home.

Banking

Credit or debit cards are widely accepted in Britain (and are necessary for renting a car and handy for booking rooms and theater and transportation tickets over the phone). For cash advances you'll find that Barclays, National Westminster, and places displaying an Access or Eurocard sign accept MasterCard. Visa is accepted at Barclays and Midland banks. In general Visa is far more widely accepted than American Express.

Many travelers also carry an ATM card. They get you a better exchange rate than traveler's checks and are as commonplace in Britain as they are in the U.S.A. Be certain your PIN is only four numbers long.

Traveler's checks work fine in Britain. Many people traveling exclusively in Britain buy traveler's checks in pounds sterling. On the road, save time and money by changing plenty of money at a time. Banks commonly charge a commission fee from £2–4 and even more. While policies vary, some British banks favor various traveler's checks by waiving the commission: Barclays and Visa checks at Barclays banks, American Express checks at Lloyds banks, and Thomas Cook checks at Midland banks or Cook offices. American Express exchange offices don't charge a commission on their checks or any others. This can save you around 2 percent. But don't let this cloud your assessment of their exchange rates.

On my last trip, I bought all my pounds in cash from a good American foreign exchange service, stowed them safely in my money belt, and never needed a bank. Even in jolly olde England you should use a money belt. Thieves target tourists. A money belt (call 425/771-8303 for our free newsletter/catalog) provides peace of mind. You can carry lots of cash safely in a money belt—and, given the high bank fees, you should.

Bank holidays bring most businesses to a grinding halt on Christmas, December 26, New Year's Day, Good Friday, Easter Monday, the first and last Monday in May, and the last Monday in August.

Travel Smart

Reread this book as you travel, and visit one of London's tourist information offices. Buy a phone card and use it for reservations and confirmations. You speak the language; use it! Enjoy the friendliness of the local people. Ask questions. Most locals are eager to point you in their idea of the right direction. Pack along a pocket-size notebook to organize your thoughts, and practice the virtue of simplicity. Those who expect to travel smart, do. Plan ahead for banking, laundry, post office chores, and picnics. Mix intense and relaxed periods. Every trip (and every traveler) needs at least a few slack days. Pace yourself. Assume you will return.

As you read this book, make note of days when sights are closed. Sundays have pros and cons, as they do for travelers in the U.S.A. (special events, limited hours, closed shops and banks, no rush hour, fewer trains and buses to outlying cities). Saturdays are virtually weekdays. Popular places are even more popular on weekends—especially sunny weekends, which are sufficient cause for an impromptu holiday in this soggy corner of Europe.

If you're planning to stay in Bath as well as London, consider a gentler small-town start in Bath, and visit London afterwards. You'll be more rested and ready to tackle Britain's greatest city. Heathrow Airport has direct connections to Bath and other cities.

Consider making the travel arrangements and reservations listed below before your trip:

• Reserve a room for London. For my recommended hotels, see Sleeping.

• If you want to book a play, you can call from the U.S.A. as easily as from London, using your credit card number to pay for your tickets. For the current schedule and phone numbers, photocopy your hometown library's London newspaper theater section or visit the Web site: www.officiallondontheatre.co.uk. For simplicity, I book plays while in London. For more information, see Entertainment.

• If you want to attend the pageantry-filled changing of the keys in the Tower of London, write to Ceremony of Keys, H.M. Tower of London, London EC3 N4AB, at least five weeks in advance, with an international reply coupon (available at U.S. post offices), requesting an invitation to the "Ceremony of the Keys" (nightly at 21:30, small group of visitors allowed). Say which night or nights you can come (it's free).

Tourist Information

In London you can pick up everything you'll need for your trip—for London or all of Britain—at the National Tourist Information Centre just off Piccadilly Circus at 1-3 Lower Regent Street (tel. 0181/846-9000). London has several other helpful tourist information offices (abbreviated "TI" in this book). For details, see the Orientation chapter. Take full advantage of TIs. Show up with a list of questions and a proposed sightseeing plan. Pick up maps, brochures, and walking-tour information. Avoid the room-finding service offered by TIs throughout Britain (bloated prices, fees, no opinions, and they take a cut from your host).

Britain's national tourist office in the U.S.A. is responsive to individual needs and offers a wealth of meaty material. Before your trip, request any information you may want, such as city maps and schedules of upcoming festivals. Their free London and Britain

maps are excellent (and the same maps are sold for £1.30 each
at TIs in Britain). Contact the **British Tourist Authority (BTA)**
at 551 5th Ave., 7th floor, New York, NY 10176, tel. 800/462-
2748 or 212/986-2200, Web sites: www.visitbritain.com and
www.londontown.com. For a listing of London's events, check the
Web sites: www.timeout.co.uk or www.thisislondon.com.

Recommended Guidebooks

For most travelers, this book is all you need. But if you'd like more
information, you may want to buy an additional guidebook. The
Michelin Green Guide to London, which is somewhat scholarly,
and the more readable Access guide for London are both well
researched. *Let's Go London* is youth-oriented with good coverage
of nightlife, hosteling, and cheap transportation deals. If you're be
traveling elsewhere in Britain, consider *Rick Steves' Great Britain &
Ireland 1999*.

Rick Steves' Books and Videos

Rick Steves' Europe Through the Back Door 1999 (John Muir Publications) gives you budget-travel skills such as minimizing jet lag,
packing light, planning your itinerary, traveling by car or train,
finding beds without reservations, changing money, avoiding rip-
offs, outsmarting thieves, hurdling the language barrier, staying
healthy, taking great photographs, and much more. The book also
includes chapters on 37 of my favorite "Back Doors," eight of
which are in Great Britain and Ireland.

   Rick Steves' Country Guides are a series of eight guidebooks
covering Europe; Great Britain & Ireland; France, Belgium & the
Netherlands; Italy; Spain & Portugal; Germany, Switzerland &
Austria (with Prague); Scandinavia; and Russia & the Baltics. All
but the last two are updated annually and come out in January.

   Rick Steves' City Guides include this book and Paris. With the
sleek Eurostar train, Paris is now just three hours from London.
Consider combining the two cities (and books) for a great visit.

   Europe 101: History and Art for the Traveler (John Muir Publications, 1996, co-written with Gene Openshaw), gives you the story
of Europe's people, history, and art. Written for smart people who
were sleeping in their history and art classes before they knew they
were going to Europe, *101* really helps Europe's sights come alive.
However, this book is more applicable to travel on the European
continent than to travel in Britain.

   Mona Winks (also co-written with Gene Openshaw, John Muir
Publications, 1998) gives you fun, easy-to-follow self-guided tours
of Europe's top 20 museums. All of the *Mona Winks* chapters on
London are included in this London guidebook. But if you'd like

similar coverage for the great museums in Paris, Amsterdam, Venice, Florence, and Rome, Mona's for you.

Of the 52 episodes in my television series, *Travels in Europe with Rick Steves*, eight shows feature Britain and Ireland. A new series of 13 shows is planned for 2000. Earlier episodes air nationally on public television and the Travel Channel. These are also available in information-packed home videos, along with my two-hour slide-show lecture on Britain (call 425/771-8303 for our free newsletter/catalog).

Rick Steves' Postcards from Europe, my new autobiographical book, packs 25 years of travel anecdotes and insights into the ultimate 3,000-mile European adventure. Through my guidebooks, I share my favorite European discoveries with you. *Postcards* introduces you to my favorite European friends. (John Muir Publications, 1999.)

Maps

The maps in this book, designed and drawn by Dave Hoerlein, are concise and simple. Dave, who is well-traveled in London and Britain, has designed the maps to help you orient quickly and get to where you want to go painlessly. In London, buy a detailed city map at the tourist information office and you're ready to travel. (Or get a free London map from the BTA in the U.S.A.; see Tourist Information, above.)

Tours of Britain and Ireland

Your travel agent can tell you about all the normal tours. But they won't tell you about ours. At ETBD we offer 20-day Britain tours and 14-day Ireland tours featuring the all-stars covered in my book on Great Britain & Ireland (call us at 425/771-8303 for details). And ETBD tour guide Roy Nicholls leads his own garden tours and south England tours all the time (call Roy in England at 44/1373-831-311, e-mail: b_____line.rednet.co.uk).

Transportation

Transportation concerns within London limited to the tube (subway), buses, and taxis, all covered in the Orientation chapter. If you have a car, stow it. You don't want to drive in London.

For all the specifics on transportation throughout Great Britain by train or car, see *Rick Steves' Great Britain 1999*. Here are a few pointers:

Regular tickets on Britain's great train system (departures from 2,400 stations daily) are the most expensive per mile in all of Europe. Those who buy in advance, go round-trip (leaving after 9:30), or ride the bus save big.

Buying Train Tickets in Advance: To save a few pounds, get a Super Advance ticket (for any journey for any day) by buying your ticket before 14:00 on the day prior to your journey. If you buy a ticket the same day you want to travel, leave after 9:30, and avoid traveling on Fridays or summer Saturdays, you'll save a little with a Super Saver ticket. There can be up to 30 different prices for the same journey. A clerk at any station (or the helpful train information staff at tel. 0345/484-950, 24 hours daily) can figure out the cheapest fare for your trip.

Buses: Buses are slower and cheaper than trains. For example, a ride on a National Express bus from London to Bath takes three hours and costs £18 one-way or £19 round-trip (ask about £8 day returns). In comparison, a London-Bath train takes 75 minutes and costs £28.50 one-way or round-trip. Bus stations are normally near train stations (in London, one block southwest of Victoria Station). The British distinguish between "buses" for local runs with lots of stops and "coaches" for long-distance express runs.

Telephones and Mail

The British telephone system is great. Easy-to-find public phone booths are either card- or coin-operated. Buy a handy BT phone card (£2, £3, £5, £10, or £20) at any newsstand, TI, or post office. (Some "credit card phones" have a slot that will take—but not accept—your BT phone card; look for a "phone card" booth.) The coin-op phones take any coin from 10p to £1, and a display shows how your money supply's doing. Only completely unused coins will be returned, so put in biggies with caution. (If money is left over, rather than hang up, push the "make another call" button.)

London is a big city. Use the telephone routinely to confirm tour times, book theater tickets, or make reservations at fancier restaurants. If you call before heading out, you'll travel more smoothly.

In London dial 999 for emergency help and 192 for directory assistance (free from public phone booths, otherwise 35p). The area code for any downtown London phone number is 0171, for suburban London, 0181. All numbers listed in this book with an area code of 0171 can be dialed directly (without the area code) within London. When dialing the suburbs (0181) from downtown (0171), you need to include the area code but it's a toll-free local call. Beware of area codes starting with 0839. These are toll numbers with recorded information—usually slow moving and very expensive.

Long distance within Britain: Calling long distance in Britain is most expensive from 8:00 to 13:00 and cheapest from 17:00 to

8:00. A short call across the country is quite inexpensive. Don't hesitate to call long distance. First dial the area code (which starts with zero), then dial the local number. Area codes are listed by city on phone booth walls or from directory assistance (free and happy to help; dial 192 in Britain).

International calls: To make an international call, dial the international access code (of the country you're calling from), the country code (of the country you're calling to), the area code (without the initial zero), and the local number. For example, London's downtown area code is 0171. To call one of my recommended London B&Bs from New York, I dial 011 (U.S.A.'s international access code), 44 (Britain's country code), 171 (London's area code without the zero), then 727-7725 (the B&B's number). To call it from Britain's old York, dial 0171/727-7725.

To call my office from Britain, I dial 00 (Britain's international access code), 1 (U.S.A.'s country code), 425 (Edmonds' area code), then 771-8303. For a listing of international access codes and country codes, see the Appendix.

Calling the USA: You have a number of options. If you dial direct from any British phone booth, you'll pay less than a dollar a minute for your call. New phone cards with PIN numbers are even cheaper, costing about 20 cents a minute—that's more than five minutes for a dollar. You buy the card (for a minimum of £5) at London's exchange bureaus and in various kiosks. The card, which lists an access number and a secret personal identification number, works great from any push-button phone. See "International calls," above, for dialing instructions.

USA Direct Services, such as AT&T, MCI, and Sprint, used to be a good value until direct-dialing rates dropped. It's cheaper to dial direct (but for your convenience, I'll list the numbers of calling card operators in Britain): AT&T: 0800-89-00-11; MCI: 0800-89-02-22; and Sprint: 0800-89-08-77). Definitely avoid using USA Direct for calls between European countries; it's far cheaper to call direct.

Mail: To arrange for mail delivery, reserve a few hotels along your route in advance and give their addresses to friends, or use American Express Company's mail services (available to anyone who has at least one Amex traveler's check). Allow 10 days for a letter to arrive. Phoning is so easy that I've dispensed with mail stops all together.

Sleeping
In the interest of smart use of your time, I favor accommodations (and restaurants) handy to your sightseeing activities. Rather than list hotels scattered throughout London, I've chosen

Sleep Code

To give maximum information with a minimum of space, I
use this code to describe accommodations listed in this book.
Prices in this book are listed per room, not per person. Breakfast is included.

S = Single room, or price for one person in a double.

D = Double or twin room (I specify double- and twin-bed
rooms only are priced differently, or if a place has only
one or the other. When reserving, you should specify).

T = Three-person room (often a double bed with a single).

Q = Four-person room (adding an extra child's bed to a T
is usually cheaper).

b = Private bathroom with toilet and shower or tub

t = Private toilet only (the shower is down the hall)

s = Private toilet only. (The shower is down the hall.)

CC = Accepts credit cards (**V** = Visa, **M** = MasterCard, **A** =
American Express). If CC isn't mentioned, assume
you'll need to pay cash.

According to this code, a couple staying at a "Db-£32,
CC:VM" hotel would pay a total of £32 (about $55) per night
for a room with a private toilet and shower (or tub). The hotel
accepts Visa, MasterCard, or cash.

three favorite neighborhoods and recommend the best accommodations values for each.

I look for places that are friendly (enjoy Americans); located in
a central, safe, quiet neighborhood; clean, with good beds; a good
value; not mentioned in other guidebooks (therefore, filled mostly
by English travelers); and willing to hold a room until 16:00 without a deposit (though more and more places are requiring a
deposit or credit-card number). In certain cases my recommendations don't meet all these prerequisites. I'm more impressed by a
handy location and a fun-loving philosophy than hairdryers and
shoe-shine machines.

I've described my recommended hotels and B&Bs with a standard code. Prices listed are for one-night stays in peak season,
include a hearty breakfast, and assume you're going direct and not
through a tourist information office. Prices may be soft for off-
season and longer stays. "Twin" means two single beds, and "double" means one double bed. If you'll take either one, let them know
or you might be needlessly turned away. Some hotels offer family
deals (I note this within their listing), which means that parents with
young children can easily get a room with an extra child's bed or a

discount for larger rooms. Call to negotiate the price. Little kids sleep almost free. Teenage kids are generally charged as adults.

B&Bs are not hotels. If you want to ruin your relationship with your hostess, treat her like a hotel clerk. Americans often assume they'll get new towels each day. The British don't, and neither will you. Hang them up to dry and reuse.

About 80 percent of the recommended B&Bs are smoke-free. While some places allow smoking in the sleeping rooms, breakfast rooms are nearly always smoke-free.

Almost every hotel or B&B has three floors of rooms, steep stairs, and no elevator. Elevators are rare. If you're concerned about stairs, call and ask about ground-floor rooms.

All rooms have sinks. Any room without a bathroom has access to a free bath or shower on the corridor. In Britain, rooms with private plumbing are called "en suite"; rooms that lack private plumbing are "standard." As more rooms go en suite, the hallway bathroom is shared with fewer standard rooms. If money's tight, ask for standard rooms.

British showers confuse (and scald) many tourists. A place built as a hotel has simple showers. But most B&Bs are retrofitted with showers, and rather than one central heating system, water is heated individually for each shower. While the switch is generally left on, in many rooms you'll have a hot water switch to consider. Any cord hanging from the ceiling is for lights (not emergencies). Once in the shower you'll find a multitude of overly clever mechanisms to somehow get the right amount and temperature of water. Good luck.

Making Reservations

Reserve your London room with a phone call or e-mail as soon as you can commit to a date. It's possible to visit London any time of year without reservations, but given the high stakes, erratic accommodations values, and the quality of the gems I've listed, I highly recommend calling ahead for rooms.

A few national holidays jam things up (especially "bank holiday" Mondays) and merit reservations long in advance. Mark these dates in red on your travel calander: Good Friday, Easter Monday, the first and last Monday in May, the last Monday in August, Christmas, December 26, and New Year's Day.

It's easy to reserve by phone. I've taken great pains to list telephone numbers with long-distance instructions (see Telephones and Mail, above; also see Appendix). A hotel receptionist will trust you and hold a room until 16:00 without a deposit, though some will ask for a credit-card number. Honor (or cancel by phone) your reservations. Long distance is cheap and easy from public phone booths. I promised my recommended places that you'd call and cancel if for some reason you won't show up. Don't let these people (or me) down. Americans are notorious for "standing up" B&Bs. If you'll be delayed or won't make it, simply call in. Trusting travelers to show up is a huge, stressful issue and financial risk to small B&B owners.

To reserve from home, call, fax, e-mail, or write the hotel. E-mail is preferred when possible. Phone and fax costs are reasonable. To fax, use the fax form in the appendix. If you're writing, add the zip code and confirm the need and method for a deposit. A two-night stay in August would be "2 nights, 16/8/99 to 18/8/99"—European hotel jargon uses your day of departure. You'll often receive a letter back requesting one night's deposit. A credit card will usually be accepted as a deposit, though you may need to send a signed traveler's check or a bank draft in the local currency. If your credit card is the deposit, you can pay with your card or cash when you arrive. If you don't show up, you'll be billed for one night. Reconfirm your reservations a day in advance for safety (or you may be bumped—really). Also, don't just assume you can extend. Consider carefully—and well in advance—how long you'll stay.

Eating

I don't mind English food. But then, I liked dorm food. True, England isn't famous for its cuisine and probably never will be, but we tourists have to eat. If there's any good place to cut corners to stretch your budget, it's in eating. Here are a few tips on budget eating:

The traditional "fry" is famous as a hearty way to start the day. Also known as a "heart attack on a plate," the breakfast is especially feasty if you've just come from the land of the skimpy continental breakfast across the Channel. Your standard fry gets off to a healthy start with juice and cereal or porridge. (Try Weetabix, a soggy English cousin of shredded wheat. Next, with tea or coffee, you get a heated plate with a fried egg, lean Canadian-style bacon, a bad sausage, a grilled tomato, and often a slice of delightfully greasy pan toast and sautéed mushrooms. Toast comes on a rack (to cool quickly and crisply) with butter and marmalade. Consider ordering kippers (herring filet smoked in an oak fire). This meal tides many travelers over until dinner. Order only what you'll eat. A B&B hostess, your temporary local mother, doesn't like to see food wasted. And there's nothing un-British about skipping the "fry"—few locals actually start their day with this heavy traditional breakfast.

These days, the best coffee is served in a cafetiere (also called a "French Press"). When your coffee has steeped as long as you like, plunge down the filter and pour. To revitalize your brew, pump the plunger again.

Many B&Bs don't serve breakfast until 8:00. If you need an early start, ask politely if it's possible. While they may not make you a cooked breakfast, they can usually put out cereal, toast, juice, and coffee.

Picnicking saves time and money. Try boxes of orange juice (pure by the liter), fresh bread, tasty English cheese, meat, a tube of Colman's English mustard, local eatin' apples, bananas, small tomatoes, a small tub of yogurt (they're drinkable), rice crackers, gorp or nuts, plain "Digestive Biscuits" (the chocolate-covered ones melt), and any local specialties. At supermarkets you can get food in small quantities. (Three tomatoes and two bananas cost me 50p.) Decent sandwiches (£2) are sold everywhere. I often munch a relaxed "meal on wheels" in a train, bus, or subway to save 30 precious minutes.

London's restaurants are fairly expensive, but cheap alternatives abound: fish-and-chips joints, Chinese and Indian take-outs, cafeterias, pubs (see below), and your typical, good old greasy-spoon cafés. Bakeries have meat pies (and microwaves), pastries, yogurt, and cartons of "semi-skimmed" milk—ideal for fresh, fast, cheap lunches. Pasties (past-eez) are "savory" (not sweet) meat pies that originated in mining country. They had big crust handles so miners with filthy hands could eat them and toss the crust. Today you'll find them in bakeries and cafés. They make a quick, cheap, hot meal.

People of leisure punctuate their day with a "Cream Tea." You'll get a pot of tea, two homemade scones, jam, and thick, creamy-as-honey clotted cream. For maximum pinky-waving taste per calorie, slice your scone thin, like a mini-loaf of bread.

Pub Grub and Beer

Pubs are a basic part of the British social scene, and whether you're a teetotaler or a beer guzzler they should be a part of your travel here. Pub is short for "public house." It's an extended living room where, if you don't mind the stickiness, you can feel the pulse of London. Unfortunately, many of London's pubs have been afflicted with an excess of brass, ferns, and video games. In any case, smart travelers use the pubs to eat, drink, get out of the rain, watch the latest sporting event, and make new friends.

Pub grub gets better each year. It's Britain's best eating value. For £5, you'll get a basic budget hot lunch or dinner in friendly surroundings. The Good Pub Guide, published annually by the British Consumers Union, is excellent. Pubs attached to restaurants often have fresher food and a chef who knows how to cook.

I recommend certain pubs, but food can spoil, and your B&B host is usually up-to-date on the best neighborhood pub grub. Ask for advice (but adjust for nepotism and cronyism, which run rampant). Locals will rarely recommend a rough pub that's a local hangout. If you want this experience (the food will be cheaper but not very good), ask for a "spit-and-sawdust" place. London's spit-and-sawdust places might not welcome tourists, but village ones do (try in Bath). They are the most interesting.

Pubs generally serve assorted meat pies such as steak and kidney pie or shepherd's pie, curried dishes, fish, quiche, vegetables, and (invariably) chips and peas. Better pubs let you substitute a "jacket potato" (baked potato) for your fries. Servings are hearty, service is quick, and you'll rarely spend more than £4 to £6 ($6–9). Your beer or cider adds another pound or two. (Free tap water is always available.) A "ploughman's lunch" is a modern "traditional English meal" that nearly every tourist tries . . . once. Pubs that advertise their food and are crowded with locals are less likely to be the kind that serve only lousy microwaved snacks.

In a pub you order your beer at the bar. Part of the experience is standing before a line of "hand pulls" and wondering which beer on tap to choose. The British take great pride in their beer. They think that drinking beer cold and carbonated, as Americans do, ruins the taste. At pubs, long hand pulls are used to pull the traditional rich-flavored "real ales" up from the cellar. These are the connoisseur's favorites: fermented naturally, varying from sweet to bitter, often with a hoppy or nutty flavor. Notice the fun names. Experiment with the obscure local microbrews. Short hand pulls at the bar mean colder, fizzier, mass-produced, and less interesting keg beers. Mild beers are sweeter with a creamy malt flavoring. Stout is dark and more bitter, like Guinness. For a cold, refreshing, basic American-style beer, ask for a "lager." Try the draft cider (sweet or dry). . . carefully. Proper English ladies like a half-beer and half-lemonade "shandy." Teetotalers can order a soft drink. Drinks are served by the pint or the half-pint. (It's almost feminine for a man to order just a half; I order mine with quiche.) There's no table service. Order drinks and meals at the bar. Pay as you order and don't tip.

Pub hours vary. The strictly limited wartime hours (designed to keep the wartime working force sober and productive) finally ended a few years ago, and now pubs can serve beer from 11:00 to 23:00, and Sunday from noon to 22:30. Children are served food and soft drinks in pubs, but you must be 18 to order a beer. A cup of darts is free for the asking. People go to a "public house" to be social. They want to talk. Get vocal with a local. Pubs are the next best thing to relatives in every town.

Stranger in a Strange Land

We travel all the way to Europe to enjoy differences—to become temporary locals. You'll experience frustrations. There are certain truths that we find God-given and self-evident, such as cold beer, ice in drinks, bottomless coffee cups, easy shower faucets, and driving on the right side of the road. One of the benefits of travel is the eye-opening realization that there are logical, civil, and even better alternatives. A willingness to go local ensures that you'll enjoy a full dose of English hospitality.

Send Me a Postcard, Drop Me a Line

If you enjoy a successful trip with the help of this book and would like to share your discoveries, please fill out and send the survey at the end of this book to me at Europe Through the Back Door, Box 2009, Edmonds, WA 98020. I personally read and value all feedback. Thanks in advance—it helps a lot.

For our latest travel information, tap into our Web site: www.ricksteves.com. My e-mail address is rick@ricksteves.com. Anyone can request a free issue of our newsletter.

Judging from the happy postcards I receive from travelers, it's safe to assume you're on your way to a great vacation—independent, inexpensive, and with the finesse of an experienced traveler. Thanks, and happy travels!

BACK DOOR TRAVEL PHILOSOPHY
As Taught in *Rick Steves' Europe Through the Back Door*

Travel is intensified living—maximum thrills per minute and one of the last great sources of legal adventure. Travel is freedom. It's recess, and we need it.

Experiencing the real Europe requires catching it by surprise, going casual . . . "Through the Back Door."

Affording travel is a matter of priorities. (Make do with the old car.) You can travel—simply, safely, and comfortably—anywhere in Europe for $60 a day plus transportation costs. In many ways, spending more money only builds a thicker wall between you and what you came to see. Europe is a cultural carnival and, time after time, you'll find that its best acts are free and the best seats are the cheap ones.

A tight budget forces you to travel close to the ground, meeting and communicating with the people, not relying on service with a purchased smile. Never sacrifice sleep, nutrition, safety, or cleanliness in the name of budget. Simply enjoy the local-style alternatives to expensive hotels and restaurants.

Extroverts have more fun. If your trip is low on magic moments, kick yourself and make things happen. If you don't enjoy a place, maybe you don't know enough about it. Seek the truth. Recognize tourist traps. Give a culture the benefit of your open mind. See things as different but not better or worse. Any culture has much to share.

Of course, travel, like the world, is a series of hills and valleys. Be fanatically positive and militantly optimistic. If something's not to your liking, change your liking. Travel is addicting. It can make you a happier American, as well as a citizen of the world. Our Earth is home to nearly 6 billion equally important people. It's humbling to travel and find that people don't envy Americans. They like us, but with all due respect, they wouldn't trade passports.

Globetrotting destroys ethnocentricity. It helps you understand and appreciate different cultures. Travel changes people. It broadens perspectives and teaches new ways to measure quality of life. Many travelers toss aside their hometown blinders. Their prized souvenirs are the strands of different cultures they decide to knit into their own character. The world is a cultural yarn shop. And Back Door Travelers are weaving the ultimate tapestry. Come on, join in!

ORIENTATION

London is more than 600 square miles of urban jungle. With 9 million struggling people—many of whom speak English—it's a world in itself and a barrage on all the senses. On my first visit, I felt very, very small.

To grasp London comfortably, see it as the old town without the modern, congested sprawl. Most of the visitor's London lies between the Tower of London and Hyde Park—about a three-mile walk.

With this orientation, you'll find London manageable and even fun. You'll get a good taste of the city's top sights, history, and cultural entertainment, as well as its ever-changing human face.

Planning Your Time

The sights of London alone could easily fill a trip to Britain. It's a great one-week get-away. After considering nearly all of London's tourist sights, I have pruned them down to just the most important (or fun) for a first visit of up to seven days. You won't be able to see all of these, so don't try. You'll keep coming back to London. After 25 visits myself, I still enjoy a healthy list of excuses to return.

Here's a suggested schedule:

Day 1: 9:00–Tower of London (Beefeater tour, crown jewels), 12:00–Munch a sandwich on the Thames while cruising from Tower to Westminster Bridge, 13:00–Follow the self-guided Westminster Walk with a quick visit to the Cabinet War Rooms, 15:30–Trafalgar Square and National Gallery, 17:30–Visit National Tourist Information Centre, near Piccadilly, to gather any information you need, 18:30–Dinner in Soho. Take in a play or 19:30 weekend concert at St. Martin-in-the-Fields.

LONDON

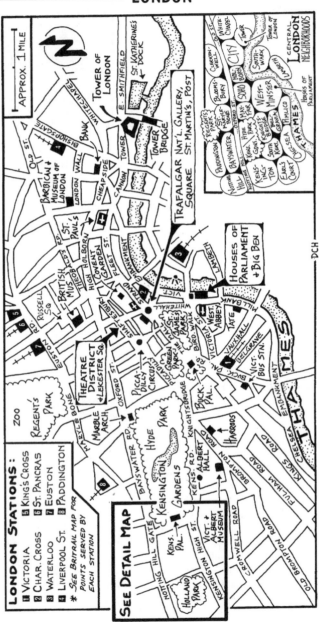

LONDON STATIONS:

1 Victoria
2 Char. Cross
3 Waterloo
4 Liverpool St.

5 King's Cross
6 St. Pancras
7 Euston
8 Paddington

* SEE BRITRAIL MAP FOR POINTS SERVED BY EACH STATION

SEE DETAIL MAP

LONDON NEIGHBORHOODS

APPROX. 1 MILE

Tower of London

St. Katherine's Dock

Trafalgar Square Nat'l. Gallery, St. Martin's Post

Houses of Parliament + Big Ben

Theatre District + Leicester Sq.

Day 2: 9:30–Take the Original London sightseeing bus tour (consider hopping off for the 11:30 Changing of the Guard at Buckingham Palace), 12:30–Covent Garden for lunch and people-watching, 14:00–Tour British Museum. Have a pub dinner before a play, concert, or evening walking tour.

Days 3 and 4: Choose among these remaining London highlights: Tour Westminster Abbey, British Library, Museum of the Moving Image, Imperial War Museum, Tate Gallery, Greenwich or Kew (via cruise), St. Paul's Cathedral, or the Museum of London. Consider another historic walking tour or some serious shopping at one of London's elegant department stores or open-air markets.

Days 5, 6, and 7: For a one-week visit to London, I'd plan five days in the city (doing the above options with more time) and two days for side-trips. To keep an England focus, side-trip out to Bath one day and Cambridge the other. For maximum travel thrills, consider a 36-hour Paris get-away. With the zippy English Channel train, Paris is only three hours away and can even be worth a long day trip. Exactly how to pull this off is explained in the Day Trip: Paris chapter.

Arrival in London

By Train: London has eight train stations, all connected by the tube (subway), all with exchange offices and luggage storage. From any station, enter the tube and head to the stop nearest your hotel.

By Bus: The bus station is one block southwest of Victoria Station, which has a TI (tourist information center) and tube entrance.

By Plane: For detailed information on getting from London's airports to downtown London, see the Transportation Connections chapter.

Tourist Information

London Tourist Information Centres (LTICs) are located at:
  • Heathrow Airport's Terminal 3 (daily 6:00–23:00, most convenient and least crowded)
  • Heathrow Airport's Terminal 1 and 2 tube (subway) stations
  • Victoria Station (daily 8:00–18:00, shorter hours in winter, crowded and commercial)
  • Waterloo International Terminal Arrivals Hall (daily 8:30–22:30).

Like the LTICs, the handier British Tourist Info Centre (described below) covers London.

Bring your itinerary and a checklist of questions. Pick up these publications: *London Planner* (a great, free monthly listing all the sights with latest hours and events), walking-tour schedule fliers, and a theater guide. Consider buying a Britain map (£1.30) and a London map (£1.30). Their fine £1.30 London map rivals the £4 maps sold in newsstands (free from BTA/British Tourist Authority in the U.S.A.: tel. 800/462-2748 or 212/986-2200, 551 5th Ave., 7th floor, New York, NY 10176, Web site: www.visitbritain.com). The TIs sell BT phone cards, passes for the tube, long-distance bus tickets and passes, British Heritage Passes (not worth it for a London-only trip), and tickets to plays (steep booking fee). They also book rooms (avoid their £5 booking fee by calling hotels direct). Smelling a new source of profit, London TIs are pushing a 50p-per-minute telephone information service. Avoid it.

The British Tourist Information Centre makes gathering information easy (Monday–Friday 9:00–18:30, Saturday and Sunday 10:00–16:00, just off Piccadilly Circus at 1–3 Lower Regent Street, tel. 0181/846-9000). Take advantage of its well-equipped London/England desk, Wales desk (tel. 0171/409-0969), and Ireland desk (tel. 0171/839-8416 or 0171/493-3201). At the center's extensive bookshop, gather whatever books, maps, and information you'll need for your entire trip. Consider the Michelin Green Guide to London or Britain (£9). Train travelers can pick up *Let's Go: Britain and Ireland* (£15, 50 percent higher than the U.S. price) and hostelers may want the *Youth Hostel Association 1999 Guide* (£5).

The Scottish Tourist Centre (19 Cockspur Street, tel. 0171/930-8661) and the slick new French National Tourist Office (Monday–Saturday 9:00–17:30, closed Sunday, 179 Piccadilly Street, tel. 0990-848-848) are nearby.

Helpful Hints

Theft Alert: Be on guard in London more than anywhere else in Britain for pickpockets and thieves, particularly on public transportation and in places crowded with tourists. Tourists, considered naive and rich, are targeted.

Changing Money: Standard transaction fees at banks are £2 to £4. American Express Offices offer a good rate and change any brand of traveler's checks for no fee. There are several offices (Heathrow Terminal 4 tube station and at 6 Haymarket near Piccadilly, Monday–Friday 9:00–17:30, Saturday 9:00–17:00, Sunday 10:00–16:00, tel. 0171/930-4411). Avoid changing money at exchange bureaus. Their latest scam: they advertise very good rates with a same-as-the-banks fee of 2 percent. But the fine print explains that the fee of 2 percent is for buying pounds. The fee for selling pounds is 9.5 percent. Ouch!

What's Up: For the best listing of what's happening (plays, movies, restaurants, concerts, exhibitions, protests, walking tours, shopping, and children's activities), and a look at the trendy London scene, pick up a current copy of *Time Out* (£1.80, www .timeout.co.uk) at any newsstand. The TI's free monthly *London Planner* lists sights, plays, and events at least as well. For a fun Web site on London's entertainment, theater, restaurants, and news, go to www.thisislondon.com.

Free Sights: The British Museum, British Library, National Gallery, National Portrait Gallery, and Tate Gallery are always free. The Imperial War Museum, Museum of London, Natural History Museum, and Victoria and Albert Museums are free from 16:30 to closing (17:30 or 18:00), saving you £5 or so.

Sunday Morning Activities: Plan your day carefully. Many sights don't open until 12:00 (14:30 for the British Museum). Possible Sunday morning activities include a church service at St. Paul's or Westminster Abbey; an Original London Sightseeing Bus Tour; Tate Gallery; Cabinet War Rooms; Globe Theater; Imperial War Museum; Museum of the Moving Image; a Thames cruise; a walking tour; or open-air markets at Petticoat Lane and Camden Market. "Speaker's Corner" in Hyde Park gets going at noon.

Travel Bookstores: Stanfords Travel Bookstore is good and stocks current editions of my guidebooks near Victoria Station (52 Grosvenor Gardens), at Covent Garden (12 Long Acre, tel. 0171/240-3611), and at 156 Regent Street. Dillons Bookstore, on the corner of Trafalgar Square, is also handy with a fine travel selection.

Getting Around London

London's taxis, buses, and subway system make a private car unnecessary. In a city this size, you must get comfortable with public transportation. Don't be timid.

By Taxi: London is the best taxi town in Europe. Big, black, carefully regulated cabs are everywhere. I never met a crabby cabbie in London. They love to talk and know every nook and cranny in town. I ride one a day just to get my London questions answered. Rides start at £1.40 and cost about £1.50 per tube stop. Connecting downtown sights is quick and easy for about £4 (e.g., St. Paul's to the Tower). For a short ride, three people in a cab travel at tube prices. Groups of four or five should taxi everywhere. If a cab's top light is on, just wave it down. (Drivers flash lights when they see you.) Wave in either direction. They have a tiny turning radius. If waving doesn't work, ask for a taxi stand. Stick with metered cabs. While telephoning a cab gets one in minutes, it's generally not necessary and adds to the cost. London is such a great wave-'em-down taxi town that most cabs don't even have a radio phone.

LONDON TUBE

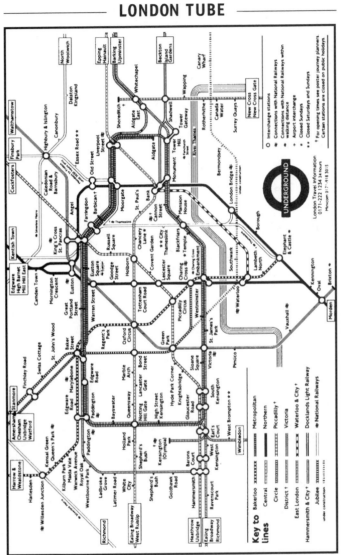

By Bus: London's extensive bus system is easy to follow if you have a map listing the routes. Get a free map from a TI or tube station. Signs at stops list routes clearly. Conductors are terse but helpful. Ask to be reminded when it's your stop. Just hop on, tell the driver where you're going, pay what he says, grab a ticket, take a seat, and relax. (The best views are upstairs.) Rides start at 90p. If the driver is not taking money, hop in, grab a seat, and the conductor will eventually sell you a ticket. If you have a transit pass, get in the habit of hopping buses for quick little straight shots (even just to get to a metro stop). During bump-and-grind rush hours (8:00–10:00 and 16:00–19:00), you'll go faster by tube.

By Tube: London's subway is one of this planet's great people-movers and the fastest (and cheapest) long-distance transport in town. Any ride in the Central Zone (on or within the Circle Line, including virtually all my recommended sights and hotels) costs £1.30. Avoid ticket window lines in tube stations by buying tickets from coin-op machines; practice on the punchboard to see how the system works (hit "adult single" and your destination). Again, nearly every ride will be £1.30. (Note: these tickets are valid only on the day of purchase.)

Every city map includes a tube map with color-coded lines and names (free at any station window). Each line has a name (such as Circle, Northern, or Bakerloo) and two directions (indicated by end stop). In stations you'll have a choice of two platforms per line. Navigate by signs leading to the platforms (usually labeled north, south, east, or west) that clearly list the stops served by each line, or ask a local or an orange-vested staff person for help. Some tracks are shared by several lines, and electronic signboards announce which train is next and the minutes remaining until various arrivals. Each train has its final destination or line name above its windshield. Read the system notices clearly posted at the platform; they explain the tube's latest flood, construction, or bomb scare. Bring something to do to pass the waits productively. And always . . . mind the gap.

You can't leave the system without feeding your ticket to the turnstile. Save time by choosing the best street exit (look at the maps on the walls). "Subway" means pedestrian underpass in "English." For tube and bus information, call 0171/222-1234.

London Tube and Bus Passes: These passes, valid on both the tube and buses, are worth considering. The "Travel Card," covering Zones 1 and 2, gives you unlimited travel for a day, starting after 9:30 and anytime on weekends, for £3.50. The all-zone version of this card costs £4.30 (and includes Heathrow airport). The "LT Card," a one-day, two-zone pass with no time restriction, costs £4.50. Families save with the one-day "Family Travel

Card." The "Weekend Travel Card," for £5.20, costs 25 percent less than two one-day cards. The "7 Day Travel Card" costs £17, covers Zone 1, and requires a passport-type photo (cut one out of any snapshot and bring it from home). All passes are available for more zones, and are purchased as easily as a normal ticket at any station. If you figure you'll take three rides in a day, get a day pass.

If you want to travel a little each day or if you're part of a group, consider buying a "carnet" for £10: you get 10 separate tickets for tube travel in Zone 1 (£1.00 each rather than £1.30).

Tours of London

▲▲▲**Original London Sightseeing Bus Tour**—This two-hour, once-over-lightly double-decker bus tour drives by all the most famous sights, providing a stressless way to get your bearings and at least see the biggies. You "hop on and hop off" at any of the 26 stops and catch a later bus (runs about every 10 minutes in summer, every 20 minutes in winter). The basic route comes with a fun, English-only, live guide. (Live guided buses have a Union Jack flag on the front of the bus. If the front has many flags, it's a tape-recorded multilingual tour—avoid it.) It's an inexpensive form of transport as well as an informative tour. There are daily departures from 9:00 (9:30 in winter) until early evening from Victoria Street (one block north of Victoria Station), Marble Arch, Piccadilly Circus, Trafalgar Square, and so on (£12; £2 off with this book—limit two discounts per book, they'll rip off the corner of this page; reservations unnecessary, buy ticket from the driver, ticket good for 24 hours, tel. 0181/877-1722). Bring a sweater and extra film. Note: if you start at Victoria at 9:30, you can hop off near the end of the two-hour loop at the Buckingham Palace stop (Bressenden Place), a five-minute walk from the Palace and the Changing of the Guard at 11:30. The many copycat tours offer about the same service and value.

▲▲**Walking Tours**—Several times every day top-notch local guides lead small groups through specific slices of London's past. Schedule fliers litter the desks of TIs, hotels, and pubs. (The beefy, plain black-and-white Original London Walks newsletter lists their extensive daily schedule). *Time Out* lists many but not all scheduled walks. Simply show up at the announced location, pay £5, and enjoy two chatty hours of Dickens, the Plague, Shakespeare, Legal London, the Beatles, Jack the Ripper, or whatever is on the agenda. "Historic" pub crawls, with a fraction of the information, are a lesser value. "Original London Walks" is the dominant company (for recorded schedule, tel. 0171/624-3978, Web site: http:\\london.walks.com). They do private tours for £70.

Chris Salaman, a semi-retired guide, loves to tailor walks for special and peculiar interests in London. He offers day-long private walking tours for just £30 per person including lunch, a tube travel card, and museum admissions (tel. 0181/871-9048).

▲▲**Cruise the Thames**—Boat tours with an entertaining commentary sail regularly between Westminster Pier (base of Westminster Bridge under Big Ben) and the Tower of London (£4.40, round-trip £5.60, 3/hrly from 10:20–21:00 in peak season, until 18:00 in winter, 30-minute cruise, tel. 0171/930-9033). Similar boats leave Westminster Pier for Greenwich (£5.80, round-trip £7, 2/hrly from 10:00–17:00, 50 min, tel. 0171/930-4097) and Kew Gardens (£6, round-trip £10, 7/day, 90 min, tel. 0171/930-2062). For pleasure and efficiency, consider combining a one-way cruise with a tube ride back.

LONDON
SIGHTS

london

These sights are arranged by neighborhood for handy sightseeing. When you see a ✪ in a listing, it means the sight is covered in much more depth in my self-guided walk or one of my museum tours.

Summer hours are listed. Many sights have slightly shorter hours off-season. Students and seniors should ask for "concessions" (discounts). Since many places run sporadic tours, make a habit of telephoning first.

From Westminster Abbey to Trafalgar Square

✪ These sights are linked by the Westminster Walk on page 40.
▲▲▲**Westminster Abbey**—England's historic coronation church is a crowded collection of famous tombs. Like a stony refugee camp waiting outside St. Peter's gates, this is an English hall of fame. Choose among tours (ours, Walkman, or live) and attend an evensong, held every weekday except Wednesday at 17:00, Saturday and Sunday at 15:00. An organ recital is held Sunday at 17:45. (£5 for abbey entry, tours extra, Monday 9:30–16:45, Tuesday–Friday 9:00–16:45, Saturday 9:00–14:45, between services on Sunday, also open for half-price on Wednesday 18:00–19:45—the only time photography is allowed, last admission 60 minutes before closing, tube: Westminster, tel. 0171/222-5152.) Praying is free; use separate marked entrance. ✪ See Westminster Tour on page 106.
▲▲**Houses of Parliament**—While Parliament is too tempting to terrorists to be opened wide to tourists, if in session, you can view debates in either the bickering House of Commons or the genteel House of Lords (Monday, Tuesday, and Thursday 14:30–22:00 with long waits until 18:00, Wednesday 9:30–22:00, Friday 9:30–15:00, use St. Stephen's entrance, tube: Westminster, tel. 0171/219-4272 for current situation).

photo: Leo de Wys Inc./Steve Vidler

While it's not worth a long wait and the actual action is generally extremely dull, it is a thrill to be inside and see the British government inaction. The House of Lords has more pageantry, shorter lines, and less-interesting debates (tel. 0171/219-3107 for schedule). If confronted with a too-long House of Commons line, see the House of Lords first. Once you've seen the Lords, you can often go directly to the Commons. If there's only one line, it's for the House of Commons. Go to the gate and tell the guard you want the Lords. You may slip right in. While other guidebooks tout the U.S. Embassy "entry cards" which get you directly in, they only give out four per day and trying to land one is most likely futile.

After passing security, slip to the left and study the big dark Westminster Hall which survived the 1834 fire. The hall is 11th century and its famous self-supporting hammer-beam roof was added in 1397. The Houses of Parliament are located in what was once the Palace of Westminster, long the palace of England's medieval kings before it was largely destroyed by fire in 1834. The palace was rebuilt in Victorian Gothic style after the 1834 fire (a move away from Neoclassicism back to England's Christian and medieval heritage, true to the Romantic age). Completed in 1860, only a few of its 1,000 rooms are open to the public. For more information about Parliament (or to get a look without actually going in), visit the Jewel Tower (across the street, 100 meters from the entry, weekdays 10:00–18:00 in summer) for a video presentation.

The clock tower (315 feet high) is named for its 13-ton bell, Ben. The light above the clock is lit when the House of Commons is sitting. For a hip HOP view, walk halfway over Westminster Bridge.

▲▲**Cabinet War Rooms**—This is a fascinating walk through the underground headquarters of the British government's fight against the Nazis in the darkest days of the Battle for Britain. The nerve center of the British war effort was used from 1939 through 1945. Churchill's room, the map room, and so on, are left just as they were in 1945. For all the blood, sweat, toil, and tears details, pick up the headsets at the entry and follow the included and excellent 45-minute Walkman tour (£4.60, daily 9:30–18:00, last admission 17:15, on King Charles Street just off Whitehall, follow the signs, tube: Westminster, tel. 0171/930-6961).

Horse Guards—The Horse Guards have an 11:00 inspection Monday–Saturday (at 10:00 on Sunday) and a colorful dismounting ceremony daily at 16:00. The rest of the day is terrible for camcorders (on Whitehall, between Trafalgar Square and #10 Downing Street, tube: Westminster). When the weather's bad, all pageantry is canceled.

▲**Banqueting House**—England's first Renaissance building (designed by Inigo Jones around 1620) and one of the few London landmarks spared by the 1666 fire, the House is the only surviving part of the original Palace of Whitehall. Don't miss its Rubens ceiling which, at Charles I's request, drove home the doctrine of the legitimacy of the divine right of kings. In 1649, divine right ignored, Charles I was beheaded on the balcony of this building by a Cromwellian parliament. Admission includes a restful 15-minute audiovisual history which shows the place in banqueting action, a 30-minute tape-recorded tour that is interesting only to history buffs, and a look at a fancy banqueting hall (£3.50, Monday–Saturday 10:00–17:00, last entry at 16:00, subject to closure for government functions, aristocratic WC, immediately across Whitehall from the Horse Guards, tube: Westminster, tel. 0171/930-4179). Just up the street is . . .

Trafalgar Square

▲▲**Trafalgar Square**—London's central square is a thrilling place to just hang out. Lord Nelson stands atop his 185-foot-tall fluted granite column, gazing out to Trafalgar, where he lost his life but defeated the French fleet. Part of this 1842 memorial is made from the melted-down cannons of his victims at Trafalgar. He's surrounded by giant lions, hordes of people, and even more pigeons. Packets of bird-pleasing seed are on sale. (When bombed, resist the impulse to wipe immediately—it'll smear. Wait for it to dry and flake off gently.) The square is the climax of most marches and demonstrations (tube: Charing Cross).

▲▲▲**National Gallery**—Wonderfully renovated, displaying Britain's top collection of European paintings from 1250 to 1900 (works by Leonardo, Botticelli, Velázquez, Rembrandt, Turner, van Gogh, and the Impressionists), this is one of Europe's classiest galleries (free, Monday–Saturday 10:00–18:00, Wednesday until 20:00, Sunday 12:00–18:00, free one-hour tours weekdays at 11:30 and 14:30 and Saturdays at 14:00 and 15:30, on Trafalgar Square, tube: Charing Cross or Leicester Square, tel. 0171/839-3321.) The CD Walkman tours are the best I've used in Europe (£3 donation requested). ✪ See National Gallery Tour on page 68.

▲**National Portrait Gallery**—Put off by halls of 19th-century characters who meant nothing to me, I used to call this "as interesting as someone else's yearbook." But a select walk through this five-centuries-long Who's Who of British history is quick, free, and puts a face on the story of England. An added bonus is the chance to admire some great art by painters such as Holbein, Van Dyck, Hogarth, Reynolds, and Gainsborough. The collection is well-described, not huge, and runs in historical sequence from the 16th century on the top floor to today's royal family on the bottom.

Highlights, in order, include: Henry VIII and wives (top floor landing); several fascinating portraits of the "Virgin Queen" Elizabeth I, Sir Francis Drake, Sir Walter Raleigh, and the only real-life portrait of Shakespeare (room 1); Charles I with his head on and Oliver Cromwell (room 2); self-portraits and other portraits by Gainsborough and Reynolds (room 9); the Romantics (Blake, Byron, Wordsworth and company, room 13); Queen Victoria and her era (rooms 17–21); and the present royal family including the late Princess Diana (first floor landing, rooms 16 and 28). For more information, follow the fine CD Walkman tours (donation requested, mostly history rather than art, actual interviews of 20th-century subjects) or the 50p quick overview guidebooklet. (Free, Monday–Saturday 10:00–18:00, Sunday 12:00–18:00, entry just off Trafalgar Square, around the corner from National Gallery, opposite Church of St. Martin-in-the-Fields, tel. 0171/306-0055.)

▲**St. Martin-in-the-Fields**—This church, built in the 1720s with a Gothic spire placed upon a Greek-type temple, is an oasis of peace on wild and noisy Trafalgar Square. St. Martin was a man who cared for the poor. "In the fields" was where the first church stood on this spot (in the 13th century), between Westminster and the City. Stepping inside, you still feel a compassion for the needs of the people in this community. The church is famous for its great concerts. Consider a free lunch-time concert (most weekdays at 13:05) or an evening concert (Thursday, Friday, and Saturday at 19:30, £6-15, tel. 0171/930-0089). Downstairs you'll find a ticket office for concerts, a good shop, brass rubbing centre, and a fine budget support-the-church cafeteria (see Eating).

More Top Squares: Piccadilly, Soho, and Covent Garden

For a "Food is Fun" dinner crawl from Covent Garden to Soho, see page 165.

▲▲**Piccadilly Circus**—London's touristy "Town Square" is surrounded by fascinating streets and swimming with youth on the rampage. The Rock Circus offers a commercial but serious history of rock music with Madame Tussaud wax stars. It's an entertaining hour under radio earphones for rock 'n' roll romantics (£8, daily 10:00– 20:00, plenty of photo ops, many enter with a beer-buzz and sing happily off-key under their headphones—nearly as entertaining as the exhibit itself, tube: Picadilly Circus). For overstimulation, drop by the extremely trashy Pepsi Trocadero Center's "theme park of the future" for its Segaworld virtual reality games, nine-screen cinema, and thundering new IMAX theater (admission to Trocadero is free; individual attractions cost £2–8; find a discount ticket before paying full price for IMAX; between Coventry and Shaftesbury, just off Piccadilly). Chinatown, to the east, has swollen since Hong Kong lost its independence. Nearby Shaftesbury Avenue and Leicester Square teem with fun-seekers, theaters, Chinese restaurants, and street singers.

Soho—North of Piccadilly, seedy Soho is becoming trendy and is well worth a gawk. Soho is London's red-light district where "friendly models" wait in tiny rooms up dreary stairways and scantily-clad con artists sell strip shows. While venturing up a stairway to check out a model is interesting, anyone who goes into any one of the shows will be ripped off. Every time. Even a £3 show comes with a £100 cover or minimum (as it's printed on the drink menu) and a "security man." The door has no handle until you pay. By the way, telephone sex is hard to avoid these days in London. Phonebooths are littered with racy fliers of busty ladies for sale. Some travelers gather six or eight phone booths' worth of fliers and take them home for kinky wallpaper.

▲▲**Covent Garden**—This boutique-ish shopping district is a people-watcher's delight with cigarette-eaters, Punch-and-Judy acts, food that's good for you (but not your wallet), trendy crafts, sweet whiffs of pot, two-tone hair (neither natural), and faces that could set off a metal detector. For the best lunch deals, walk a block or two away from the eye of this touristic tornado (check out the places along Neal Street and Endell Street—each a block north of the tube station, see "Eating." Tube: Covent Garden).

North London

▲▲▲**British Museum**—This is the greatest chronicle of our civilization anywhere. Visiting this immense museum is like hiking through Encyclopedia Britannica National Park (free, £2 donation requested, Monday–Saturday 10:00–17:00, Sunday 14:30– 18:00, least crowded weekday mornings, guided 1.5 hour £6 tours offered daily—3/day on Sunday, 2/day in winter—call museum for times, tube: Tottenham Court Road, tel. 0171/636-1555, Web site: www. british-museum.ac.uk). ✪ See British Museum Tour on page 48.

▲▲▲**British Library**—Wander through the manuscripts that have enlightened and brightened our lives for centuries in the new and impressive British Library (free, Monday–Saturday 9:30–18:00, Sunday 11:00–17:00, tube to King's Cross/St. Pancras, leaving station, turn right and walk a block to 96 Euston Road, tel. 0171/412-7332, Web site: www.bl.uk). ✪ See British Library Tour on page 96.

Madame Tussaud's Waxworks—This is expensive but dang good (£10, children £6.60, under five free, daily from 9:30, last admission at 17:30, Marylebone Road, tube: Baker Street, tel. 0171/935-6861; combined ticket for Tussaud's and Planetarium is £12 for adults, £8 for kids). Buy your ticket at the TI—no more than 24 hours in advance—to save a little money and get in with no wait.

Sir John Soane's Museum—Architects and fans of eclectic knick-knacks love this quirky place (free, Tuesday–Saturday 10:00–17:00, closed Sunday and Monday, 13 Lincoln's Inn Fields, five blocks east of British Museum, tube: Holborn, tel. 0171/405-2107).

Buckingham Palace

▲**Buckingham Palace**—In order to pay for the restoration of fire-damaged Windsor Castle, the royal family is opening its lavish home to the public until 2000 (£10 to see the state apartments and throne room, open August and September only, daily 9:30–16:30, limited to 8,000 visitors a day—come early to get an appointed visit time, tube: Victoria, call tel. 0171/930-4832 and reserve a ticket with your credit card).

▲**Changing of the Guard at Buckingham Palace**—Overrated but almost required (daily April–July at 11:30, generally every even-numbered day August–March, no band when wet). Join the mob at the back side of the palace (the front faces a huge and extremely private park). The pageantry and parading are colorful and even stirring, but the actual changing of the guard is a non-event. It is interesting, however, to see nearly every tourist in London gathered in one place at the same time. Hop into a big black taxi and say, "To Buck House, please." For all the color with none of the crowds, see the Inspection of the Guard Ceremony at 11:00 in front of the Wellington Barracks, east of the palace on Birdcage Walk. Afterwards, stroll through nearby St. James's Park. For guards' schedule, call 0171/930-4832 (tube: Victoria, St. James' Park, or Green Park).

West London: Hyde Park and Nearby

▲**Hyde Park and Speakers' Corner**—London's "Central Park" has more than 600 acres of lush greenery, a huge man-made lake, the royal Kensington Palace (not worth touring), and the ornate neo-Gothic Albert Memorial across from the Royal Albert Hall. Early afternoons on Sunday, Speaker's Corner offers soapbox oratory at its best (tube: Marble Arch). "The grass roots of democracy" is actually a holdover from when the gallows stood here and the criminal was allowed to say just about anything he wanted to before he swung. I dare you to raise your voice and gather a crowd—it's easy to do.

▲▲**Victoria and Albert Museum**—The world's top collection of decorative arts is a gangly (150 rooms over 12 acres) but surprisingly interesting assortment of artistic stuff from the West as well as Asia and Islam. The V&A grew out of the Great Exhibition of 1851—that ultimate festival celebrating the industrial revolution and the greatness of Britain—and was originally for manufactured art. But after much support from Queen Victoria and Prince Albert, it was renamed after the royal couple and its present building was opened in 1909. The idealistic Victorian notion that anyone can be continually improved by education and example remains the driving force behind this museum.

While just wondering works well here, consider catching one of the regular 60-minute orientation tours, buying the fine *Hundred Highlights* guidebook, or walking through these ground-floor highlights: Medieval Treasury (room 43, well-described treasury of Middle Age European art), the finest collection of Indian decorative art outside India (room 41), the Dress Gallery (room 40, 400 years of English fashion corseted into 40 display cases), the Raphael Gallery (room 48a, seven huge watercolor "cartoons" painted as designs for tapestries to hang in the Sistine Chapel, among the greatest art treasures in Britain and the best works of the High Renaissance), reliefs by the Renaissance sculptor Donatello (room 16), a close-up look at medieval stained glass (room 28, much more upstairs), the fascinating Cast Courts (46a and 46b, two giant rooms filled with plaster copies of the greatest art of our civilization—such as *Trajan's Column* and Michelangelo's *David*—made for the benefit of 19th-century art students who couldn't afford to travel), and a hall lined with "great" fakes and forgeries (room 46). Upstairs you can walk through the British Galleries for centuries of aristocratic living rooms. (£5, Monday 12:00–18:00, Tuesday–Sunday 10:00–18:00, and usually Wednesday evenings until 21:30 in summer, free after 16:30, pleasant garden café, tube: South Kensington, a long tunnel leads directly from the tube station to the museum, tel. 0171/938-8500.)

▲**Natural History Museum**—Across the street from the Victoria and Albert Museum, this mammoth museum is housed in a giant and wonderful Victorian neo-Romanesque building. Built in the 1870s specifically to house the huge collection (50 million specimens), it presents itself in two halves: the Life Galleries (creepy-crawlies, human biology, origin of the species, "our place in evolution," and awesome dinosaurs) and the Earth Galleries (meteors, volcanoes, earthquakes, and so on). Exhibits are wonderfully explained with lots of creative interactive displays (£6, families £16, free after 16:30 and after 17:00 on weekends, Monday–Saturday 10:00–18:00, Sunday 11:00–18:00, a long tunnel leads directly from the South Kensington tube station to the museum, tel. 0171/938-9123, Web site: www.nhm.ac.uk).

East London: "The City"
▲▲**The City of London**—When Londoners say "The City," they mean the one-square-mile business, banking, and journalism

THE CITY

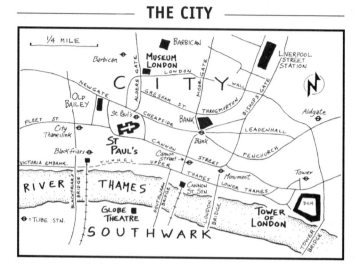

center that 2,000 years ago was Roman Londinium. The outline
of the Roman city walls can still be seen in the arc of roads from
Blackfriars Bridge to Tower Bridge. Within the City are 24
churches designed by Christopher Wren. It's a fascinating district
to wander, but since nobody actually lives there, it's a ghost town
on Saturday and Sunday. An hour in the City's Central Criminal
Courts, known as "Old Bailey," is always interesting (Monday–
Friday 10:30–13:00, 14:00–16:30, quiet in August, no cameras, no
bags, no cloakroom, no kids under 14, at Old Bailey and Newgate
Streets, tube: St. Paul's, tel. 0171/248-3277).

▲▲▲**St. Paul's Cathedral**—Wren's most famous church is the
great St. Paul's, its elaborate interior capped by a 365-foot dome.
St. Paul's was Britain's World War II symbol of resistance, as
Nazi bombs failed to blow it up. The crypt (free with admission)
is a world of historic bones and memorials, including Admiral
Nelson's tomb and interesting cathedral models. This was the
wedding church of Prince Charles and the late Princess Diana.
Climb the dome for a great city view (£4 entry, free on Sunday
but restricted viewing due to services, £3.50 extra to climb dome,
allow an hour to climb up and down the dome—open daily
9:30–16:30, last entry 16:00, £3.50 for guided 90-minute cathedral and crypt tours offered at 11:00, 11:30, 13:30, and 14:00, or
£3 for a Walkman tour anytime, Sunday services at 8:00, 8:45,
11:00, and 15:15, evensongs weekdays at 17:00, tube: St. Paul's,
tel. 0171/236-4128). ✪ See St. Paul's Tour on page 113.

▲**Museum of London**—Stroll through London history—from pre-Roman times to the Blitz up through today (£4.30, free after 16:30, Monday–Saturday 10:00–18:00, Sunday 12:00–18:00, tube: Barbican or St. Paul's, tel. 0171/600-3699). This regular stop for the local schoolkids gives the best overview of London history in town.

▲▲**Tower of London**—The Tower has served as a castle in wartime, a king's residence in peace and, most notoriously, as the prison and execution site of rebels. This historic fortress is host to more than 3 million visitors a year. Enjoy the free, fun 50-minute Beefeater tour (leaves regularly from inside the gate, last one is usually at 15:30). The crown jewels, dating from the Restoration, are the best on earth. To avoid the crowds, arrive at 9:00 and go straight for the jewels, doing the tour and tower later—or do the jewels after 16:30 (£9, Monday–Saturday 9:00–18:00, Sunday 10:00–18:00, the long but fast-moving line is worst on Sundays, last entry at 17:00, tube: Tower Hill, tel. 0171/709-0765). ★ See Tower of London Tour on page 118.

Ceremony of Keys: Every night at 21:30, with pageantry-filled ceremony, the Tower of London is locked up (as it has been every night for the last 700 years). To attend this free event, you need to request an invitation at least five weeks before your visit. Write to: Ceremony of Keys, H.M. Tower of London, London EC3N 4AB. Include your name, number of people (up to seven), requested date, alternative dates, and an international reply coupon (buy at a U.S. post office).

Sights Next to the Tower—The best remaining bit of London's Roman Wall is just north of the tower (at the Tower Hill tube station). Freshly painted and restored, **Tower Bridge** has an 1894–1994 history exhibit (£5.70, daily 10:00–18:30, last entry at 17:15, good view, poor value, tel. 0171/403-3761). **St. Katherine Yacht Harbor**, chic and newly renovated, just east of the Tower Bridge, has mod shops and the classic old Dickens Inn, fun for a drink or pub lunch. If you cross the bridge you'll find the trendy new Butler's Wharf area with happening restaurants and the Bramah Tea and Coffee Museum (see below). From here it's a pleasant riverside walk up to the Globe Theater passing many sights along the South Bank. **The Docklands** is the latest rage in London's growth. Since the weather blows in from west, London's bad air ended up in the east. Before pollution was conquered, gritty east London was home only to the poor and a huge harbor (the largest 19th-century port in the world). Newly cleaned up and enjoying fine air, the east end is now trendy.

Geffrye Decorative Arts Museum—Walk through British front rooms from 1600 to 1930 (free, Tuesday–Saturday 10:00–17:00,

Sunday 14:00–17:00, closed Monday, tube: Liverpool Street, then
bus 149 or 242 north, tel. 0171/739-9893).

South London, on the North Bank

▲▲**Tate Gallery**—One of Europe's great art houses, the Tate
specializes in British painting: 14th-century through contemporary, including pre-Raphaelites, Impressionism, and the modern
art of Matisse, van Gogh, Monet, and Picasso. Learn about the
mystical Blake and romantic Turner (free, daily 10:00–18:00, fine
£2 CD Walkman tours, free tours weekdays: 11:30–Turner,
14:30–British, and 15:30–Modern, confirm schedule by phone at
0171/887-8000, tube: Pimlico). In 2000 the Tate's modern collection will be moving to the new Tate Modern Art Gallery (on the
South Bank) and the current museum will become the Tate
Gallery of British Art. ✪ See Tate Gallery Tour on page 85.

South London, on the South Bank

The South Bank is rapidly becoming gentrified and a thriving arts
and cultural center. From Westminster Bridge to the Tower of
London bridge, a slick Jubilee Promenade is a trendy jogging, yuppie pub-crawling walk.

▲▲**Globe Theater**—The original Globe Theater has been
rebuilt—half-timbered and thatched—exactly as it was in Shakespeare's time. It's open as a museum and hosts authentic old-time
performances of Shakespeare's plays. The theater and exhibit are
open to tour when there are no plays (£5, daily 9:00–12:15,
14:00–16:00, includes guided 30-minute tour offered on the half
hour; if a play is scheduled, the museum is open only 9:00–12:30;
on the south bank directly across the Thames over Southwark
Bridge from St. Paul's, tube: Mansion House, tel. 0171/902-1500,
for details on seeing a play, see Entertainment chapter).

▲▲**Imperial War Museum**—This impressive museum covers
the wars of this century, from heavy weaponry to love notes and
Varga Girls, from Monty's Africa campaign tank to Schwartzkopf's
Desert Storm uniform. You can trace the development of the
machine gun, watch footage of the first tank battles, hold your
breath through the gruesome WWI trench experience, and buy
WWII-era toys in the fun museum shop. Rather than glorify war,
the museum does its best to shine a light on the powerful human
side of one of mankind's most persistent traits (£5, daily 10:00–
18:00, free after 16:30, 90 minutes is enough time for most visitors,
tube: Lambeth North, tel. 0171/416-5000).

▲▲**Museum of the Moving Image**—This high-tech, interactive,
hands-on museum traces the story of moving images from a cave-
man's flickering fire to modern TV. There's great footage of the

earliest movies and TV shows. Turn-of-the-century-clad staff speak as if silent films are the latest marvel. Don't miss Agit-Train (1919 propaganda film train which brought indoctrination to the far reaches of the early USSR) or the breathtaking 50-years-in-10-minutes montage of magic MGM moments (big screen above the Odeon marquee). Brit movie buffs will enjoy the montage of British cinematic highlights in the large theater. And children will enjoy making their own animated cartoon (£6.25, daily 10:00–18:00, last ticket sold at 17:00, from Embankment tube stop walk across the Thames pedestrian bridge and turn left, it's under the Waterloo bridge, tel. 0171/928-3535).

Bramah Tea and Coffee Museum—Aficionados of tea or coffee will find this small museum fascinating. It tells the story of each drink almost passionately. The owner, Mr. Bramah, comes from a big tea family and wants the world to know how the advent of commercial television with breaks not long enough to brew a proper pot of tea required a faster hot drink. In came the horrible English instant coffee. Tea countered with finely chopped leaves in tea bags and it's gone downhill ever since. (£3.50, daily 10:00–18:00, in the Butlers Wharf complex just across the bridge from the Tower, tel. 0171/378 0222).

Outer London

▲**Kew Gardens**—For a fine riverside park and a palatial greenhouse jungle to swing through, take the tube or the boat to every botanist's favorite escape, Kew Gardens. While to most visitors, the Royal Botanic Gardens of Kew is simply a delightful opportunity to wander among 33,000 different types of plants, it is a hardworking organization committed to understanding and preserving the botanical diversity of our planet. The Kew tube station drops you in an herbal little business community a two-block walk to Victoria Gate (the main garden entry). Watch the five-minute orientation video and pick up a map brochure with a monthly listing of best blooms.

Garden lovers could easily spend all day exploring Kew's 300 acres. For a quick visit, spend a fragrant hour wandering through three buildings: the Palm House—a humid Victorian world of iron, glass and tropical plants, built in 1844; a Waterlily House that Monet would swim for; and the Temperate House—a modern greenhouse with many different climate zones growing countless cactus, bug-munching carnivorous plants and more (£4.50, Monday–Saturday 9:30–18:00, Sunday 9:30–19:00, until 16:30 in off-season, galleries and conservatories close a half-hour earlier, entry discounted to £3 late in day, tube: Kew Gardens, tel. 0181/940-1171). For tea, consider the Maids of Honor (280 Kew Road, near garden entrance, tel. 0181/940-2752).

Hampton Court Palace—Fifteen miles up the Thames from downtown (£16 taxi ride from Kew Gardens) is the 500-year-old palace of Henry VIII. Actually, it was the palace of his minister, Cardinal Wolsey. When Wolsey, a clever man, realized Henry VIII was experiencing a little palace envy, he gave it to his king. The Tudor palace was also home to Elizabeth I and Charles I. And parts were updated by Christopher Wren for William and Mary. The palace stands stately overlooking the Thames with some impressive Tudor rooms including a Great Hall with its magnificent hammer-beam ceiling. The industrial-strength Tudor kitchen was capable of keeping 600 schmoozing courtesans thoroughly—if not well—fed. The sculpted garden features a rare Tudor tennis court and a popular maze. The palace, fully restored since its 1986 fire, tries very hard to please, but it falls flat to me. The costumed guides seem low energy. The Walkman tours are slow and boring. From the information center in the main courtyard, visitors book times for guided tours or grab Walkmans for taped tours (all free). The Tudor Kitchens, Henry VIII's Apartments, and the King's Apartments are most interesting. The Georgian Rooms are pretty dull. The maze in the nearby garden is a curiosity some find fun. The train (2/hrly, 30 min) from London's Waterloo station drops you just across the river from the palace (£10, daily 10:15–18:00, until 16:30 November to March, tel. 0181/781-9500).

Thames Barrier—East of Greenwich, the world's largest movable flood barrier welcomes visitors with an informative and entertaining exhibition (£3.40, Monday–Friday 10:00–17:00, weekends 10:30–17:30; catch 70-minute boat from Westminster Pier, or take 30-minute boat from Greenwich pier, or train from London's Charing Cross station to Charlton, then a 15-minute walk, tel. 0181/305-4188).

Disappointments of London

The venerable BBC broadcasts from Broadcasting House. Of all its productions, its new **"BBC Experience"** tour for visitors is the worst. Avoid it. On the South Bank, the **London Dungeon**, a much-visited but amateurish attraction, is just a highly advertised, over-priced haunted house—certainly not worth the £10 admission, much less your valuable London time. Wait for Halloween and see one in your hometown to support a better cause. The **Design Museum** (next to Bramah Tea and Coffee Museum) and **"Winston Churchill's Britain at War Experience"** (next to London Dungeon) waste your time.

WESTMINSTER WALK

From Big Ben to Trafalgar Square

Just about every visitor to London strolls the historic Whitehall boulevard from Big Ben to Trafalgar Square. This quick nine-stop guided walk gives meaning to that touristy ramble. Under London's modern traffic and big city bustle lies 2,000 fascinating years of history. You'll get a whirlwind tour as well as a practical orientation to the London.

Start halfway across Westminster Bridge, first looking upstream (Parliament) and then downstream. Allow an hour for this leisurely ¾-mile walk.

1. Westminster Bridge: View of Big Ben and Parliament

Ding dong ding dong. Dong ding ding dong. Yes indeed, you are in London. Big Ben is actually "Not the clock, not the tower, but the bell that tolls the hour." However, since the 14-ton bell is not visible, everyone just calls the whole tower Big Ben. Although Ben (named for a fat bureaucrat) is scarcely older than my great-grandmother, it has quickly become the city's symbol. The tower is 320 feet high and the clock faces are 23 feet across. The 14-foot minute hands sweep the length of your body every five minutes.

Big Ben is the north tower of a long building, the Houses of Parliament, stretching along the Thames.

Britain is ruled from this building. For centuries, it was the home of kings and queens. Then, as democracy was foisted on tyrants, a parliament of nobles was allowed to meet in some of the rooms. Soon, commoners were elected to office, the neighborhood was shot, and royalty moved down the road to Buckingham Palace. The current building, though it looks medieval, was built in the 1800s after a fire gutted old Westminster Palace.

Today, the House of Commons, which is more powerful than the Queen and Prime Minister combined, meets in the north half

WESTMINSTER BRIDGE

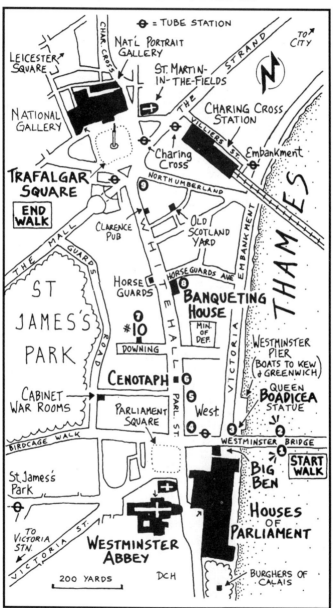

⊖ = TUBE STATION

Leicester Square

CHAR. CROSS

Nat'l Portrait Gallery

St. Martin-in-the-Fields

THE STRAND

TO CITY

National Gallery

Charing Cross Station

VILLIERS ST.

Embankment

Charing Cross

TRAFALGAR SQUARE

NORTHUMBERLAND

THAMES

END WALK

Clarence Pub

Old Scotland Yard

EMBANKMENT

THE MALL

GUARDS

Horse Guards Ave

Horse Guards

BANQUETING HOUSE

ST JAMES'S PARK

WHITEHALL

#10 DOWNING

MIN. OF DEF.

VICTORIA

Westminster Pier (Boats to Kew & Greenwich)

CENOTAPH

PARL. ST.

West.

QUEEN BOADICEA STATUE

Cabinet War Rooms

Parliament Square

BIRDCAGE WALK

WESTMINSTER BRIDGE

START WALK

St. James's Park

BIG BEN

TO VICTORIA STN.

VICTORIA ST.

WESTMINSTER ABBEY

DCH

HOUSES OF PARLIAMENT

BURGHERS OF CALAIS

200 YARDS

of the building. The rubber-stamp House of Lords grumbles and snoozes in the south end of this 1,000-room complex.

• *Look downstream (north).*

2. Westminster Bridge: City View

Until 1750 only London Bridge crossed the Thames. Then a bridge was built here. Downstream and on the other side of the river stands the huge former city hall (GLC, or Greater London Council building). In a monumental conflict with conservative Prime Minister Margaret Thatcher, the liberal city government was basically shut down. The GLC building, while now a hotel complex, still seems to snarl across the river at the home of the national government.

(Margaret Thatcher made a huge impact on London life. Until her administration, the standard litmus test to see if someone was insane was to ask "Who's the prime minister?" But in the time of "The Iron Lady," even the certifiably nuts knew who was at the helm.)

The GLC building marks the start of London's vibrant new gentrified arts and cultural zone. A pleasant riverside jogging path leads downhill from here past several miles of trendy new restaurants, theaters, and museums including the new Globe Theater. The new Tate Gallery of Modern Art will open here in 2000 (and the old Tate will house British art).

On the Big Ben side of the river, notice the Westminster Pier; boats depart here for the Tower of London, Greenwich, and Kew (fine free public WC). Beyond the pier are little green copper lions' heads with rings for tying up boats. Before the construction of the Thames Barrier (the world's largest movable flood barrier, downstream near Greenwich), floods were a recurring London problem. The police measured the river by these lions. "When the lions drink, the city's at risk."

London's history is tied to the Thames, the highway that links the interior of England with the North Sea. Early in the morning of September 3, 1803, William Wordsworth stood where you're standing and described what he saw:

"This city now doth like a garment wear

The beauty of the morning; silent, bare,

Ships, towers, domes, theaters, and temples lie

Open unto the fields, and to the sky;

All bright and glittering in the smokeless air."

• *Walk to the edge of the bridge to the black statue of a lady on a chariot.*

3. Boadicea, Queen of the Iceni

Riding in her two-horse chariot, daughters by her side, this Celtic Xena leads her people against Roman invaders. Julius Caesar had

been the first Roman to cross the
Channel, but even he was weirded
out by the island's strange inhabitants who worshipped trees, sacri-
ficed virgins, and went to war
painted blue. Later Romans subdued and civilized them, building
roads and making this spot on the
Thames—"Londinium"—into a
major urban center.

But Boadicea refused to be
Romanized. In A.D. 60, after Roman soldiers raped her daughters,
she rallied her people, liberated London and massacred 70,000
Romans. But the brief revolt was snuffed out, and she and her family took poison rather than surrender.

• *There's a civilized public toilet down the stairs, behind Boadicea. Now*
cross the street and take the subway (underpass) to the busy intersection.
You should be standing kitty-corner across from a big black statue of
Winston Churchill.

4. Parliament Square

The Houses of Parliament and the two big towers of Westminster
Abbey are the heart of the medieval city of Westminster. Like
Buda and Pest, London is two cities which grew into one. The City
of London (formerly Londinium) was the place to live. But Edward
the Confessor decided to build the Abbey here, outside the city
walls, in Westminster. And to oversee its construction, he moved
his court here and built the Palace of Whitehall at Westminster . . .
or Westminster Palace. Here in Westminster, the abbey came first,
then the palace. And when the king needed to sort out a problem
with his subjects, he provided them with a place where their repre-
sentatives could meet with the king. Gradually this evolved into the
Parliament buildings, which to this day are in what's called the
"Palace of Westminster."

The cute little church, which snuggles under the Abbey "like a
baby lamb under a ewe," is St. Margaret's Church. Since 1480 this
has been the place for a high society wedding.

Parliament Square, the small park between Westminster Abbey
and Big Ben, is filled with statues of famous Brits. The statue of
Winston Churchill, the man who saved Britain from Hitler, is
shown wearing the military coat he wore as he stepped victoriously
onto the beaches at Normandy after D-Day. According to tour
guides, the statue has a current of electricity running through it to
honor Churchill's wish that if a statue is made of him, his head
shouldn't be soiled by pigeons.

In 1868, the world's first traffic light was installed on the corner where you stand. And speaking of lights, the little yellow lamp atop the concrete post marking the street corner closest to Parliament says "taxi." When a member of Parliament needs a taxi, this blinks to hail one.

• *Turn right and walk away from the Houses of Parliament, down Parliament Street which becomes Whitehall. For the rest of this walk you'll be walking along the edge of what was a sprawling palace complex called Whitehall—and a street by that name.*

5. Walking Along Whitehall

Today, Whitehall is the most important street in Britain, lined with the ministries of finance, treasury, and so on. As you walk, notice the security measures. For example, iron grates seal off the concrete ditches between the buildings and sidewalks for protection against explosives. Notice also the ornamental arrow-head tops of the iron fences. Originally these were colorfully painted. When Prince Albert died in 1861, Queen Victoria ordered them all painted black. Probably the world's most determined mourner, when her beloved Albert died ("the only one who called her Vickie") she wore black for the standard two-and-a-half year period of mourning for a Victorian widow—and added an extra 38 years.

• *Continue toward the tall, square concrete monument in the middle of the road. On your right is a colorful pub, the Red Lion. Across the street a 225-yard detour down King Charles Street leads to the Cabinet War Rooms, the underground bunker of 20 rooms which was the nerve center for Britain's campaign against Hitler (see page 29).*

6. Cenotaph

The big white stone monument in the middle of Parliament Street honors those who died in two events that most shaped modern Britain—World Wars I and II. The monumental devastation of these wars helped turn a colonial superpower into a cultural colony of an American superpower.

The actual "cenotaph" is the tomb-shaped slab that sits atop the obelisk. You'll notice no religious symbols on this memorials. The dead honored by this monument came from many creeds and all corners of Britain's empire.

It's hard for an American to understand the impact of the Great War on Europe. It's said that if all the WWI dead from the British Empire were to march four abreast past the Cenotaph, the sad parade would last for seven days.

The equestrian statue in the street just beyond the Cenotaph is of Earl Haig. As commander-in-chief of the British army from 1916 to 1918, he led Britain into the killing fields of WWI.

• *Continue up Parliament Street. Just past the Cenotaph, look across Whitehall at Downing Street, blocked off by an iron security gate.*

7. #10 Downing Street and the Ministry of Defense

Britain's version of the White House is where the Prime Minister and his family live at #10—a hundred yards down the blocked-off street on the right. It looks modest, but the entryway does open up into fairly impressive digs. There's not much to see here unless a VIP happens to drive up. Then the bobbies check credentials, the gates open, the traffic barrier midway down the street drops into its bat-cave, the car drives in, and then . . . the bobbies go back to joking with the tourists again.

The huge bleak building across Whitehall from Downing Street is the Ministry of Defense (MOD). This place looks like a Ministry of Defense should. When the building was being built, in the 1930s, they discovered and restored Henry VIII's wine cellar. English soldiers and politicians have drunk together here for 500 years . . . that's continuity.

One more security note: the drapes of the MOD are too long for good reason. They come with lead weights on the bottom. If a bomb blew out the windows, the drapes would billow in and contain the flying glass.

In front of the MOD are statues of illustrious defenders of Britain. "Monty" is Field Marshal Montgomery, the great British general of WWII fame. Monty beat the Nazis in North Africa (defeating "the Desert Fox" at El Alamein). Along with Churchill, Monty breathed confidence back into a demoralized British army, persuading them they could ultimately beat Hitler.

Nearby, the statue of Walter Raleigh marks the spot where he was presented to Queen Elizabeth. Nothing marks the spot—a few hundred yards back towards Big Ben—where he was beheaded a few years later. He's buried in St. Margaret's Church.

You may be enjoying the shade of London's plane trees. They do well in polluted London: roots which work well in clay, waxy leaves which self-clean in the rain, and bark that sheds so the pollution doesn't get into its vascular system.

• *At the equestrian statue you're flanked by the Welsh and Scottish government offices. At the next corner you find the Banqueting House.*

8. Banqueting House

The Banqueting House is just about all that remains of what was once the biggest palace in Europe, stretching from here to the current Halls of Parliament. Henry VIII, Elizabeth I, Charles I, and others lived here. The Banqueting House was the only part of the palace to survive a great fire in 1698.

At 110 feet wide by 55 feet tall by 55 feet deep, the Banqueting House is a perfect double cube. London's first Renaissance building must have been a wild contrast to the higgledy-piggledy sprawl of the Whitehall palace complex of which it was just one segment.

On January 27, 1649, a man dressed in black appeared at one of the Banqueting House's first floor windows and looked out at a huge crowd that surrounded the building. He stepped out the window and onto a wooden platform. It was King Charles I. He gave a short speech to the crowd, framed by the magnificent backdrop of the Banqueting House. His final word was, "Remember." Then he knelt and laid his neck on a block as another man in black approached. It was the executioner—who cut off the King's head.

With a plop, the concept of divine monarchy in Britain died. But there would still be kings after Cromwell. In fact, the royalty was soon restored and Charles' son, Charles II, got his revenge here in the Banqueting Hall . . . by living well. His elaborate parties under the chandeliers of the Banqueting House celebrated the Restoration of the monarchy. But from now on, every king would know that he rules by the grace of Parliament.

Charles I is remembered today with a statue at one end of Whitehall (in Trafalgar Square, at the base of the tall column), while his killer, Oliver Cromwell, is given equal time with a statue at the other—at the Halls of Parliament.

• *Cross the street for a close look at the Horse Guards (11:00 inspection Monday–Saturday, at 10:00 on Sunday, and a dismounting ceremony daily at 16:00). Until the Ministry of Defense was created, the Horse Guards were the headquarters of the British Army. It's still the home of the queen's private guard.*

Continue up Whitehall, dipping into the guarded entry court of the next big building with the too-long Ionic columns. This holds the offices of the Old Admiralty, headquarters of the British navy. Ponder the scheming that must have gone on behind these walls as the British navy built the greatest empire the earth has ever seen. Across the street behind the old Clarence Pub stood the original Scotland Yard, headquarters of London's crack police force in the days of Sherlock Holmes. Finally, Whitehall opens up into the grand, noisy, traffic-filled . . .

9. Trafalgar Square

London's "Times' Square" bustles around the monumental column with Admiral Horatio Nelson standing 170 feet tall in the crow's nest. Nelson saved England at a time as dark as World War II. In 1805, Napoleon (the Hitler of his day) was poised on the other side of the Channel, preparing to invade England. Meanwhile, a thousand miles away, the one-armed, one-eyed, daring—sometimes reckless—Lord Nelson attacked the French fleet off the coast of Spain at Trafalgar. The French were routed, Britannia ruled the waves, and the once-invincible French army would be slowly worn down and defeated at Waterloo.

Nelson—while victorious—was shot by a sniper in the battle. He died gasping, "Thank God, I have done my duty."

Surrounding the column are four huggable lions—cast from melted-down enemy cannons—dying to have their photo taken with you. The artist had never seen a lion before so he used his dog as a model. The legs look like doggie paws. At least his kitten might have had them crossed like felines do.

In front of the column (nearer you) stands the statue of Charles I. Directly behind Charles is a pavement stone marking the center of London.

In medieval times, Westminster was the seat of government but the city action was downstream in London. When people from "The City" and the government needed to meet halfway, it was here. Today, Trafalgar is the center of modern London.

Trafalgar Square feels cohesive because of a bannister which cuts from building to building right around the square. Follow it counter-clockwise from the South Africa house on the right, along St. Martin-in-the-Fields church, across the National Gallery, and finally along the Canada house on the left. Harmony.

St. Martin-in-the-Fields was built in 1722. Many Americans feel at home with this church because its style—a church spire atop a classical building—inspired many town churches in New England.

You may see me at the top of Trafalgar Square on December 31, 1999, gazing down Whitehall, waiting for Big Ben to ring me into the future.

BRITISH MUSEUM TOUR

In the 19th century, the British flag flew over one-fourth of the world. London was the global capital, where women in saris walked the streets with men in top hats. And England collected art as fast as it collected colonies. In the British Museum, you'll see much of the world's greatest art from ancient Egypt, Assyria, and Greece. The British Museum is the chronicle of Western civilization. History is a modern invention. Three hundred years ago people didn't care about crumbling statues and dusty columns. Nowadays, we value a look at past civilizations, knowing that "those who don't learn from history are condemned to repeat it."

The British Museum is the only place I know where you can follow the rise and fall of three great civilizations in a few hours with a coffee break in the middle. And, while the sun never set on the British Empire, it will on you, so on this tour, we'll see just the most exciting two hours.

Orientation

Hours: Monday–Saturday 10:00–17:00, Sunday 2:30–18:00; closed on Good Friday, the first Monday in May; December 24, 25, and 26; and January 1.

Cost: Free but £2 donation requested

Tour length: Two hours

Getting there: Tube to Russell Square, Tottenham Court Road, or Holborn, and a four-block walk. Bus 7, 8, 10, 19, 22b, 24, 25, 29, 38, 55, 68, 73, 91, 98, 134, or 188. Taxis are reasonable if you buddy up.

Information: Main lobby information booth (English spoken) serves a free museum plan. The monthly events flier lists free tours and lectures given most lunch times. Tel. 0171/636-1555, recorded information tel. 0171/580-1788, or visit the museum's Web site at

——— BRITISH MUSEUM OVERVIEW ———

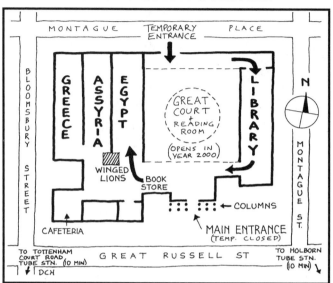

www.british-museum.ac.uk. Rainy days and Sundays always get me down because they're most crowded.

Cloakroom: Check your bags—anything left lying around that looks like a bomb will be treated as one. If the line is long and not moving, the cloakroom may be full.

Photography: Photos are allowed, flash okay, no tripod.

Cuisine art: Cheap and decent museum café and restaurant. The more comfortable and less crowded restaurant has a good salad bar and free water. There are lots of fast, cheap, and colorful cafés, pubs, and markets along Great Russell Street. Covent Garden is nearby. Marx picnicked on the benches near the entrance.

Starring: Rosetta Stone, Egyptian mummies, Assyrian lions, and Elgin Marbles.

The Tour Begins

Our tour starts at the two huge winged Assyrian lions who stand guard over the exhibit halls covering Egypt, Assyria, and Greece. Expect construction until the year 2000, when the museum opens its new "Great Court" entrance hall with the round Reading Room in the center. If you enter from the north side (Montague Place), you may be routed upstairs in order to traverse the building.

Once you reach the southern lobby, pass through the bookshop.

THE ANCIENT WORLD

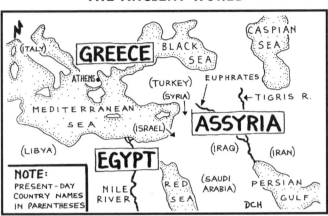

At the end, turn right and look down the long Egyptian Gallery. Introduce yourself to the two large, winged Assyrian lions (with bearded human heads) on your left. We'll rendezvous here after our hikes through Egypt, Assyria, and Greece.

EGYPT (3000 B.C.–A.D. 1)

Egypt was one of the world's first "civilizations," that is, a group of people with a government, religion, art, and written language. The Egypt we think of—pyramids, mummies, pharaohs, and guys who walk funny—lasted from 3000–1000 B.C. with hardly any change in the government, religion, or arts. Imagine two millennia of Eisenhower.

• *Enter the Egyptian Gallery (Room 25), walking between the two black statues of pharaohs on their thrones. On your left you'll see a crowd of people surrounding a big black rock with writing on it.*

The Rosetta Stone (196 B.C.)

When this rock was unearthed in the Egyptian desert in 1799, it caused a sensation in Europe. Picture a pack of scientists (I think of the apes in that scene from *2001: A Space Odyssey*) screeching with amazement, dancing around it, and poking curiously with their fingers. This black slab caused a quantum leap in the evolution of history. Finally, Egyptian writing could be decoded.

EGYPT

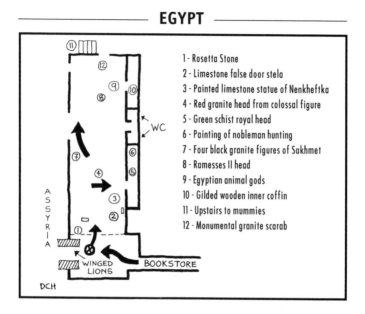

1 - Rosetta Stone
2 - Limestone false door stela
3 - Painted limestone statue of Nenkheftka
4 - Red granite head from colossal figure
5 - Green schist royal head
6 - Painting of nobleman hunting
7 - Four black granite figures of Sakhmet
8 - Ramesses II head
9 - Egyptian animal gods
10 - Gilded wooden inner coffin
11 - Upstairs to mummies
12 - Monumental granite scarab

The writing in the upper part of the stone is known as hieroglyphics. For a thousand years, no one knew how to read this mysterious ancient language. Did, say, a picture of a bird mean "bird"? Or was it a sound, forming part of a larger word, like "burden"? As it turned out, hieroglyphics were a complex combination of the two.

The Rosetta Stone allowed them to break the code. It contains a single inscription repeated in three languages. The bottom third is plain old Greek (find your favorite frat or sorority), while the middle is more modern Egyptian. By comparing the two known languages with the one they didn't know, they figured it out.

The breakthrough came from the large oval in the sixth line from the top. They found out that the bird symbol represented the sound "a," part of the name Cleo-pa-tra. Simple.

• *Move on, passing between two lion statues. On the wall to your right you'll find . . .*

Limestone False Door from the Tomb of Bateti (c. 2400 B.C.)

In ancient Egypt, you could take it with you. They believed that after you died, your soul lived on, enjoying its earthly possessions. This small statue represents the soul of a dead man.

It decorated his tomb, which contained all that he'd need in the next life: his mummified body, a résumé of his accomplishments on earth, and his possessions—sometimes including his servants who might be buried alive with their master. The great pyramids, besides being UFO psychic power stations, were also elaborate tombs for the rich and powerful. But most tombs were small rectangular rooms of brick or stone.

"False doors" like this were slapped on the outside of the tomb. The soul of the deceased, like the statue, could come and go through the "door" as he pleased—grave robbers couldn't. The deceased's relatives placed food outside the door to nourish such spirits who woke up in the middle of eternity with the munchies.

• *Just a few steps farther down the gallery, in a glass case on the right, you'll find the . . .*

Painted Limestone Statue of Nenkheftka (2400 B.C.)

After a snack the soul might wander through the nether lands (somewhere north of Belgium) searching for paradise, meeting

strange beings and weird situations. If things got too hairy, the soul could always find temporary refuge in statues like this one. It was helpful to have as many statues of yourself as possible to scatter around the earth, in case your soul needed a safe resting place.

This statue, like most Egyptian art, is not terribly lifelike—the figure is stiff, hands at the sides, left leg forward, mask-like face, stylized anatomy, and an out-of-date skirt. And talk about uptight—he's got a column down his back! But it does have all the essential features, like the simplified human figures on international traffic signs. To a soul caught in the fast lane of astral travel, this symbolic statue would be easier to spot than a detailed one.

You'll see the same rigid features in almost all the statues in the gallery.

• *Head past two tall columns which give a sense of the grandeur of the Egyptian temples. About 30 yards farther down the gallery, you'll find a huge head with a broken-bowling-pin hat.*

Red Granite Head from a Colossal Figure of a King

Art also served as propaganda for the pharaohs, kings who called themselves gods on earth. Put this head on top of an enormous body (which still stands in Egypt) and you have the intimidating

image of an omnipotent ruler who demands servile obedience. Next to the head is, appropriately, the pharaoh's powerful fist—the long arm of the law.

The crown is also symbolic. It's actually two crowns in one. The pointed upper half is the royal cap of Upper Egypt. This rests on the flat fez-like crown symbolizing Lower Egypt. A pharaoh wearing both crowns together is bragging that he rules a united Egypt.

• *Enter Room 25a, to the right. In a glass case you'll find . . .*

Green Schist Royal Head (c. 1490 B.C.)

This pharaoh has several symbols of authority—the familiar pointed crown of Upper Egypt, a cobra-headed "hat pin" on the forehead and a stylized "chin strap" beard. These symbols tell us clearly he's a powerful pharaoh, but which one?

Scholars aren't even sure if he's a he. Is it bearded King Tuthmosis III . . . or the smooth-skinned Queen Hatshepsut, one of phour phemale pharaohs who actually did wear ceremonial "beards" as symbols of royal power?

• *Ponder the mystery of this AC/DC monarch, then turn to the painting at the end of the room.*

Painting of a Nobleman Hunting in the Marshes (1425 B.C.)

This nobleman walks like Egyptian statues look—stiff. We see his torso from the front and everything else—arms, legs, face—in profile, creating the funny walk that has become an Egyptian cliché. (Like an early version of Cubism, we see various perspectives at once.)

But the stiffness is softened by a human-ness. It's a family scene, a snapshot of loved ones from a happy time to be remembered for all eternity. The nobleman, taking a break from his courtly duties, is hunting. He's standing in a reed boat, gliding through the marshes. His arm is raised, ready to bean a bird with a snake-like hunting stick. On the right, his wife looks on, while his daughter crouches between his legs, a symbol of fatherly protection.

Though this two-dimensional hunter looks as if he were just run over by a pyramid, the painting is actually quite realistic. The birds above and fish below are painted like encyclopedia entries. The first "paper" came from papyrus plants like the bush on the left. The only truly unrealistic element is the house cat (thigh-high, in front of the man), acting as a retriever—just possibly the only cat in history that ever did anything useful.

• *Back in the main gallery, cross over to find four black lion-headed statues.*

Four Black Granite Figures of the Goddess Sakhmet (1400 B.C.)

This goddess was a good one to have on your side. She looks pretty sedate here, but this lion-headed woman could spring into a fierce crouch when crossed. Gods were often seen as part animal, admired

for being stronger, swifter, or more fierce than puny homo sapiens.

The gods ruled the Egyptian cosmos like a big banana republic (or the American Congress). To get a favor, Egyptians bribed their gods with offerings of food, animals, or money, or by erecting statues like these to them.

Notice the ankh that Sakhmet is holding. This key-shaped cross was the hieroglyph meaning "life," and was a symbol of eternal life. Later, it was adopted as a Christian symbol because of its cross shape and religious overtones.

• *Catch the happy couple nearby, seated hand in hand waiting for the Eternity Express. Then continue to the big glass case in the middle with leftovers from an ancient Egyptian arts-and-crafts fair. Respect that bronze cat with the nose ring. Cats were the sacred cows of Egypt. You could be put to death for harming one. Walk farther on to the big eight-foot granite head and torso.*

Upper Half of Colossal Statue of Rameses II of Granite (1270 B.C.)

When Moses told the king of Egypt, "Let my people go!" this was the stone-faced look he got. Rameses II (reigned c. 1290–1223 B.C.)

was likely in power when Moses led the Israelites out of captivity in Egypt to their homeland in Israel. According to the Bible, Moses, a former Egyptian prince himself, appealed to the pharaoh to let them go peacefully. When the pharaoh refused, Moses cursed the land with a series of plagues. Finally, the Is-

raelites just bolted with the help of their God, Yahweh, who drowned the Egyptian armies in the Red Sea. Egyptian records don't exactly corroborate the tale, but this Ramesses here looks enough like Yul Brynner in *The Ten Commandments* to make me a believer.

This statue, made from two different colors of granite, is a fragment from a temple in Thebes. Rameses was a great builder of temples, palaces, tombs, and statues of himself. There are probably more statues of him in the world than there are cheesy fake Davids. He was so concerned about achieving immortality that he even chiseled his own name on other people's statues. Very rude.

Imagine, for a second, what the archaeologists saw when they came upon this—a colossal head and torso separated from the enormous legs, toppled into the sand, all that remained of the works of a once-great pharaoh. Kings, megalomaniacs, and workaholics, take note.

• *Say, "Ooh, heavy," and climb the ramp behind Ramesses, looking for animals.*

Various Egyptian Gods as Animals

Before technology made humans the alpha animal on earth, it was easier to appreciate our fellow creatures. The Egyptians saw the superiority of animals, and worshipped them as incarnations of the gods. The lioness was stronger, so she portrayed (as we saw earlier) the fierce goddess Sakhmet.

The clever baboon is Thoth, the god of wisdom, and Horus has a falcon's head. The standing hippo is Theoris, protectress of childbirth. See her stylized breasts and pregnant belly supported by ankhs, the symbol of life. The god Amun, a powerful ram, protects a puny pharaoh under his powerful head.

• *Continuing up the ramp into Room 25b, you'll come face to face with a golden coffin.*

Gilded Wooden Inner Coffin of the Chantress of Amen-Re Henutmehit (1290 B.C.)

Look into the eyes of the deceased, a well-known singer, painted on the coffin. The Egyptians tried to cheat death by preserving

their corpses. In the next life, the spirit was homeless without its body. They'd mummify the body, place it in a wooden coffin like this one and, often, put that coffin inside a larger stone one. The result is that we now have Egyptian bodies that are as well-preserved as Dick Clark.

The coffin is decorated with scenes of the deceased praising the gods, as well as magical spells to protect the body from evil and to act as crib notes for the confused soul in the nether world.

• *You can't call Egypt a wrap until you visit the mummies upstairs. If you can handle four flights of stairs (if not, cut straight to the Assyria section from here), head on down to the end of the gallery past the giant stone scarab (beetle) and up the stairs lined with Roman mosaics, then left into Rooms 59 and 60. Snap a death mask photo of your partner framed by an open coffin, then step into the action . . . Room 60.*

Mummies

To mummify a body, disembowel it, fill the body cavities with pitch or other substances, and dry the body with natron, a natural form of sodium carbonate (and, I believe, the active ingredient in Twinkies). Then carefully bandage it head to toe with fine linen strips. Place in a coffin, wait 2,000 years, and, *voilà!* Or just dump the corpse in the desert and let the hot, dry Egyptian sand do the work—you'll get the same results.

The mummies in the glass cases here are from the time of the Roman occupation. The X-ray photos on the cases tell us more about these people. On the walls are murals showing the Egyptian burial rites as outlined in the *Book of the Dead*. In Roman times Egyptians painted a fine portrait in wax on the wrapping. And don't miss the animal mummies.

• *Linger here, but remember that eternity is about the amount of time it takes to see this entire museum. Head back down the stairs to the huge stone beetle in the center of the room at the end of the gallery . . .*

Monumental Granite Scarab (200 B.C.)

This species of beetle would burrow into the ground then reappear—like dying and rebirth—a symbol of resurrection.

Like the scarab, Egyptian culture was buried, first by Greece, then by Rome. Knowledge of the ancient writing died, condemning the culture to obscurity. But since the discovery of the Rosetta Stone, Egyptology is booming and Egypt has come back to life.

• *Backtrack to the Rosetta Stone. Meet you on a bench in the shadow of those bearded Assyrian human-headed lions.*

ASSYRIA (1000–600 B.C.)

Assyria was the lion, the king of beasts of early civilizations. From its base in northern Mesopotamia (northern Iraq), it conquered and dominated the Middle East—from Israel to Iran—for more than three centuries. The Assyrians were a nation of warriors—hardy, disciplined and often cruel conquistadors—whose livelihood depended on booty and slash-and-burn expansion.

Two Winged Lions with Human Heads (c. 870 B.C.)

These lions stood guard at key points in Assyrian palaces to intimidate enemies and defeated peoples. With lion body, eagle

wings and human head, these magical beasts—and therefore the Assyrian people—had the strength of a lion, the speed of an eagle, the brain of a man, and the beard of Z.Z. Top. They protected the palace from evil spirits and they scared the heck out of foreign ambassadors and left-wing newspaper reporters.

(What has five legs and flies? Take a close look. These quintrupeds appear complete from both the front and the side.)

On the stone between the bearded lions' loins, you can see one of civilization's most impressive achievements— writing. This wedge-shaped ("cuneiform") script is the world's first written language, invented five thousand years ago by the Sumerians and passed down to their less-civilized descendants, the Assyrians.

• *Walk between the lions, glance at the large reconstructed wooden gates from an Assyrian palace, and turn right into the narrow red gallery lined with brown relief panels.*

ASSYRIA

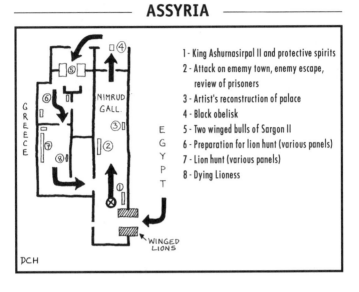

1 - King Ashurnasirpal II and protective spirits
2 - Attack on ememy town, enemy escape, review of prisoners
3 - Artist's reconstruction of palace
4 - Black obelisk
5 - Two winged bulls of Sargon II
6 - Preparation for lion hunt (various panels)
7 - Lion hunt (various panels)
8 - Dying Lioness

Nimrud Gallery (9th century B.C.)

This gallery is a mini-version of the main hall of Ashurnasirpal II's palace. It was decorated with these pleasant sand-colored gypsum relief panels (which were, however, originally painted, as you'll see illustrated halfway down the hall).

That's Ashurnasirpal himself in the first panel on your right, with braided beard and fez-like crown, flanked by his supernatural hawk-headed henchman. The bulging muscles tell us that Ashurnasirpal was a conqueror's conqueror who enjoyed his reputation as a savage, merciless warrior who tortured and humiliated the vanquished. The following panels chronicle his bloody career.

• *Walk 15 yards farther. On your left find an upper panel labeled . . .*

Attack on an Enemy Town

Many "nations" conquered by the Assyrians consisted of little more than a single walled city. Here, the Assyrians lay siege with the aid of a movable tower that gives them protection as they advance to the city walls. The king is shooting arrows from high atop that battering-ram "tank."

• *Next, to the right, you'll find . . .*

Enemy Escape
Though this may represent enemies fleeing the Assyrians by swimming across the Euphrates, it's more likely the Assyrians themselves with a unique amphibious assault technique. The soldiers inflate animal skins to keep them afloat as they sneak downstream to an enemy city.
• *Below, you'll see . . .*

Review of Prisoners
The Assyrian economy depended on booty. Here a conquered nation is paraded before the Assyrian king. Above their heads the sculptor shows the rich spoils of war—elephant tusks, metal cauldrons, and so on.
• *Notice the painted reconstruction on the opposite wall, then find the black obelisk.*

Black Obelisk of Shalmaneser III (c. 840 B.C.)
The Assyrians demanded annual tribute from the conquered lands. The obelisk shows people bringing tribute to Shalmaneser from all corners of the empire. The second band from the top shows the tribute from Israel. Parts of Israel were under Assyrian domination from the 9th century B.C. on. Old Testament prophets like Elijah and Elisha constantly warned their people of the corrupting influence of the Assyrian gods.

Also check out the parade of exotic animals on the third band, especially the missing-link monkeys.
• *Exit the gallery at the far end and hang a U-turn left into Room 16. More winged beasts.*

Two Winged Bulls from the Khorsabad Palace of Sargon II (c. 710 B.C.)
These 16-ton bulls guarded the palace of Sargon II. And speaking of large amounts of bull, "Sargon" wasn't his real name. It's obvious to savvy historians that Sargon must have been an insecure usurper to the throne, since the name meant "true king."
• *Sneak past these bulls, veering right into the small Room 17 where horses are being readied for the big hunt.*

Royal Lion Hunts
Lion hunting was Assyria's sport of kings. On the right wall we see horses being readied for the hunt. On the left wall, hunting dogs. And next to them are beautiful lions. They rest peacefully in their idyllic garden, unaware that they will shortly be rousted, stampeded, and slaughtered.

Lions lived in Mesopotamia up until modern times, and it had

long been the duty of kings to keep the lion population down to protect farmers and herdsmen. This duty soon became sport as the kings of men proved their power by taking on the king of beasts. They actually bred lions to stage hunts. As we'll see, these "hunts" were as sporting as shooting fish in a barrel. Later Assyrian kings had grown soft and decadent, hardly the raging warriors of Ashurnasirpal's time.
• *Enter the larger lion-hunt room. Reading the panels like a comic strip, start in the right corner and gallop counter-clockwise.*

The Lion-Hunt Room (c. 650 B.C.)

They're releasing the lions from their cages. Above, soldiers on horseback herd them into an enclosed arena. The king has them cornered. Let the slaughter begin.

The chariot carries old King Ashurbanipal himself. The last of Assyria's great kings, he's ruled now for 50 years. He shoots ahead while spearmen hold off lions attacking from the rear.
• *At about the middle of the long wall . . .*

The fleeing lions, shot through with arrows and weighed down with fatigue, begin to fall, tragically. The lead lion carries on valiantly even while vomiting blood.

This, perhaps the low point of Assyrian cruelty, is the high point of their artistic achievement. It's a curious coincidence that civilizations often produce their greatest art in their declining years. Hmm.

Dying Lioness

• *On the wall opposite the vomiting lion . . .*
A dying lioness roars in pain and frustration, trying to run, but her body is too heavy. Her muscular hind legs, once the source of her

power, are now paralyzed, a burden dragging her down.

Did the sculptor sense the coming death of his own civilization? Like these brave, fierce lions, Assyria's once-great warrior nation was slain. Shortly after Ashurbanipal's death, Assyria was conquered, sacked, and looted by an ascendent Babylon. The mood of tragedy, of dignity, of proud struggle in a hopeless cause makes this Dying Lioness simply one of the most beautiful of all human creations.

• *Return to the winged lions (where we started) by exiting the lion-hunt room at the far end, soon connecting up with familiar territory. Take a break.*

To reach the Greek section, enter the doorway opposite the bookstore (Room 1), walking past early Greek Barbie and Ken dolls from the Cycladic period (2500 B.C.). Just before the cafe, restaurant, and WCs, turn right, passing through rooms 3 and 4 to the long Room 5. Relax on a bench and read, surrounded by vases and statues.

GREECE (600 B.C.–A.D. 1)
The history of ancient Greece could be subtitled "making order out of chaos." While Assyria was dominating the Middle Eastern world, "Greece" was floundering in darkness—a gaggle of warring tribes roaming the Greek peninsula. But by around 700 B.C. these tribes began settling down, experimenting with democracy, forming self-governing city-states and making ties with other city-states. Scarcely two centuries later, they would be a united community and the center of the civilized world.

During its "Golden Age" (500–430 B.C.), Greece set the tone for all of Western civilization to follow. Modern democracy, theater, literature, mathematics, philosophy, science, art, and architecture, as we know them, were all virtually invented by a single generation of Greeks in a small town of maybe 80,000 citizens.
• *On the wall in Room 5, find . . .*

Map of Greek World (500–30 B.C.)
Athens was the most powerful of the city-states and the center of the Greek world. Golden Age Greece was never really a full-fledged empire, but more a common feeling of unity among Greek-speaking peoples on the peninsula.

A century after the Golden Age, Greek culture was spread still farther as the Macedonian Alexander the Great conquered the Mediterranean world and beyond. By 300 B.C., the "Greek" world stretched from Italy to India to Egypt (including most of what used to be the Assyrian Empire). Two hundred years later this Greek-speaking "Hellenistic Empire" was conquered by the Romans.
• *There's a nude male to the left of the map.*

Boy (Kouros) (490 B.C.)
The Greeks saw the human body as a perfect example of the divine orderliness of the universe. For the Greeks, even the gods themselves had human forms. The ideal man was a balance of opposites, the "Golden Mean." In a statue, that meant finding the right balance between motion and stillness, between realistic human anatomy

—— EARLY GREECE ——

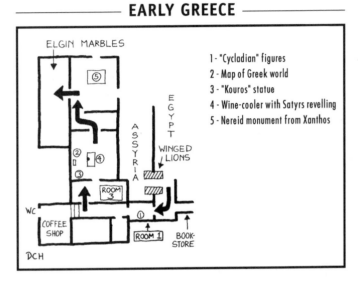

ELGIN MARBLES

⑤

E
G
Y
P
T

A
S
S
Y
R
I
A

WINGED
LIONS

② ④
③

ROOM
3

WC

COFFEE
SHOP

①

ROOM 1

BOOK-
STORE

DCH

1 - "Cycladian" figures
2 - Map of Greek world
3 - "Kouros" statue
4 - Wine-cooler with Satyrs revelling
5 - Nereid monument from Xanthos

(with human flaws) and the perfection of a Greek god. This Boy is still a bit uptight, stiff as the rock he's carved from. But—as we'll see—in just a few short decades, the Greeks would cut loose and create realistic statues that seemed to move like real humans.

• *Look in the glass case by the map, filled with decorated vases. One in the center is marked . . .*

Red-figured Psykter (Wine Cooler) with Satyrs Revelling (490 B.C.)

This clay wine cooler, designed to float in a bowl of cooling water, is decorated with satyrs holding a symposium, or drinking party. These half-man/half-animal creatures (notice their tails) had a reputation for lewd behavior, reminding the balanced and moderate

Greeks of their rude roots.

The revelling figures painted on this jar are more realistic, more three-dimensional, and suggest more natural movements than even the literally three-dimensional but quite stiff Kouros statue. The Greeks are beginning to conquer the natural world in art. The art, like life, is more in balance. And speaking of "balance," if that's a Greek sobriety test, revel on.

• *Carry on into Room 7 and sit facing the Greek temple at the far end.*

Nereid Monument from Xanthos (c. 400 B.C.)

Greek temples (like this reconstruction of a temple-shaped tomb) housed a statue of a god or goddess. Unlike Christian churches,

which serve as meeting places, Greek temples kept worshippers gathered outside, so the most impressive part of the temple was its exterior. Temples were rectangular, surrounded by rows of columns, topped by a slanted roof.

The triangle-shaped roof, filled in with sculpture (reliefs or statues), is called the "pediment." The crossbeams that support the roof are called "metopes" (MET-o-pees). Now look through the columns to the building itself. Above the doorway is another set of relief panels running around the building (under the "eaves") called the "frieze."

Next, we'll see pediment, frieze, and metope decorations from Greece's greatest temple.

• *Leave the British Museum. Take the Tube to Heathrow and fly to Athens. In the center of the old city, on top of the high, flat hill known as the Acropolis, you'll find . . .*

The Parthenon

The Parthenon—the temple dedicated to Athena, goddess of wisdom and the patroness of Athens—was the crowning glory of an enormous urban renewal plan during Greece's Golden Age. After Athens was ruined in a war with Persia, the city, under the bold leadership of Pericles, constructed the greatest building of its day. The Parthenon was a model of balance, simplicity and harmonious elegance, the symbol of the Golden Age. Phidias, the greatest Greek sculptor, decorated the exterior with statues and relief panels.

While the building itself remains in Athens, many of the Parthenon's best sculptures are right here in the British Museum—the so-called Elgin Marbles, named for the

shrewd British ambassador who acquired them in the early 1800s. Though the Greek government complains about losing its marbles, the Brits feel they rescued and preserved the sculptures.

• *Enter through the glass doors labeled "Sculptures of the Parthenon."*

THE ELGIN MARBLES (450 B.C.)

The marble panels you see lining the walls of this large hall are part of the frieze that originally ran around the exterior of the Parthenon. The statues at either end of the hall once filled the Parthenon's triangular-shaped pediments. Near the pediment sculptures, we'll also find the relief panels known as metopes. Let's start with the frieze.

The Frieze

These 56 relief panels show Athens' "Fourth of July" parade, celebrating the birth of their city. On this day, citizens marched up the Acropolis to symbolically present a new robe to the 40-foot gold and ivory statue of Athena housed in the Parthenon.

• *Start at the panels to your right (#134) and work counter-clockwise.*

Men on horseback, chariots, musicians, animals for sacrifice, and young maidens with offerings are all part of the grand parade, all heading in the same direction. Prance on.

Notice the muscles and veins in the horses' legs (#128) and the intricate folds in the cloaks and dresses (#115). Some panels (#103) have holes drilled in them, where gleaming bronze reins were fitted to heighten the festive look. Despite the bustle of figures posed every which way, the frieze has one unifying element—all the heads are at the same level, creating a single ribbon around the Parthenon.

• *Cross to the opposite wall.*

A three-horse chariot (#59) cut out of only two inches of marble is more lifelike and three-dimensional than anything the Egyptians achieved in a free-standing statue.

The procession culminates (#35) in the presentation of the robe to Athena. A man and a child fold the robe for the goddess while the rest of the gods look on. There's Zeus and Hera (#29), the king and queen of the gods, seated, enjoying the fashion show and wondering what length hemlines will be this year.

• *Head for the set of pediment sculptures at the right end of the hall.*

The Pediment Sculptures

These statues nestled nicely in the triangular pediment above the columns at the Parthenon's east entrance. The missing statues at the peak of the triangle once showed the birth of Athena. Zeus had his head split open, allowing Athena, the goddess of wisdom, to rise from his brain fully grown and fully armed.

ELGIN MARBLES

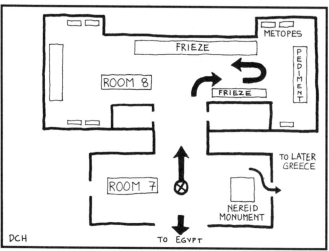

The other gods at this Olympian banquet slowly become aware of the amazing event. The first to notice is the one closest to them, Hebe, the cup-bearer of the gods (tallest surviving fragment). Frightened, she runs to tell the others, her dress whipping behind her. A startled Demeter (just left of Hebe) turns toward Hebe.

The only one that hasn't lost his head is laid-back Dionysus (the cool guy on the far left). He just raises another glass of wine to his lips. Over on the right, Aphrodite, goddess of love, leans back luxuriously into the lap of her mother, too busy posing to even notice the hubbub. A horse screams, "These people are nuts—let me out of here!"

The scene had a message. Just as wise Athena rose above the lesser gods who are scared, drunk, or vain, so would her city, Athens, rise above her lesser rivals.

This is amazing workmanship. Compare Dionysus, with his natural, relaxed, reclining pose, to all those stiff Egyptian statues standing eternally at attention. The realism of the muscles is an

improvement even over the Kouros we saw, sculpted only 50 years earlier.

Appreciate the folds of the clothes on the female figures (on the right half), especially Aphrodite's clinging, rumpled robe. Some sculptors would build a model of their figure first, put real clothes on it, and study how the cloth hung down before actually sculpting in marble. Others found inspiration at the tavern on wet T-shirt night.

Even without their heads, these statues with their detailed anatomy and expressive poses speak volumes.

Wander behind. The statues originally sat 40 feet above the ground. The backs of the statues—which were never intended to be seen—are almost as detailed as the fronts. That's quality control . . .

• *The metopes are the panels on the walls to either side. Start with "South Metope XXXI" on the right wall, center.*

The Metopes

In #XXXI, a Centaur grabs a man by the throat while the man pulls his hair. The human Lapiths have invited some Centaurs—wild half-man/half-horse creatures—to a wedding feast. All goes well until the brutish Centaurs, the original party animals, get too drunk and try to carry off the Lapith women. A battle ensues.

The Greeks prided themselves on creating order out of chaos. Within just a few generations, they went from nomadic barbarism to the pinnacle of early Western civilization. These metopes tell the story of this struggle between the forces of civilization (Lapiths) and barbarism (Centaurs).

In #XXVIII (opposite wall, center), the Centaurs start to get the upper hand as one rears triumphant over a fallen man. The lion skin draped over the Centaur's arm roars a taunt at the prone man. The humans lose face.

In #XXVII (to the left), the humans finally rally and drive off the brutish Centaurs. A Centaur, wounded in the back, tries to run, but the man grabs him by the neck and raises his right hand (missing) to deliver the final blow. Notice how the Lapith's cloak drapes a rough-textured background that highlights the smooth skin of this graceful,

Centaurs slain around the world. *Dateline 500 B.C.—Greece, China, India: Man no longer considers himself an animal. Bold new ideas are exploding simultaneously around the world. Socrates, Confucius, Buddha, and others are independently discovering a non-material, unseen order in nature and in man. They say man has a rational mind or soul. He's separate from nature and different from the other animals.*

ideal man. The Centaurs have been defeated. Civilization has triumphed over barbarism, order over chaos, and rational man over his half-animal alter-ego.

Why are the Elgin Marbles so treasured? The British of the 19th century saw themselves as the new "civilized" race subduing "barbarians" in their far-flung Empire. Maybe these rocks made them stop and wonder—will our great civilization also turn to rubble?

NATIONAL GALLERY TOUR

6

london

The National Gallery lets you tour Europe's art without ever crossing the Channel. With so many exciting artists and styles, it's a fine overture to art if you're just starting a European trip, and a pleasant reprise if you're just finishing. Anytime, the "National Gal" is a welcome interlude from the bustle of London sightseeing.

Orientation

Hours: Monday-Saturday 10:00–18:00, Sunday 12:00–18:00, Wednesdays until 20:00. Closed on Good Friday, December 24, 25, 26 and January 1.

Cost: Free

Tour length: Ninety minutes

Getting there: It's central as can be, overlooking Trafalgar Square, a 15-minute walk from Big Ben, 10 minutes from Piccadilly. Tube: Charing Cross or Leicester Square. Bus: 3, 6, 9, 11, 12, 13, 15, 23, 24, 29, 53, 88, 91, 94, 109.

Information: Information desk with a free and handy floor plan brochure in lobby. Excellent CD Walkman tours (£3) let you dial up info on any painting in the museum. The latest events schedule and a listing of free lunch lectures is in the free National Gallery News flier. Free one-hour general overview tours are offered most weekdays at 11:30 and 14:30. Don't miss the "Micro Gallery," a computer room even your dad could have fun in (closes 30 minutes earlier than museum). You can study any artist, style, or topic in the museum and even print out a tailor-made tour map. Tel. 0171/839-3321, recorded information 0171/747-2885.

Cloakroom: Free cloakrooms at each entrance welcome your coat and umbrella but probably not your bag. You can take in a bag.

Photography: Strictly forbidden.

Cuisine art: The Brasserie (first floor, Sainsbury Wing) is classy with reasonable prices and a petite menu. The Café (near the end of this tour, just before the Impressionists) is a bustling, inexpensive self-service cafeteria with realistic salads, Rubens sandwiches, and Gauguin juices. A block away, there's a good cafeteria in the crypt of St. Martin-in-the-Fields church (facing Trafalgar Square). For pub grub, walk a block toward Big Ben and dip into the Clarence.

Starring: You name it—Leonardo, Van Eyck, Raphael, Titian, Caravaggio, Rembrandt, Rubens, Velázquez, Monet, Renoir, and van Gogh.

The Tour Begins

Of the two entrances that face Trafalgar Square, enter through the smaller building (fifty yards left of the main entrance as you face it). Pick up the free map and climb the stairs. At the top, turn left and grab a seat in room 51 facing Leonardo's Virgin of the Rocks.

The National Gallery offers a quick overview of European art history. We'll stay on one floor, and after a brief preview of Leonardo, we'll work chronologically through medieval holiness, Renaissance realism, Dutch detail, Baroque excess, British restraint, and the colorful French Impressionism that leads to the modern world. Cruise like an eagle with wide eyes for the big picture, seeing how each style progresses into the next.

THE ITALIAN RENAISSANCE (1400–1550)

Leonardo da Vinci —*The Virgin of the Rocks*

Mary, the mother of Jesus, plays with her son and little Johnny the Baptist (with cross, at left) while John's mother looks on. Leonardo brings this holy scene right down to earth. But looking closer we see that Leonardo has deliberately posed them into a pyramid shape, with Mary's head at the peak, creating an oasis of maternal stability and serenity amid the hard rock of the earth. Leonardo, who was illegitimate, may have sought after the young mother he never knew, in his art. Freud thought so.

The Renaissance—or "rebirth" of the culture of ancient Greece

NATIONAL GALLERY OVERVIEW

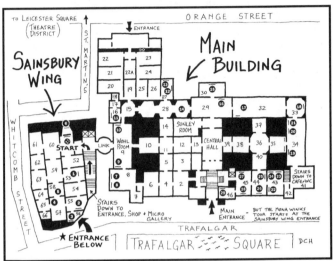

Medieval and Early Renaissance
1. Wilton Diptych
2. UCCELLO—Battle of San Romano
3. VAN EYCK—Arnolfini Marriage
4. CRIVELLI—Annunciation With St. Emidius
5. BOTTICELLI—Venus and Mars

High Renaissance
6. LEONARDO DA VINCI— Virgin and Child (painting and cartoon)
7. ICHELANGELO—Entombment
8. RAPHAEL—Pope Julius II

Venetian Renaissance
9. TINTORETTO—Origin of the Milky Way
10. TITIAN—Bacchus and Ariadne

Northern Protestant Art
11. VERMEER—Young Woman Standing at a Virginal
12. REMBRANDT—Self-Portrait
13. REMBRANDT—Belshazzar's Feast

Baroque and Rococo
14. RUBENS—The Judgment of Paris
15. VAN DYCK—Charles I on Horseback
16. VELÁZQUEZ—The Rokeby Venus
17. CARAVAGGIO—Supper at Emmaus
18. BOUCHER—Pan and Syrinx

British
19. CONSTABLE—The Hay Wain
20. TURNER—The Fighting Téméraire
21. TURNER—Rain, Steam, Speed

Impressionism and Beyond
22. MONET—Gare St. Lazare
23. MANET—The Waitress (La Servante de Bocks)
24. DEGAS— Miss La La at the Cirque Fernando
25. RENOIR—The Umbrellas
26. SEURAT—Bathers at Asnieres
27. VAN GOGH—Sunflowers
28. CÉZANNE—Bathers
29. MONET—Water Lilies

and Rome—was a cultural boom that changed people's thinking about every aspect of life. In politics, it meant democracy. In religion, a move away from Church dominance and toward the assertion of man (humanism) and a more personal faith. Science and secular learning were revived after centuries of superstition and ignorance. In architecture, it was a return to the balanced columns and domes of Greece and Rome.

In painting, the Renaissance meant realism. Artists rediscovered the beauty of Nature and the human body. With pictures of beautiful people in harmonious surroundings they expressed the optimism and confidence of this new age.

• *We'll circle back around to Leonardo in a couple hundred years. But first, turn your back on the Renaissance and cruise through the medieval world in Rooms 52, 53, and 54.*

Medieval and Early Renaissance (1260–1510)

Shiny-gold paintings of saints, angels, Madonnas, and crucifixions. One thing is very clear: Middle Ages art was religious, dominated by the Church. The illiterate faithful could meditate on an altarpiece and visualize heaven.

Medieval heaven was different from medieval earth. The holy wore gold plates on their heads. Faces were serene and generic. People posed stiffly, facing directly out or to the side, never in-between. Saints are recognized by symbols they carry (a key, a sword, a book), rather than human features. They floated in an ethereal nowhere of gold leaf. In other words, medieval artists had no need to master the techniques of portraying the "real" world of rocks, trees, and distinguished noses, because their world was . . . otherworldly.

• *One of the finest medieval altarpieces is in a glass case in Room 53.*

The Wilton Diptych—anonymous (c. 1395)

In this two-paneled altarpiece, a glimmer of human realism peeks through the gold leaf. The kings on the left have distinct, down-to-earth faces as they adore Mary and the baby on the right. And the back side shows—not a saint, not a god, not a symbol—but a real-life deer lying down in the grass of this earth.

Still, the anonymous artist is struggling with reality. Look at the left panel—John the Baptist is holding a "lamb of God" that looks more like a chihuahua. Nice try. In the right panel, the angels with their flame-like wings and cloned faces bunch together

single file across the back rather than receding realistically into the distance. Mary's exquisite fingers hold an anatomically impossible little foot. The figures are flat, scrawny, and sinless with cartoon features—far from flesh-and-blood human beings.

• *Walking straight into Room 55, you'll leave this gold leaf peace and you'll find . . .*

Uccello—*Battle of San Romano* (c. 1450)

This colorful battle scene shows the victory of Florence over Siena— and the battle for literal realism on the canvas. It's an early Renaissance attempt at a realistic, non-religious, three-dimensional scene.

Uccello challenges his ability by posing the horses and soldiers at every conceivable angle. The background of farmyards, receding hedges and tiny soldiers creates a 3-D illusion of distance. In the foreground, Uccello actually constructs a 3-D grid out of fallen lances, then places the horses and warriors within it. Still, Uccello hasn't quite worked out the bugs—the figures in the distance are far too big, and the fallen soldier on the left isn't much bigger than the fallen shield on the right.

• *In Room 56, you'll find . . .*

Van Eyck—*The Arnolfini Marriage* (1434)

Called by some "The Shotgun Wedding," this painting of a simple ceremony (set in Bruges, Belgium) is a masterpiece of down-to-earth details. Van Eyck has built us a medieval dollhouse, then invites us to linger over the finely crafted details. Feel the texture of the fabrics, count the terrier's hairs, trace the shadows generated by the window. In fact, each object is painted at an ideal angle, with the details you'd see if you were only a foot away. So the strings of beads hanging on the back wall are as crystal-clear as the bracelets on the bride.

And to top it off, look into the round mirror on the far wall—the whole scene is reflected backwards in miniature, showing the loving couple and two mysterious visitors. Is it the concerned parents? The minister? Van Eyck himself at his easel? Or has the artist painted you, the home viewer, into the scene?

In medieval times (this was painted only a generation after The Wilton Diptych) everyone could read the hidden meaning of certain symbols—the chandelier with its one lit candle (love), the fruit on the windowsill (fertility), the whiskbroom (the bride's domestic responsibilities), and the terrier (Fido—fidelity).

By the way, she may not be pregnant. The fashion of the day was to wear a pillow to look pregnant in hopes you'd soon get that way. At least, that's what they told their parents.

The surface detail is extraordinary, but the painting lacks true Renaissance depth. The tiny room looks unnaturally narrow, cramped, and claustrophobic, making us wonder: where will the mother-in-law sleep?

• *Continue into Room 57.*

Crivelli—*The Annunciation with Saint Emidius*

Mary, in green, is visited by the dove of the Holy Ghost who beams down from the distant heavens in a shaft of light.

Like Van Eyck's wedding, this is a brilliant collection of realistic details. Notice the hanging rug, the peacock, the architectural minutiae that lead you way way back, then, bam, you've got a giant pickle in your face.

It's detail combined with Italian spaciousness. The floor tiles and building bricks recede into the distance. We're sucked right in, accelerating through the alleyway, under the arch and off into space. The Holy Ghost spans the entire distance, connecting heavenly background with earthly foreground. Crivelli creates an Escher-esque labyrinth of rooms and walkways that we want to walk through, around, and into, or is that just a male thing?

Renaissance Italians were interested in—even obsessed with— portraying 3-D space. Perhaps they focused their spiritual passion away from heaven, and toward the physical world. With such restless energy, they needed lots of elbow room. Space, the final frontier.

• *In Room 58 . . .*

Botticelli—*Venus and Mars*

Mars takes a break from war, succumbing to the delights of Love (Venus), while impish satyrs play innocently with the discarded tools of death. In the early spring of the Renaissance, there was an optimistic mood in the air, the feeling that enlightened Man could solve all problems, narrowing the gap between mortals and the Greek gods. Artists felt free to use the pagan Greek gods as symbols of human traits, virtues, and vices. Venus has sapped man's medieval stiffness and welcomed him roundly out of the darkness and into the Renaissance.

• *Now return through Room 59 to the Leonardo in Room 51, where we started.*

The High Renaissance (1500)

With the "Big Three" of the High Renaissance—Leonardo, Michelangelo, and Raphael—painters had finally conquered realism. But these three Florentine artists weren't content to just copy Nature, cranking out photographs-on-canvas. Like Renaissance architects (which they also were), they carefully composed their figures on the canvas, "building" them into geometrical patterns that reflected the balance and order they saw in Nature.

• *Enter the small dark cave behind the Rocks.*

Leonardo da Vinci—*Virgin and Child with St. John the Baptist and St. Anne*

At first glance this chalk drawing, or cartoon, looks like a simple snapshot of two loving moms and two playful kids. The two children play—oblivious to the violent deaths they'll both suffer—beneath their mothers' Mona Lisa smiles.

But follow the eyes: shadowy-eyed Anne turns toward Mary who looks tenderly down to Jesus who blesses John who gazes back dreamily. As your eyes follow theirs, you're led back to the literal and psychological center of the composition—Jesus. Without resorting to heavy-handed medieval symbolism, Leonardo drives home a theological concept in a natural, human way. Leonardo the perfectionist rarely finished paintings. This sketch gives us an inside peek at his genius.

• *Enter the large Room 9. We'll return to these big, colorful canvases, but first, turn right into Room 8.*

Michelangelo—*Entombment* (unfinished)

Michelangelo, the greatest sculptor ever, proves it here in this "painted sculpture" of the crucified Jesus being carried to the tomb. The figures are almost like chiseled statues of Greek gods, especially the musclehead in red rippling beneath his clothes. Christ's naked body, shocking to the medieval Church, was completely acceptable in the Renaissance world where classical nudes were admired as an expression of the divine.

In true Renaissance style, balance and symmetry reign. Christ is the center of the composition, flanked by two equally leaning people who support his body with strips of cloth. They in turn are flanked by two more.

Where Leonardo gave us expressive faces, Michelangelo lets the bodies do the talking. The two supporters strain to hold up Christ's body, and in their tension we, too, feel the great weight and tragedy of their dead god. Michelangelo expresses the divine through the human form.

Raphael—*Pope Julius II* (1511)

The new worldliness of the Renaissance even reached the Church. Pope Julius II, who was more a swaggering conquistador than a pious pope, set out to rebuild Rome in Renaissance style (including hiring Michelangelo to paint the Vatican's Sistine Chapel).

Raphael has captured this complex man with perfect realism and psychological insight. On the one hand the pope is an imposing pyramid of power, with fancy rings boasting of wealth and success. But at the same time he's a bent and broken man, his throne backed into a corner, with an expression that seems to say, "Is this all there is?"

In fact, the great era of Florence and Rome was coming to an end. With Raphael's death in 1520, the Renaissance shifted to Venice.

• *Return to the long Room 9.*

Venetian Renaissance (1510–1600)

Big change. The canvases are bigger, the colors brighter. Madonnas and saints are being replaced by goddesses and heroes. And there are nudes—not Michelangelo's lumps of noble, knotted muscle, but smooth-skinned, sexy, golden centerfolds.

Venice got wealthy by trading with the luxurious and exotic East. Its happy-go-lucky art style shows a taste for the finer things in life. But despite all the flashiness and fleshiness, Venetian art still keeps a sense of Renaissance balance.

Titian—*Bacchus and Ariadne* (1523)

In this Greek myth, Bacchus, the God of Wine, comes leaping into the picture, his red cape blowing behind him, to cheer up

Ariadne (far left), who has been jilted by her lover. Bacchus' motley entourage rattles cymbals, bangs on tambourines, and literally shakes a leg.

Man and animal mingle in this pre-Christian orgy, with leopards, a snake, a dog, and the severed head and leg of an ass ready for the barbecue. Man and animal also literally "mix" in the satyrs—part man, part goat. The fat, sleepy guy in the background has had too much.

Titian uses a pyramid composition to balance an otherwise unbalanced scene. Follow Ariadne's gaze up to the peak of Bacchus' flowing cape, then down along the snake handler's spine to the lower right corner. In addition he "balances" the picture with harmonious colors—most everyone is dressed/undressed in greens and golds that blend into the landscape, while the two main figures stand out with loud splotches of red.

Tintoretto—*The Origin of the Milky Way*

In another classical myth, the god Jupiter places his illegitimate son, baby Hercules, at his wife's breast. Juno says, "Wait a minute.

That's not my baby!" Her milk spurts upward, becoming the Milky Way, and downward, becoming lilies.

Tintoretto places us right up in the clouds, among the gods who swirl around at every angle. An "X" composition unites it all—Juno slants one way while Jupiter slants the other. The result is more dramatic and complex than the stable pyramids of Leonardo and Raphael. Also, notice how Jupiter appears to be flying almost right at us. Such shocking 3-D effects hint at the Baroque art we'll see later.

• *Exit Room 9 at the far end, turning left into the small Room 16 for Dutch art.*

Northern Protestant Art (1600–1700)

We switch from CinemaScope to a nine-inch TV—smaller canvases, subdued colors, everyday scenes, and not even a bare shoulder.

Money shapes art. While Italy had wealthy aristocrats and the powerful Catholic Church to purchase art, the North's patrons were middle-class, hardworking, Protestant merchants. They wanted simple, cheap, no-nonsense pictures to decorate their homes and offices. Greek gods and Virgin Marys were out, hometown folks and hometown places were in—portraits, landscapes, still-lifes, and slice-of-life scenes. Painted with great attention to detail, this is art meant not to wow or preach at you, but to be enjoyed and lingered over. Sightsee.

Vermeer—*A Young Woman Standing at a Virginal*

Here we have a simple interior of a Dutch home with a prim virgin playing a "virginal." We've surprised her and she pauses to look up at us. Contrast this quiet scene with, say, Titian's bombastic, orgiastic Bacchus and Ariadne.

The Dutch took (and still take) great pride in the orderliness of their small homes. Vermeer, by framing off such a small world to look at—from the blue chair in the foreground to the wall in

back—forces us to appreciate the tiniest details, the beauty of everyday things. We can meditate on the shawl, the tiles lining the floor, the subtle shades of the white wall and, most of all, the pale diffused light that soaks in from the window. The painting of a nude cupid on the back wall only strengthens this virgin's purity.
• *Stroll down the long Room 28, turning left into Room 27.*

Rembrandt—*Belshazzar's Feast*
The wicked king has been feasting with God's sacred dinnerware when the meal is interrupted.

Belshazzar turns to see the finger of God, burning an ominous message into the wall that Belshazzar's number is up. As he turns, he knocks over a goblet of wine. We see the jewels and riches of his decadent life.

Rembrandt captures the scene at the most ironic moment. Belshazzar is about to be ruined. We know it, his guests know it, and judging by the look on his face, he's coming to the same conclusion.

Rembrandt's flair for the dramatic is accentuated by the strong contrast between light and dark. Most of his canvases are a rich, dark brown, with a few crucial details highlighted by a bright light.

Rembrandt—*Self-Portrait Aged 63*

Rembrandt throws the light of truth on . . . himself. This craggy self-portrait was done the year he died. Contrast it with one done three decades earlier (hanging nearby). Rembrandt, the greatest Dutch painter, started out as the successful, wealthy young genius of the art world. But he refused to crank out commercial works. Rembrandt painted things that he believed in but no one would invest in—family members, down-to-earth Bible scenes, and self-portraits like these.

Here, Rembrandt surveys the wreckage of his independent life. He was bankrupt, his mistress had just died, and he had also buried several of his children. We see a disillusioned, well-worn, but proud old genius.
• *Return to the long Room 28.*

BAROQUE (1600–1700)

Rubens

This room is full of big, colorful, emotional works by Peter Paul Rubens and others from Catholic Flanders (Belgium). While Protestant and democratic Europe painted simple scenes, Catholic and aristocratic countries turned to the style called "Baroque." Baroque art took what was flashy in Venetian art and

made it flashier, gaudy and made it gaudier, dramatic and made it shocking.

Rubens painted anything that would raise your pulse—battles, miracles, hunts and, especially, fleshy women with dimples on all four cheeks. The Judgment of Paris, for instance, is little more than an excuse for a study of the female nude, showing front, back, and profile all on one canvas.

• *Exit Room 28 at the far end. To the left, in Room 30, you'll see the large canvas of . . .*

Van Dyck—*Charles I on Horseback*

Kings and bishops used the grandiose Baroque style to impress the masses with their power. This portrait of England's Catholic, French-educated, Divine Right king portrays him as genteel and refined, yet very much in command. Charles is placed on a huge horse to accentuate his power. The horse's small head makes sure that little Charles isn't dwarfed.

Charles ruled firmly as a Catholic king in a Protestant country until England's Civil War (1648), when Charles' genteel head was separated from his refined body by Cromwell and company.

Van Dyck's portrait style set the tone for all the stuffy, boring portraits of British aristocrats who wished to be portrayed as sophisticated gentlemen—whether they were or not.

• *For the complete opposite of a stuffy portrait bust, backpedal into Room 29 for . . .*

Velázquez—*The Rokeby Venus*

Though horny Spanish kings bought Titian-esque centerfolds by the gross, this work by the king's personal court painter is the first (and, for over a century, the only) Spanish nude. Like a Venetian model, she's posed diagonally across the canvas with flaring red, white, and grey fabrics to highlight her white skin and inflame our passion. About the only concession to Spanish modesty is the false reflection in the mirror—if it really showed what the angle should show, Velázquez would have needed two mirrors . . . and a new job.

• *Turning your left cheek to hers, tango into Room 32.*

Michelangelo Merisi de Caravaggio—*The Supper at Emmaus*

After Jesus was crucified, he rose from the dead and appeared without warning to some of his followers. Jesus just wants a quiet meal, but the man in green, suddenly realizing who he's eating with, is

about to jump out of his chair in shock. To the right, a man spreads his hands in amazement, bridging the distance between Christ and us by sticking his hand in our face.

Baroque took reality and exaggerated it. Most artists amplified the prettiness, but Caravaggio exaggerated the grittiness. He shocked the public by using real, ugly, unhaloed people in Bible scenes. Caravaggio's paintings look like a wet dog smells. Reality.

We've come a long way since the first medieval altarpieces that wrapped holy people in a golden foil. From the torn shirts, to the five o'clock shadows, to the uneven part in Jesus' hair, we are witnessing a very human miracle.

• *Leave the Caravaggio room under the sign reading "East Wing, painting from 1700–1900," into Room 33.*

FRENCH ROCOCO (1700–1800)

As Europe's political and economic center shifted from Italy to France, Louis XIV's court at Versailles became its cultural hub. Every aristocrat spoke French, dressed French and bought French

paintings. The Rococo art of Louis's successors was as frilly, sensual, and suggestive as the decadent French court at Versailles. We see their rosy-cheeked portraits and their fantasies: lords and ladies at play in classical gardens, where mortals and gods cavort together.
• *One of the finest examples is the tiny . . .*

Boucher—*Pan and Syrinx* (1739)

Rococo art is like a Rubens that got shrunk in the wash—smaller, lighter pastel colors, frillier and more delicate than the Baroque style. Same dimples, though.
• *Enter Room 34.*

BRITISH (1800–1850)

Constable—*The Hay Wain*

The more reserved British were more comfortable cavorting with nature rather than with the lofty gods. Come-as-you-are poets like Wordsworth found the same ecstasy just being outside.

Constable spent hours in the out-of-doors, capturing the simple majesty of billowing clouds, billowing trees, and everyday human activities. Even British portraits (by Thomas Gainsborough and others) placed refined lords and ladies amid idealized greenery.

This simple style—believe it or not—was considered shocking in its day. The rough, thick paint and crude country settings scandalized art lovers used to the high-falutin', prettified sheen of Baroque and Rococo.
• *Take a hike and enjoy the English country garden ambience of this room.*

Turner—*The Fighting Téméraire*

Constable's landcape was about to be paved over by the Industrial Revolution. Soon, machines began to replace humans, factories belched smoke over Constable's hay cart, and cloud gazers had to punch the clock. Romantics tried to resist it, lauding the forces of nature and natural human emotions in the face of technological "progress." But, alas, here a modern steamboat symbolically drags a famous but obsolete sailing battleship off into the sunset to be destroyed.

Turner—*Rain, Steam and Speed*

A train emerges from the depths of fog, rushing across a bridge toward us. The red-orange glow of the engine's furnace burns like embers of a fire. (Turner was fascinated by how light penetrates haze.)

Through the blur of paints, the outline of a bridge is visible, while in the center, shadowy figures (spirits?) head down to the river.

Turner's messy, colorful style gives us our first glimpse into the modern art world—he influenced the Impressionists. Turner takes an ordinary scene (like Constable), captures the play of light with messy paints (like Impressionists), and charges it with mystery (like wow).

• *London's Tate Gallery (see page 85) has an enormous collection of Turner's work. For now, enter Room 41, past some interesting Pre-Raphaelite paintings (more in the Tate, as well). Pass the door that leads downstairs to the café and WC, and turn right, into Room 43. The Impressionist paintings are scattered through Rooms 43-46.*

IMPRESSIONISM AND BEYOND (1850–1910)

For 500 years, a great artist was someone who could paint the real world with perfect accuracy. Then along came the camera and, click, the artist was replaced by a machine. But unemployed artists refused to go the way of the Fighting Téméraire.

They couldn't match the camera for painstaking detail, but they could match it—even beat it—in capturing the fleeting moment, the candid pose, the play of light and shadow, the quick impression a scene makes on you. A new breed of artists burst out of the stuffy confines of the studio. They set up their canvases in the open air or carried their notebooks into a crowded café, dashing off quick sketches in order to catch a momentary . . . impression.

• *Start with the misty Monet train station.*

Monet—*Gare St. Lazare* (1877) *(bottom of page 82)*
Claude Monet, the father of Impressionism, was more interested in
the play of light off his subject than the subject itself. Here, the sun
filters through the glass roof of the train station and is refiltered
through the clouds of steam.

Renoir—*The Umbrellas* (1880s)
View this from about 15 feet away. It's a nice
scene of many-colored umbrellas. Now move
in close. The "scene" breaks up into almost
random patches of bright colors. The "gray"
dress of the woman in the foreground is actually built from blotches of lavender, blue,
green, yellow and orange. Up close it looks
like a mess, but when you back up to a proper
distance, Voilà! It shimmers. This kind of
rough, coarse brushwork (where you can actually see the brushstroke) is one of the telltale
signs of Impressionism.

Manet—*The Waitress (Corner of a Café-Concert)*
Imagine how mundane (and therefore shock-
ing) Manet's quick "impression" of this café
must have been to a public that was raised on
Greek gods, luscious nudes, and glowing
Madonnas.

Degas—*Miss La La at the Cirque Fernando* (1879)
Degas, the master of the candid snapshot, enjoyed catching every-
day scenes at odd angles.
• *Into Room 44, the biggest canvas, on your left, is . . .*

Seurat—*Bathers at Asnieres* (1883)
Seurat took the Impressionist
color technique to its logical
extreme. These figures are
"built," dot by dot, like newspaper photos, using small
points of different colors.
Only at a distance do they
blend together to make a hat,
a patch of "green" grass, or a
bather.

Van Gogh—*Sunflowers* (1888)

In military terms, van Gogh was the point-man of his culture. He went ahead of his co-horts, explored the unknown, and caught a bullet young. He added emotion to Impressionism, infusing his love of life even into inanimate objects. These sunflowers, painted with characteristic swirling brush-strokes, shimmer and writhe in either agony or ecstasy—depending on your own mood.

Van Gogh painted these during his stay in southern France, a time of frenzied painting when he himself hovered between agony and ecstasy, bliss and madness. Within two years of painting this, he shot himself.

In his day van Gogh was a penniless nobody, selling only one painting in his whole career. Today, a *Sunflowers* (one of a half dozen versions he did) sells for $40 million (a salary of about $5,000 a day for 70 years), and it's not even his highest-priced painting. Hmm.

Cézanne—*Bathers* (*Les Grandes Baigneuses)*

These Bathers are arranged in strict triangles *à la* Leonardo—the five nudes on the left form one triangle, the seated nude on the right forms another, and even the background trees and clouds are triangular patterns of paint.

Cézanne uses the Impressionist technique of building a figure with dabs of paint (though his "dabs" are often larger-sized "cube" shapes) to make more solid, 3-D geometrical figures in the style of the Renaissance. In the process, his cube shapes helped inspire a radical new art style—"Cube"-ism—bringing us into the 20th century.

Monet—*Water Lilies* (1916)

We've traveled from medieval spirituality to Renaissance realism to Baroque elegance and Impressionist colors. Before you spill out into the 21st-century hubbub of busy London, relax for a second in Monet's garden at Giverny near Paris. Monet planned an artificial garden, rechanneled a stream, built a bridge, and planted these water lilies—a living work of art, a small section of order and calm in a hectic world.

TATE GALLERY TOUR

7

The Tate is the world's best collection of British art. This is people's art, with realistic paintings rooted in the people, landscape, and stories of the British Isles.

Orientation

Hours: Monday–Saturday 10:00–17:50, Sunday 14:00–17:50, closed on December 24, 25, 26.
Cost: Free
Tour length: One hour
Getting there: Subway to Pimlico (and seven-minute walk) or bus 88 or 77A, or ten-minute walk along Thames from Big Ben.
Information: Free current map at information desk. Free tours offered (normally 11:00–British, Noon–Impressionism, 14:00–Turner, 15:00–20th century). Tel. 0171/887-8000, recorded information 0171/887-8008, e-mail: information@tate.org.uk. Great bookshop.
Cloakroom: Free
Photography: Without a flash is permitted.
Cuisine art: Coffee shop (affordable gourmet buffet line) and restaurant (expensive, but delightful atmosphere).
Starring: Hogarth, Gainsborough, Reynolds, Blake, Constable, Pre-Raphaelites, and Turner.

The Tour Begins

Orient yourself from the rotunda near the entrance, facing the long central sculpture gallery. The traditional British collection—the core of what we'll see—is in the left half of the museum. The 20th century is to the right. The Turner collection in the Clore Gallery is also to the right.

Warning: Expect changes. The Tate is shedding its wacky

TATE GALLERY OVERVIEW

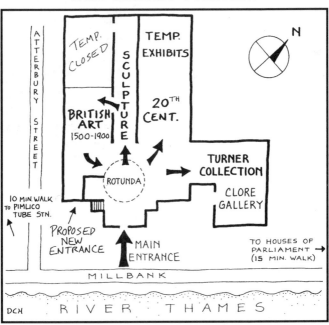

modern collection (to be housed in a new museum—opening in May 2000—on London's South Bank) and focusing on what it does best: British art. Until the Tate settles down after the millennium, a painting-by-painting tour is impossible. In this chapter, we'll keep the big picture, seeing the essence of each artist and style, then let the Tate surprise us with its ever-changing wardrobe of paintings.

• *From the rotunda, walk down the central gallery, turn left and find Room 1.*

EARLY BRITISH ART (1500–1800)

British artists painted people, horses, countrysides, and scenes from daily life, all done realistically and without the artist passing judgment. (Substance over style.) What you won't see here is the kind of religious art so popular elsewhere. The largely Protestant English abhorred the "graven images" of Catholic saints and the Virgin Mary. Many were even destroyed during the 16th-century Reformation. They preferred landscapes of the quaint English countryside and flesh-and-blood English folk.

Portrait of Lord and Lady Whoevertheyare

These stuffy portraits of a beef-fed society try to make uncultured people look delicate and refined. English country houses often had a long hall built specially to hang family portraits. You could stroll along and see your noble forebears looking down their noses at you. Britain's upper crust in the 1600s had little interest in art other than as a record of themselves along with their possessions—their wives, children, clothes and guns.

You'll see plenty more portraits in the Tate, right up to modern times. Each era had its own style, some stern and dignified, some more relaxed and elegant.

Stubbs—Various Pictures of Horses

In the 1700s, as British art came into its own, painters started doing more than just portraits. Stubbs was the Michelangelo of horses, studying their anatomy and painting them with incredible detail and realism. Normally, he'd paint the horses first on a blank canvas, then fill in the background landscape around them.

William Hogarth (1697–1764)

Hogarth loved the theatre. "My picture is my stage," he said, "and my men and women my players." The curtain goes up and we see

one scene that tells a whole story, often satirizing English high society. Hogarth often painted series based on popular novels of the time.

William Hogarth revelled in the darker side of "merry olde England." An 18th-century Charles Dickens, Hogarth's best paintings were slices of real England. Not content to paint just pretty portraits, he chose models from real life and put them into real-life scenes.

A born Londoner, Hogarth loved every gritty aspect of the big city. You could find him in seedy pubs and brothels, at the half-price ticket booth in Leicester Square, at prizefights, cockfights, duels and public executions—sketchpad in hand. With biting satire, he exposed the hypocrisy of the upper class . . . and exposed the upper classes to the hidden poverty of society's underbelly.

BRITISH COLLECTION

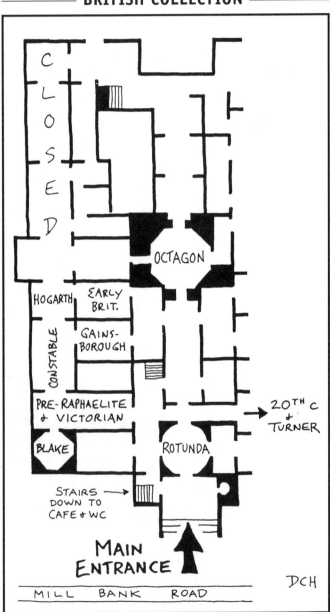

C
L
O
S
E
D

OCTAGON

HOGARTH

EARLY BRIT.

CONSTABLE

GAINS-BOROUGH

PRE-RAPHAELITE & VICTORIAN

20TH C & TURNER

BLAKE

ROTUNDA

STAIRS → DOWN TO CAFE & WC

MAIN ENTRANCE

DCH

MILL BANK ROAD

Thomas Gainsborough (1727–1788)

Portraits were still the bread and butter for painters, and Thomas Gainsborough was one of the best. His specialty was showcasing the elegant, educated women of his generation. The results were always natural and never stuffy. The cheeks get rosier, the poses more relaxed, the colors brighter and more pastel, showing the influence of the refined French culture of the court at Versailles. His models' clear, Ivory-soap complexions stand out from the swirling greenery of the background.

Reynolds and the "Grand Style" (1750–1800)

Real life wasn't worthy to be painted. So said Britain's Royal Academy. People, places, and things had to be gussied up with Greek columns, symbolism, and great historic moments, ideally from classical Greece.

By combining history and portraits, they could turn Lord Milquetoast into a heroic Greek patriot, or Lady Bagbody into the Vénus de Milo. Combining the Grand Style with landscapes, you got Versailles-type settings of classical monuments amid landscaped greenery.

Sir Joshua Reynolds, the pillar of England's art establishment, stood for all that was noble, upright, tasteful, rational, brave, clean, reverent, and boring. According to Reynolds, art was meant to elevate the viewer, appealing to his rational nature and filling him with noble sentiment.

Since so much of the art we'll see from here on was painted in the looming shadow of Reynolds, and since his technique and morals are flawless, let's dedicate a minute's silence to his painting. Fifty-nine. Fifty-eight. I'll be in the next room.

Constable's Landscapes (1776–1837)

While the Royal Academy thought Nature needed makeup, Constable thought She was just fine. He painted the English landscape just as it is, realistically, and without idealizing it.

Constable's style became more "Impressionistic" near the end of

his life—messier brushwork. He often painted full-scale "sketches" of works he'd perfect later (such as the Salisbury cathedral).

It's rare to find a Constable (or any British) landscape that doesn't have the mark of man in it—a cottage, hay cart, country lane, or field-hand. For him, the English countryside and its people were one.

Cloudy skies are one of Constable's trademarks. Appreciate the effort involved in sketching ever-changing cloud patterns for hours on end. His subtle genius wasn't fully recognized in his lifetime, and he was forced to paint portraits for his keep. The neglect caused him to tell a friend: "Can it therefore be wondered at that I paint continual storms?"

Other Landscapes

Compare Constable's unpretentious landscapes with others you'll find in the Tate. Some artists mixed landscapes with intense human emotion to produce huge, colorful canvases of storms, burning sunsets, towering clouds, crashing waves, all dwarfing puny humans. Others made supernatural, religious fantasy-scapes. Artists in the "Romantic" style saw the most intense human emotions reflected in the drama and mystery in Nature. God is found within Nature, and Nature is charged with the grandeur and power of God.

THE INDUSTRIAL REVOLUTION (1800–1900)

Think of England at mid-century. New-fangled inventions were everywhere. Railroads laced the land. You could fall asleep in Edinburgh and wake up in London, a trip that used to take days or weeks. But along with technology came factories coating towns with soot, urban poverty, regimentation, and clock-punching. Machines replaced honest laborers, and once-noble Man was viewed as a naked ape.

Strangely, you'll see little of the modern world in paintings of the time—except in reaction to it. Many artists rebelled against "progress" and the modern world. They looked back to ancient Greece as a happier, more enlightened time (Neo-classicism of Reynolds). Or to the Middle Ages (Pre-Raphaelites). Or they escaped the dirty cities to commune with nature (Romantics). Or found a new spirituality in intense human emotions (dramatic scenes from history or literature). Or they left our world altogether. (Which brings us to . . .)

William Blake

At the age of four, Blake saw the face of God. A few years later, he ran across a flock of angels swinging in a tree. Twenty years later he was living in a rundown London flat with an illiterate wife, scratching out a thin existence as an engraver. But even in this squalor, ignored by all but a few fellow artists, he still had his heavenly visions, and he described them in poems and paintings.

One of the original space cowboys, Blake was also a unique painter who is often classed with the "Romantics" because he painted in a fit of ecstatic inspiration rather than by studied technique. He painted angels, archangels, thrones, and dominions rather than the dull material world. While Britain was conquering the world with guns and Nature with machines, and while his fellow Londoners were growing rich, fat, and self-important, Blake turned his gaze inward, painting the glorious visions of the soul.

Blake's work hangs in a darkened room to protect the watercolors. Enter his mysterious world and let your pupils dilate opium-wide.

His pen and watercolor sketches glow with an unearthly aura. In visions of heaven and hell, his figures have superhero musculature. The colors are almost translucent.

Blake saw the material world as bad, trapping the divine spark inside each of our bodies and keeping us from true communion with God. Blake's prints illustrate his views on the ultimate weakness of material, scientific man. Despite their Greek-god anatomy, his men look noble, but tragically lost.

A famous poet as well as painter, Blake summed up his distrust of the material world in a poem addressed to "The God of this World," that is, Satan:

> *Though thou art worshipped by the names divine*
> *Of Jesus and Jehovah, thou art still*
> *The son of morn in weary night's decline,*
> *The lost traveler's dream under the hill.*

PRE-RAPHAELITES (1850–1880)

Millais, Rossetti, Waterhouse, Burne-Jones, etc.

You'll see medieval damsels in dresses and knights in tights, legendary lovers from poetry, and even a very human Virgin Mary as a delicate young woman. The women wear flowing dresses, with

long wavy hair and delicate, elongated, curving bodies. Beautiful.

You won't find Pre-Raphaelites selling flowers at the airport, but this "Brotherhood" of young British artists had a cult-like intensity. (You may see the initials P.R.B. (Pre-Raphaelite Brotherhood) by the artist's signature in some paintings.) After generations of the pompous Grand Style art, the Pre-Raphaelites finally said enough's enough.

They returned to a style "Pre-Raphael." Their art was intended to be "medieval" in its simple style, in the melancholy mood, and often in subject matter. "Truth to Nature" was their slogan. Like the Impressionists who followed, they donned their scarves, barged out of the stuffy studio and set up outdoors, painting trees, streams, and people as they really were. Despite the Pre-Raphaelite claim to paint life just as it is, this is so beautiful it hurts. Be prepared to suffer, unless your heart is made of stone.

This is art from the cult of femininity, worshipping Woman's haunting beauty, compassion, and depth of soul. (Proto-feminism or retro-chauvinism?) The artists' wives and lovers were their models and muses, and the art echoed their love lives. The people are surrounded by nature at its most beautiful, with every de-

tail painted crystal-clear. Even without the people, there is a mood of melancholy.

The Pre-Raphaelites hated gushy sentimentality and overacting. Their subjects—even in the face of great tragedy, high passions, and moral dilemmas—barely raise an eyebrow. Outwardly, they're reflective, accepting their fate. But subtle gestures and sinuous posture speak volumes. These volumes were footnoted by small objects with symbolic importance placed around them: red flowers denoting passion, lilies for purity, pets for fidelity, and so on.

The colors—greens, blues, and reds—are bright and clear, with everything evenly lit so we see every detail. To get the luminous color, they painted a thin layer of bright paint over a pure white undercoat, which subtly "shines" through. These canvases radiate a pure spirituality, like stained glass windows.

Victorian (1837–1901)

Middle-class Brits loved to see Norman Rockwell-style scenes from everyday life. The style has Pre-Raphaelite realism, but is too sentimental for Pre-Raphaelite tastes.

We see families and ordinary people eating, working, and relaxing. Some works tug at the heartstrings, with scenes of parting couples, the grief of death, or the joy of families reuniting. Dramatic scenes from popular literature get the heart beating. There's the occasional touching look at the plight of the honest poor, reminiscent of Dickens. And many paintings warn us to be good little boys and girls, by showing the consequences of a life of sin.

Stand for a while and enjoy the exquisite realism and human emotions of these Victorian works . . . real people painted realistically. Get your fill, because beloved Queen Victoria is about to check out, the modern world is coming, and with it, new art to express modern attitudes.

• *To help ease the transition . . .*

The Turner Collection

J. M. W. Turner (1775–1851)

The Tate has the world's best collection of Turners. Walking through his life's work, you can trace his progression from a painter of realistic historical scenes, through his wandering years, to "Impressionist" paintings of color-and-light patterns.

• *The Turner Collection is in the Clore Gallery, the wing that juts out to the right of the Tate. The main entrance is outside, but you can also enter through Room 18, on the other side of the rotunda.*

Start in the large square Room T1, marked "High Art, History, and the Sublime." From these early paintings, the collection runs roughly chronologically as you work your way through to Room T9.

Room T1—High Art, History, and the Sublime

Trained in the Reynolds school of grandiose epics, Turner painted the obligatory big canvases of great moments in history—The Battle of Waterloo, Hannibal in the Alps, Destruction of Sodom, The Lost Traveler's Checks, Jason and the Argonauts, and various shipwrecks. Not content to crank them out in the traditional staid manner, he sets them in expansive landscapes. Nature's stormy mood mirrors the human events, but is so grandiose it dwarfs them.

THE TURNER COLLECTION

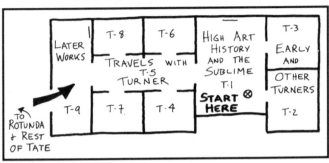

LATER WORKS

T-8   T-6

TRAVELS WITH T-5 TURNER

HIGH ART HISTORY AND THE SUBLIME T-1
START ⊗ **HERE**

T-3 EARLY AND

OTHER TURNERS

T-9   T-7   T-4

T-2

TO ROTUNDA & REST OF TATE

Room T2
See his self-portrait as a young man, and read details of his life.

Room T3—Travels with Turner
Turner's true love was Nature. And he was a born hobo. Oblivious to the wealth and fame that his early paintings gave him, he set out traveling—mostly on foot—throughout England and the Continent, with a rucksack full of sketchpads and painting gear.

He found the "Sublime" not in the studio or in church, but in the overwhelming power of Nature. The landscapes throb with life and motion.

• *Walk up the hallway (T5) back towards the Tate, popping into the four rooms along the way.*

Room T5—Italy: Landscape and Antiquity
Turner visited the great museums of Italy, drawing inspiration from the Renaissance masters. He painted the classical monuments and Renaissance architecture. He copied masterpieces, learned, assimi-

lated, and fused a great variety of styles—a true pan-European vision.

Room T7—Venice
I know what color the *palazzo* is. But what color is it at sunset? Or after filtering through the watery haze that hangs over Venice? Can I

paint the glowing haze itself? Maybe if I combine two different colors, and smudge the paint on . . .

Venice titilated Turner's lust for reflected light. This room contains both finished works and unfinished sketches . . . uh, which is which?

Room T8 - Marine and Coastal Subjects
Seascapes were his specialty, with waves, clouds, mist, and sky churning and mixing together, all driven by the same forces.

Turner used oils like many painters use watercolors. First he'd lay down a background (a "wash") of large patches of color, then add a few dabs of paint to suggest a figure. The final product lacked photographic clarity but showed the power and constant change in the forces of Nature. He was perhaps the most prolific painter ever, with some 2,000 finished paintings and 20,000 sketches and watercolors.

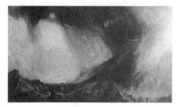

Room T9—Later Works
The older he got, the messier both he and his paintings became. He was wealthy, but died in a rundown dive where he'd set up house with a prostitute. Yet the colors here are brighter and the subjects less pessimistic than in the dark brooding early canvases. His last works—whether landscape, religious, or classical scene—are a blur and swirl of colors in motion, lit by the sun or a lamp burning through the mist. They're "modern," in that the subject is less important than the style. You'll have to read the title to "get" it.

You could argue that an Englishman helped invent Impressionism, a generation before Monet and ilk boxed the artistic ears of Paris in the 1880s. Turner's messy use of paint to portray reflected light "chunneled" its way to France to inspire the Impressionists.

BRITISH
LIBRARY
TOUR

8

london

The British Empire built its greatest monuments out of paper. It's in literature that England has made her lasting contribution to history and the arts. Opened in 1998 in a fine new building, this national archives of Britain has more than 12 million books, 180 miles of shelving, and the deepest basement in London. We'll concentrate on a handful of documents—literary and historical—that changed the course of history. Start with the top 12 stops (described in this tour), then stray according to your interests.

Orientation

Open: Monday–Saturday 9:30–18:00, Sunday 11:00–17:00
Cost: Free
Tour length: One hour
Getting there: Tube to King's Cross/St. Pancras Station. Leaving the station, turn right and walk a block to 96 Euston Road. (Note that the British Library is no longer housed within the British Museum but has moved to its new location near King's Cross station.)
Information: Tours are offered usually Monday, Wednesday, Friday, and Sunday at 15:00, Saturday at 10:30 and 15:00 (one hour, £3, for schedule and to reserve, call 0171/412-7332 or see www.bl.uk; library telephone: 0171/412-7000).
Cloakroom: Free
No-no's: No photography, smoking, or chewing gum.
Cuisine art: The library's restaurant and café, while nothing special from an eating point of view, have a 50-foot-tall wall of 65,000 old books given to the people by King George IV in 1823. This mother of all bookshelves is pretty high-tech behind glass, movable and with movable lifts.
Starring: Magna Carta, Bibles, Shakespeare, and the Beatles.

BRITISH LIBRARY TOUR

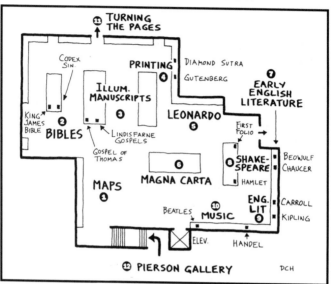

The Tour Begins

Entering the library courtyard you'll see a huge statue. It depicts the poet William Blake's vision of Isaac Newton bending forward to plot—with a pair of dividers—the immensity of the universe. This statue, symbolizing the union of nature and science, poetry and art, expresses the library's purpose: to preserve the record of our endless search for truth.

Stepping inside you'll see the information desk. The cloakroom, WC, and café are to the right. The tiny but exciting area you'll tour is to the left under a sign marked Exhibitions.

The priceless literary and historical treasures of the collection are in this one carefully designed and well-lit room. The adjoining "Turning the Pages" computer room is in the back. Down a few steps you'll find the history of printing "workshop" and the Pierson Gallery (with its recommended History of Children's Lit exhibit).

1. Maps

Navigate the wall of historic maps from left to right. One shows Britain in 1250. Another is the Christian world of 1260 with Jerusalem in the middle and Jesus on top. Below that, a 1490 map shows the best map Columbus could get. And then a 1506 map shows the first depiction of America . . . as part of Asia. By 1562 the eastern coast of North America was fairly accurate. And you could plan your next trip with Mercator's 1570 map of Europe.

2. Bibles

My favorite excuse for not learning a foreign language is: "If English was good enough for Jesus Christ, it's good enough for me!" I don't know what that has to do with anything, but obviously Jesus didn't speak English—nor did Moses or Isaiah or Paul or any other Bible authors or characters. As a result, our present-day English Bible is not directly from the mouth and pen of these religious figures, but the fitful product of centuries of evolution and translation.

The Bible is not a single book; it's an anthology of books by many authors from different historical periods writing in different languages (usually Hebrew or Greek). So there are three things that editors must consider in compiling the most accurate Bible: 1) deciding which books actually belong; 2) finding the oldest and most accurate version of each book; and 3) translating it accurately.

Codex Sinaiticus (c. A.D. 350)

The oldest complete "Bible" in existence (along with one in the Vatican), this is one of the first attempts to collect various books together into one authoritative anthology. It's in Greek, the language in which most of the New Testament was written. The Old Testament portions are Greek translations from the original Hebrew. This particular Bible, and the nearby *Codex Alexandrus* (A.D. 425), contain some books not included in most modern English Bibles. (Even today Catholic Bibles contain books not found in Protestant Bibles.)

Fragment of an Unknown Gospel and The Gospel of Thomas

Here are pieces—scraps of papyrus—of two such books that didn't make it into our modern Bible. The "unknown" Gospel (an account of the life of Jesus of Nazareth) is as old a Christian manuscript as any in existence. Remember, the Gospels weren't written down for a full generation after Jesus died, and the oldest surviving manuscripts are from later than that. So why isn't this early version of Jesus' life part of our Bible right up there with Matthew, Mark, Luke, and John? Possibly because some early Bible editors didn't like the story it told about Jesus not found in the four accepted Gospels.

The "Gospel of Thomas" gives an even more radical picture of Jesus. This Jesus preaches enlightenment by mystical knowledge. He seems to be warning people against looking to gurus for the answers, a Christian version of "If you meet the Buddha on the road, kill him." This fragment dates from A.D. 150, more than a century after Jesus' death, but that's probably not the only reason why it's not in our Bible (after all, the Gospel of John is generally dated at A.D. 100). Rather, the message, which threatened established church leaders, may have been too scary to include in the Bible— whether Jesus said it or not.

The Authorized Version, or King James Bible (1611)

Jesus spoke Aramaic, a form of Hebrew. His words were written down in Greek. Greek manuscripts were translated into Latin, the language of medieval monks and scholars. By 1400 there was still no English version of the Bible, though only a small percentage of the population understood Latin. A few brave reformers risked death to make translations into English and print them with Gütenberg's new invention. Within two centuries English translations were both legal and popular.

The King James version (done during his reign) has been the most popular English translation. Fifty scholars worked for four years, borrowing heavily from previous translations, to produce the work. Its impact on the English language was enormous, making Elizabethan English something of the standard, even after all those *thees* and *thous* fell out of fashion in everyday speech.

In our century, many new translations are both more accurate (based on better scholarship and original manuscripts) and more readable, using modern speech patterns.

3. Lindisfarne Gospels (A.D. 698) and Illuminated Manuscripts

Throughout the Middle Ages, Bibles had to be reproduced by hand. This was a painstaking process usually done by monks for a rich patron. This beautifully illustrated ("illuminated") collection of the four Gospels is the most magnificent of medieval British monk-u-scripts. The text is in Latin, the language of scholars ever since the Roman empire, but the elaborate decoration mixes Irish, classical, and even Byzantine forms.

These Gospels are a reminder that Christianity almost didn't make it in Europe. After the Fall of Rome (which had established Christianity as the official religion), much of Europe reverted to its pagan ways. This was the time of

Beowulf, when people worshiped woodland spirits, smurfs, and terrible Teutonic gods. It took dedicated Irish missionaries 500 years to re-establish the faith on the Continent. Lindisfarne, an obscure monastery of Irish monks on an island off the east coast of England, was one of the few beacons of light after the Fall of Rome, tending the embers of civilization through the long night of the Dark Ages. (You can virtually flip through the Lindisfarne Gospels in the adjacent "Turning the Pages" computer room.)

Browse through more illuminated manuscripts (in the cases behind the Lindisfarne Gospels). This is some of the finest art from what we call the "Dark Ages." The little intimate details offer a rare and fascinating peek into medieval life.

4. Printing

Diamond Sutra—a scroll from 868—is the earliest dated printed document. Printing was common in Asia from the mid-eighth century—700 years before Gutenberg "invented" the printing press in Europe. In texts such as the Buddhist *Diamond Sutra*, carved blocks with Chinese characters were dipped into paint or ink to print. Notice also the fine wood block illustration. This was discovered in China in 1907.

The Gütenberg Bible (c. 1455)

It looks like just another monk-made Latin manuscript, but it's the first book printed in Europe. Printing is one of the most revolutionary inventions in history. Johann Gütenberg (c. 1397–1468), a German goldsmith, devised a convenient way to reproduce written materials quickly, neatly and cheaply—by printing with movable type. You scratch each letter onto a separate metal block, then arrange them into words, ink them up and press them onto paper. When one job was done you could reuse the same letters for a new one.

This simple idea had immediate and revolutionary consequences. Knowledge became cheap and accessible to a wide audience, not just the rich. Books became the "mass media" of Europe, linking people by a common set of ideas. And, like a drug, this increased knowledge only created demand for still more.

Suddenly the Bible was available for anyone to read. Church authorities, more interested in "protecting" than spreading the word of God, passed laws prohibiting the printing of Bibles. As the Church feared, when people read the Bible, they formed their own opinions of God's message, which was often different from the version spoon-fed to them by priests. In the resulting Reformation, Protestants broke away from the Catholic Church, confident they could read the Bible without a priest's help.

5. Leonardo da Vinci's Notebook

Pages from Leonardo's notebook show his genius for invention, his powerful curiosity, and his famous backward and inside-out handwriting.

6. Magna Carta

How did Britain, a tiny island with a few million people, come to rule a quarter of the world? Not by force but by law. The Magna Carta was the basis for England's constitutional system of government.

In the year 1215, England's barons rose in revolt against the slimy King John. After losing London, John was forced to negotiate. The barons presented him with a list of demands. John, whose rule was worthless without the support of the barons, had no choice but to fix his seal to it.

This was a turning point in the history of government. Kings had ruled by God-given authority. They were above the laws of men, acting however they pleased. Now for the first time there were limits—in writing—on how a king could treat his subjects. More generally, it established the idea of "due process"—that is, the government can't infringe on people's freedom without a legitimate legal reason. This small step became the basis for all constitutional governments, including yours.

A few days after John agreed to this original document, it was rewritten in legal form, and some 35 copies of this final version of the "Great Charter" were distributed around the kingdom (with two displayed here). You'll also see letters from the Pope supporting John and annulling Magna Carta. The Pope knew what a radical principle Magna Carta represented—the questioning of church-ordained authorities by the common rabble.

So what did this radical piece of paper actually say? Not much by today's standards. (Read the translated bit in the center case.) The specific demands had to do with things like inheritance taxes, the king's duties to widows and orphans, and so on. It wasn't the specific articles that were important, but the simple fact that the king had to abide by them as law.

Around the corner there are many more historical documents in the Library—letters by Queen Elizabeth I, Isaac Newton, Wellington, Gandhi, and so on. But for now, let's trace the evolution of . . .

7. Early English Literature

Four out of every five English words have been borrowed from other languages. The English language, like English culture (and London today), is a mix derived from foreign invaders. Some of the historic ingredients that make this cultural stew are:

1. The original Celtic tribesmen
2. Romans (A.D. 1–500)
3. Germanic tribes called Angles and Saxons (making English a Germanic language and naming the island "Angle-land"—England)
4. Vikings from Denmark (A.D. 800)
5. French-speaking Normans under William the Conqueror (1066–1250).

Beowulf (c. 1000)

This Anglo-Saxon epic poem written in Old English, the early version of our language, almost makes the hieroglyphics on the Rosetta Stone look easy. The manuscript here is from A.D. 1000, although the poem itself dates to about 750. This is the only existing medieval manuscript of this first English literary masterpiece.

In the story, the young hero Beowulf (BAY-uh-wolf) defeats two half-human monsters threatening the kingdom. Beowulf symbolized England's emergence from Dark Age chaos and barbarism.

Canterbury Tales (c. 1410)

Six hundred years later, England was Christian but it was hardly the pious, predictable, Sunday-school world we might imagine. Geoffrey Chaucer's bawdy collection of stories, told by pilgrims on their way to Canterbury, gives us the full range of life's experiences—happy, sad, silly, sexy, and pious. (Late in life, Chaucer wrote an apology for those works of his "that tend toward sin.")

While most serious literature of the time was written in scholarly Latin, *The Canterbury Tales* was written in Middle English, the language that developed when the French invasion (1066) added a Norman twist to Old English.

8. Shakespeare

William Shakespeare (1564–1616) is the greatest author in any language. Period. He expanded and helped define modern English. In one fell swoop, he made the language of everyday people as important as Latin. In the process, he gave us phrases like "one fell swoop" that we quote without knowing it's Shakespeare.

Perhaps as important was his insight into humanity. With his stock of great characters—Hamlet, Othello, Macbeth, Falstaff, Lear, Romeo and Juliet—he probed the psychology of human beings 300 years before Freud. Even today, his characters strike a familiar chord.

Shakespeare as a Collaborator

Shakespeare co-wrote a play titled *The Booke of Sir Thomas More*. Some scholars have wondered if maybe Shakespeare had help on other plays as well. After all, they reasoned, how could a journeyman actor, with little education, have written so many masterpieces? Modern scholars, though, unanimously agree that Shakespeare did indeed write the plays ascribed to him.

The Good and Bad Quarto of *Hamlet*

Shakespeare wrote his plays to be performed, not read. He published a few, but as his reputation grew, unauthorized "bootleg" versions also began to circulate. Some of these were written out by actors, trying (with faulty memories) to recreate a play they'd been in years before. Here are two different versions of *Hamlet*: "good" and "bad."

The Shakespeare First Folio (1623)

It wasn't until seven years after his death that this complete-works collection of his plays came out. The editors were friends and fellow actors.

The engraving of Shakespeare on the title page is one of only two likenesses done during his lifetime. Is this what he really looked like? No one knows. The best answer probably comes from his friend and fellow-poet Ben Jonson in the introduction on the facing page. He concludes: "Reader, look not on his picture, but his book."

9. Other Greats in English Literature

The rest of the "Beowulf/Chaucer wall" is a greatest hits sampling of British literature featuring the writing of Wordsworth, Blake, Dickens, and James Joyce. Especially interesting may be:

Coleridge—Xanadu, an Earthly Paradise
from *Kubla Khan*

One day Samuel Taylor Coleridge took opium. He fell asleep while reading about the fantastic palace of the Mongol emperor, Kubla Khan. During his three-hour drug-induced sleep, he composed in his head a poem of "from two- to three-hundred lines." When he woke up, he grabbed a pen and paper and "instantly and eagerly wrote down the lines that are here preserved." But just then, a visitor on business knocked at the door and kept Coleridge busy for an hour. When Coleridge finally kicked him out, he discovered that he'd forgotten the rest! The poem *Kubla Khan* is only a fragment, but it's still one of literature's masterpieces.

Coleridge (aided by his Muse-in-the-medicine-cabinet) was one of the Romantic poets. Check out his fellow Romantics—Keats, Shelley, and Wordsworth—nearby.

Dickens

In 1400, only a select few could read. By 1850 in England, almost everyone could and did. Charles Dickens (1812–1870) gave them their first taste of "literature." His books were serialized in periodicals and avidly read by the increasingly educated masses. The story is told of American fans gathering in mobs at the docks waiting with "Who shot J.R?" enthusiasm for the ship from England with the latest news of their favorite character.

Dickens also helped raise social concern for the underprivileged—of whom England had more than her share. When Dickens was 12 years old, his father was thrown into debtor's prison, and young Charles was put to work to support the family. The ordeal of poverty scarred him for life and gave him experiences he'd draw on later for books such as *Oliver Twist* and *David Copperfield*.

Lewis Carroll—The Original
Alice in Wonderland

I don't know if Lewis Carroll ever dipped into Coleridge's medicine jar or not, but his series of children's books makes Kubla Khan read like the phone book. Carroll was a stammerer, which made him uncomfortable around everyone but children. For them he created a fantasy world where grown-up rules and logic were turned upside-down.

10. Music

The Beatles

Future generations will have to judge whether this musical quartet ranks with artists like Dickens and Keats, but no one can deny its historical significance. The Beatles burst onto the scene in the early 1960s to unheard-of popularity. With their long hair and loud music, they brought counterculture and revolutionary ideas to the middle class, affecting the values of a whole generation.

Here are photos of John Lennon, Paul McCartney, and George Harrison before their fame (the fourth Beatle was Ringo Starr).

Most interesting are the manuscripts of song lyrics written by Lennon and McCartney, the two guiding lights of the group. "I

Wanna Hold Your Hand" was the song that launched them to superstardom. John's song, "Help," was the quickly written title song for one of the Beatles' movies. "Yesterday," by Paul, was recorded with guitar and voice backed by a string quartet—a touch of sophistication by the producer George Martin. Also glance at the rambling, depressed, cynical but humorous letter by John on the left. Is that a self-portrait at the bottom?

Music Manuscripts
Kind of an anti-climax after the Fab Four, I know, but here are manuscripts by Handel, Mozart, Beethoven, Schubert, and others.

11. Turning the Pages—Virtual Reality Room
For a chance to virtually flip though the pages of a few of the most precious books in the collection, drop by the Turning the Pages room. Grab a computer and let your fingers do the walking.

12. Pierson Gallery and Printing Workshop
As you leave, browse through the Pierson Gallery for a chance to trace the story of writing, the evolution of printing and bookmaking, and a great exhibit on the history of children's books. "W is for the woman, who not overly nice, made very short work of the three blind mice."

WESTMINSTER ABBEY TOUR

Westminster Abbey is the greatest church in the English-speaking world. England's kings and queens have been crowned and buried here since 1066. The history of Westminster Abbey and of England are almost the same. A thousand years of English history—3,000 tombs, the remains of 29 kings and queens, and hundreds of memorials—lie within its walls and under its stone slabs.

Orientation

Hours: Monday 9:30–16:45, Tuesday–Friday 9:00–16:45, Saturday 9:00–14:45, between services on Sunday, also open for half-price on Wednesday 18:00–19:45; last admission 60 minutes before closing. Mornings are most crowded. On weekdays, 15:00 is less crowded; come then and stay for the 17:00 evensong (not held on Wednesday).

Cost: £5, half-price Wednesday evening. Praying is free, thank God; use separate marked entrance.

Tour length: 90 minutes

Getting there: Near Big Ben and Houses of Parliament (tube: Westminster).

Information: Informative walkman tours cost £2 (offered until 15:00 weekdays or until 13:00 Saturdays). Vergers, the church equivalent of a bat boy, give more entertaining guided tours for £3 (up to 6/day, 90 min, tel. 0171/222-7110 to get times). Tour themes are the historic church, the personalities buried here, and the great coronations.

Evensong is on Mondays, Tuesdays, Thursdays, and Fridays at 17:00, Saturday and Sunday at 15:00, and an organ recital is held Sunday at 17:45 (confirm times, tel. 0171/222-5152).

Photography: Prohibited, except on Wednesday evening.

Starring: Edwards, Elizabeths, Henrys, Annes, Richards, Marys, and the Poets' Corner.

——— WESTMINSTER ABBEY TOUR ———

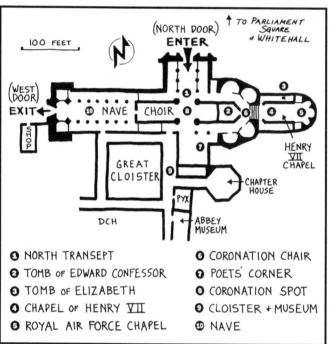

❶ NORTH TRANSEPT
❷ TOMB of EDWARD CONFESSOR
❸ TOMB of ELIZABETH
❹ CHAPEL of HENRY VII
❺ ROYAL AIR FORCE CHAPEL

❻ CORONATION CHAIR
❼ POETS' CORNER
❽ CORONATION SPOT
❾ CLOISTER + MUSEUM
❿ NAVE

The Tour Begins

You'll have no choice but to follow the steady flow of tourists in through the north transept, wandering among tombstones, circling behind the altar, into Poets' Corner in the south transept, detouring through the cloisters and finally back out through the west end of the nave. It's all one way and the crowds can be a real crush. If you have 90 minutes and an interest in English kings and characters, rent the headphones or follow one of the vergers on a live guided tour. They are great. If you prefer to float through at your own tempo, here are the Abbey's top 10 stops:

• *Walk straight in, pick up the map flier which locates the most illustrious tombs, and belly up to the barricade in the center.*

1. North Transept

Look down the long, narrow center aisle of the church. Lined with the praying hands of the Gothic arches, glowing with light from the stained glass, it's clear that this is more than a museum. With saints in stained glass, heroes in carved stone, and the bodies of England's greatest under the floorstones, Westminster Abbey is the religious heart of England.

The tomb of the church's founder, King Edward the Confessor, is at the high altar. He felt God wanted him to go to St. Peter's Basilica at the Vatican. But—with Normans thinking conquest—it was too dangerous for him to leave England. Instead, he built this grand church and dedicated it to St. Peter.

The first Abbey was finished just in time to bury Edward (1065) and to crown his foreign rival, William the Conqueror (1066). People prayed on Edward's tomb and after getting fine results, Edward was canonized—the only English king ever to be sainted.

For the next 250 years the Abbey was built and remodeled to become essentially the church you see today, not withstanding an extensive resurfacing in the 19th century. Thankfully, later architects—ignoring building trends of their generation—honored the vision of the original planner and the building was completed in one relatively harmonious style. The nave is the tallest in England. The chandeliers, 10 feet tall, look small in comparison. (Sixteen were given to the Abbey by the Guinness family.)

The north transept (through which you entered) is nicknamed "Statesmen's Corner" and specializes in famous prime ministers. The musicians are to the right.

• *Now turn left and follow the crowd. Walk under Robert Peel, the prime minister whose policemen were nicknamed "bobbies" and stroll a few yards into the land of dead kings and queens. Stop at the blocked wooden staircase on your right.*

2. Tomb of Edward the Confessor

The most holy part of the church is above you (where the wooden staircase leads, behind the canopied medieval coffins). Step back to look over the tomb of Henry III (with its lower gold mosaic stones picked clean by thieving hands) and you can see a bit of the black and green coffin of Edward the Confessor. This elevated, central tomb is surrounded by the tombs of eight kings and queens.

• *Continue on. At the top of the large staircase, detour left into the private burial chapel of Elizabeth I.*

3. Tomb of Queen Elizabeth I

Although there's only one effigy on the tomb (Elizabeth's), there are two queens buried beneath it, each daughters of Henry VIII (by different mothers). Mary—meek, pious, sickly, and Catholic—enforced Catholicism during her reign by burning "heretics" at the stake. Elizabeth—strong, clever, "virginal," and Protestant—steered England on an Anglican course. Her long reign was one of the greatest in English history: a time when England ruled the seas and Shakespeare explored human emotions. The effigy, taken from Elizabeth's death mask, is considered very accurate. Now these two half-sisters who disliked each other in life lie side-by-side for eternity—with a prayer for Christians of all persuasions to live peacefully together.

• *Go with the flow, continuing into the ornate room behind the main altar. Take a seat in . . .*

4. Chapel of King Henry VII

The light from the stained-glass windows and the colorful banners overhead give the room the festive air of a medieval tournament. The prestigious Knights of Bath meet here, under the magnificent ceiling studded with gold pendants. Unless you're going to Cambridge's King's College Chapel, this ceiling is the finest English Perpendicular Gothic and fan vaulting you'll see. The brilliant stone ceiling was built in 1509 at the end of the Gothic period.

The knights sit in the wooden stalls with churches on their heads, capped by their own insignia. When the queen worships here, she sits in the corner chair under the carved wooden throne.

Behind the fine painting of a Madonna and Child is an iron cage housing tombs of the old warrior Henry VII of Lancaster and his wife, Elizabeth of York. Their love and marriage finally settled the "War of the Roses" between the two clans. The combined red-and-white rose symbol decorates the ironwork. Henry VII was the first Tudor king. (Later Tudors included Henry VIII and Elizabeth I.) This exuberant chapel heralds a new optimistic post-war era in English history.

• *Walk past Henry and Elizabeth to the far end of the church. Stand at the banister in front of the bright modern set of stained-glass windows.*

5. Royal Air Force Chapel

Saints in robes and halos mingle with pilots in bomber jackets and parachutes in this tribute to World War II flyers who earned their angel wings in the Battle of Britain. These were the fighters about whom Churchill said, "Never has so much been owed by so many to so few."

The Abbey survived the blitz virtually unscathed. As a memorial, a tiny bit of bomb-damage—the little glassed-over hole in the wall— is left below the windows in the lower left-hand corner. The book of remembrances lists each of the casualties of the Battle of Britain.

Hey. Look down at the floor. You're standing on the grave of Oliver Cromwell, leader of the rebel forces in England's Civil War. Or rather, Cromwell was buried here from 1658 to 1661.

Then his corpse was exhumed, hanged, drawn, quartered, and decapitated, with the head displayed on a stake as a warning to future king-killers.

• *Circulate back through the Chapel of Henry VII, pass the side chapel with the tomb of Mary Queen of Scots. Step out of the flow at the top of the stairs to stand before the old chair. Immediately behind the chair is the tomb of Henry VII. Behind that, again, is the tomb of the church's founder, Edward the Confessor.*

6. Coronation Chair

The gold-painted wooden chair waits here—with its back to the high altar—for the next coronation. For every English coronation since 1296, it's been moved to its spot before the high altar to receive the royal buttocks. The chair's legs rest on lions, England's symbol.

• *Continue through the golden gates, out of the royal chapels. Turn left into the south transept. You're in Poets' Corner.*

7. Poets' Corner

England's greatest contribution to art is not painting, sculpture, or music. It's the written word. Here lie buried the masters of (arguably) the world's most complex and expressive language. (Many writers are honored with plaques and monuments; relatively few are actually buried here.)

Geoffrey Chaucer is often considered the father of English literature (1340–1400; buried eye-level in the wall under the blue windows). He was buried here first. Later, Poets' Corner was built around his tomb. His *Canterbury Tales* told of earthy people speaking everyday English. The plaques on the floor before Chaucer are memorials to England's literary greats.

Although Shakespeare is not buried here, a fine statue of this greatest of English writers stands at the end of the transept, overlooking the others. High on the wall opposite Shakespeare, with another death mask–accurate face, is George Frederick Handel (most famous for composing the *Messiah*). His tomb is on the floor next to Charles Dickens (whose serialized novels brought "literature" to the masses). You'll also find tombs of Samuel Johnson (wrote first English dictionary), Alfred Lord Tennyson (conscience of the Victorian age), and the great English actor Lawrence Olivier. (Olivier disdained the "Method" style of experiencing intense emotions in order to portray them. When his co-star stayed up all night in order to appear haggard for a scene, Olivier said, "My dear boy, why don't you simply try acting?")

• *Walk to the center of the Abbey in front of the high altar. Stand directly under the central spire.*

8. The Coronation Spot

The area between the choir (with the elaborately carved wooden chairs) and the altar is bigger than normal because this is the site where kings and queens are crowned.

Here is where every English coronation since 1066 has taken place. The nobles, in robes and powdered wigs, look on from the choir area. The archbishop stands at the high altar (the table with the candlesticks). The coronation chair is placed in the center of the church, directly below the cross on the ceiling high in the middle of the central tower. Surrounding the whole area are temporary bleachers for VIPs, creating a "theatre" for this unique spectacle. For Queen Elizabeth's 1953 coronation, seating was created for 7,000 with bleachers going halfway up the rose windows of each transept.

Imagine the day when Prince William becomes king. Long silver trumpets hung with banners will be raised and sound a fanfare, as the monarch-to-be enters the church from the main entrance and parades slowly down the center of the nave and up the steps to the altar. After a church service, he'll be seated in the chair, facing the nobles. A royal scepter and orb will be placed in his hands, and—dut, dutta dah—the archbishop lowers the Crown of St. Edward the Confessor onto his royal head. Finally, King William will stand up, descend the steps and be presented to the people for their approval. The people will cry, "God save the king!"

• *Before leaving, pause in the center and remember that royalty are also given funerals here. Princess Diana's coffin lay here before the funeral service attended by 2,000. She was then buried on her family estate. Exit the church at the south door, leading to . . .*

9. Cloisters and Museum

The church is known as the "Abbey" because it was the headquarters of Benedictine monks—until Henry VIII kicked them out in 1540. The buildings that adjoin the church housed the monks. Cloistered courtyards gave them a place to meditate on God's creation.

Look back at the church through the cloisters. Notice the flying buttresses, the stone bridges that push in on the church walls, allowing Gothic architects to build so high.

If you're interested in all of this history, pay £1 extra for three more rooms. The Chapter House, where the monks had daily meetings, features fine architecture with faded but well-described medieval art. The tiny Pyx Chamber has an exhibit about the King's Treasury. The Abbey Museum, formerly the monks' lounge with a cozy fireplace and snacks, now has fascinating exhibits on royal coronations, funerals, and abbey history.

Consider the shop, cafeteria, and WC before continuing back into the church for the last stop.

10. Nave

On the floor near the west entrance of the Abbey is the flower-lined Tomb of the Unknown Warrior, one ordinary WWI soldier buried in soil from France with lettering made from melted-down weapons from that war. Hanging on a column next to it is the United States Congressional Medal of Honor presented to England's WWI dead by General Pershing in 1921. Closer to the door is a memorial to Winston Churchill.

Look back down the nave of the Abbey, filled with the remains of the people who made Britain great. Now step back outside into a city filled with the same kind of people.

ST. PAUL'S
TOUR

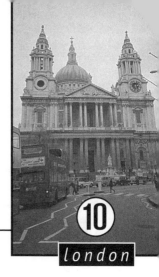

No sooner was Christopher Wren selected to refurbish Old St. Paul's church than the Great Fire of 1666 incinerated it. Within six days, Wren had a plan for a whole new building . . . and for the city around it, complete with some 50 new churches. For the next four decades he worked to achieve his vision—a spacious church, topped by a dome, surrounded by a flock of Wrens.

St. Paul's is England's national church. There's been a church on this spot since 604. It was the symbol of London's rise from the Great Fire of 1666 and of London's survival of the Blitz of 1940.

Orientation

Hours: Daily 9:30–16:30; last entry is at 16:00.

Cost: £4, free on Sunday but restricted viewing due to services, £3.50 extra to climb dome (allow an hour for the climb up and down).

Tour length: One hour (two if you climb dome).

Getting there: Located in "The City" in east London, tube: St. Paul's.

Information: Guided 90-minute cathedral and crypt tours are offered at 11:00, 11:30, 13:30, and 14:00. Walkman tours cost £3. Sunday services are at 8:00, 8:45, 11:00, and 15:15; evensongs are weekdays at 17:00. Tel. 0171/236-4128.

Photography: Allowed without a flash.

Starring: Christopher Wren, Wellington, and WWII.

The Tour Begins

Even now, as skyscrapers encroach, the 365-foot dome of St. Paul's rises majestically above the rooftops of the neighborhood. The tall dome is set on classical columns, capped with a lantern, topped by a six-foot ball, and iced with a cross. As the first Catholic cathedral

ST. PAUL'S TOUR

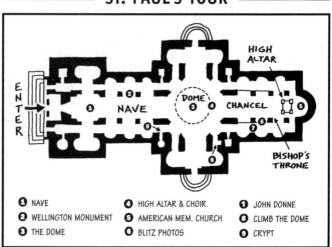

❶ NAVE   **❹** HIGH ALTAR & CHOIR   **❼** JOHN DONNE
❷ WELLINGTON MONUMENT   **❺** AMERICAN MEM. CHURCH   **❽** CLIMB THE DOME
❸ THE DOME   **❻** BLITZ PHOTOS   **❾** CRYPT

built in London after the Reformation, it is Baroque: St. Peter's filtered through clear-eyed English reason.

• *Enter, buy your ticket, and stand at the back of the nave.*

1. Nave

Look down the nave through the choir stalls to the stained glass at the far end. This big church feels big. Its spaciousness is accentuated by the lack of decoration. The simple cream-colored ceiling and the clear glass in the windows light everything evenly. Wren wanted this: a simple, open church with nothing to hide. Unfortunately, only this entrance area keeps his original vision—the rest was crusted with Baroque decoration after his death.

• *Glance up and behind. The organ trumpets say come to the 17:00 evensong. Ahead and on the left is the towering . . .*

2. Wellington Monument

It's so tall that even Wellington's horse has to duck to avoid bumping his head. Wren would have been appalled, but his church has become so central to England's soul that many national heroes are buried here (in the basement crypt). General Wellington, Napoleon's conqueror and the embodiment of British stiff-upper-lippedness, was honored here in a funeral packed with 13,000 fans.

• *Stroll up the same nave Prince Charles and Lady Diana walked on their 1981 wedding day. Grab a chair underneath the dome.*

3. The Dome

The dome you see, painted with scenes from the life of St. Paul, is only the innermost of three domes. Look up through the hole in the center and you'll see the light-filled lantern, which is supported by dome #2 (the dome itself isn't visible). Covering it all is dome #3, the outer shell of lead-covered wood, which is what you see from the outside. Wren's ingenious 3-in-1 design was psychological as well as functional—he wanted a low inner dome so the worshipper wouldn't feel dwarfed.

You'll see tourists walking around the base of the dome, the "Whispering Gallery." The dome is constructed with such precision that whispers from one side of the dome are heard on the other side, 170 feet away.

Christopher Wren (1632–1723) was the right man at the right time. While the 31-year-old math professor had never built a major building in his life when he got the commission for St. Paul's, his reputation for brilliance and a unique ability to work with others carried him through. The church has the clean lines and geometric simplicity of the age of Newton, when reason was holy and God set the planets spinning in perfect geometrical motion.

For over 40 years Wren worked on this site, overseeing every detail. At age 75, he got to look up and see his son place the cross on top of the dome, completing the masterpiece.

On the floor directly beneath the dome is a brass grate—part of a 19th-century attempt to heat the church. Encircling it is Christopher Wren's name and epitaph, written in Latin: *Lector, si monumentum requiris circumspice* (Reader, if you seek his monument, look around you).

Now review the ceiling: behind is Wren simplicity and ahead is Baroque ornate.

• *The choir area blocks your way to the altar at the far end, but belly up to the entrance between two sets of organ pipes and look at the far end under a golden canopy.*

4. High Altar and Choir

The altar (the marble slab with crucifix and candlesticks—you'll get a close-up look later) was destroyed in WWII. Today it lies under a huge canopy with corkscrew columns. It looks ancient, but was actually built in 1958 according to sketches by Wren.

English churches, unlike most in Europe, often have an area like this in the center of the church known as the choir (or quire or chancel) where church officials sit, along with the singers. St. Paul's—a cathedral since 604—is home to the local bishop, who presides in the chair closest to the altar on the south or right side (the carved bishop's hat hangs over the chair).

The ceiling above the choir is a riot of glass mosaic representing God and his creation.

• *Walk down the left side of the choir, pausing at the modern statue of "Mother and Child" by Britain's greatest modern sculptor, Henry Moore. After donating this to St. Paul's, he was rewarded with a burial spot in the crypt. Continue to the far end of the church where you'll find three bright and modern stained-glass windows.*

5. American Memorial Church

Each of the three windows has a central core of religious scenes, but the brightly colored panes that arch around them have some unusual iconography: American. Spot the American eagle, and look for George Washington (right window, upper right corner). In the carved wood beneath the windows you'll see birds and foliage native to the States. And at the very far right, check out the tiny tree "trunk" beneath the bird behind the carved leaves—it's a U.S. rocket circa 1958, shooting up to the stars.

Britain is very grateful to its WWII saviors, the Yanks, and remembers them religiously here immediately behind the altar with the Roll of Honor. This book under glass lists the names of 28,000 U.S. servicemen based in Britain who gave their lives.

• *Take a close look at the high altar and the view back to the entrance from here, then continue on around the altar where you'll find a glass case of . . .*

6. Blitz Photos

Nazi planes firebombed a helpless London in 1940. While "The City" around it burned to the ground, St. Paul's survived, giving hope to the citizens. Some swear that bombs bounced miraculously off Wren's dome, while others credit the heroic work of local firefighters. (There's a memorial chapel to the heroic firefighters who kept watch over St. Paul's with hoses cocked.)

• *Across the aisle, standing white in a black niche, is a statue of . . .*

7. John Donne

This statue survived the Great Fire of 1666. Donne, shown here wrapped in a burial shroud, was a passionate preacher in Old St. Paul's as well as a great poet.

Imagine hearing Donne deliver a funeral sermon here, with the huge church bell tolling in the background: "No man is an island . . . Any man's death diminishes me, because I am involved in Mankind. Therefore, never send to know for whom the bell tolls—it tolls for thee."

• *And also for dozens of people who lie buried beneath your feet, in the crypt where you'll end your tour. But first . . .*

8. Climb the Dome

There are no elevators, and you must pay extra, but the 530-step climb is worthwhile. First you get to the Whispering Gallery (with views of the church interior). Have fun in the gallery and whisper sweet nothings into the wall; your partner (and anyone else) on the far side can hear you. Then, after another climb you're at the Stone Gallery (views of London, high enough if you're exhausted). Finally a long tight metal 150-step staircase takes you to the very top of the cupola for stunning unobstructed views of the city. A tiny window allows you to peek directly down on the church floor.

9. Crypt

Grand tombs of General Wellington and Admiral Nelson dominate the center of the crypt. Nelson, who defeated the French fleet in 1805 and ensured that Britannia ruled the waves, lies buried directly beneath the dome (and heating grate). Christopher Wren's tomb is in the far corner (left of the stairs as you enter, right of chapel altar). Also find painters Turner, Reynolds, and others (near Wren), Florence Nightingale (near Wellington), and memorials to many others (including George Washington, who lies buried back in old Virginny.) There are interesting exhibits about the building of the cathedral, a cafeteria, fine gift shop, and WC.

TOWER OF LONDON TOUR

William I, still getting used to his new title of "the Conqueror," built the stone "White Tower" (1077–1097) to keep the Londoners in line. The tower served as an effective lookout for invaders coming up the Thames. His successors enlarged it to its present 18-acre size. Because of the security it provided, it has served over the centuries as the Royal Mint, the Royal Jewel House, and most famously, as the prison and execution site of those who dare oppose the crown. The Tower's hard stone and glittering jewels represent the ultimate power of the king. So does the executioners' block. You'll find more bloody history per square inch in this original tower of power than anywhere in Britain.

Orientation

Hours: Monday–Saturday 9:00–18:00, Sunday 10:00–18:00, last entry at 17:00. To avoid the crowds, arrive at opening time and go straight for the jewels, doing the tour and tower later (or do the jewels after 16:30). The crowd hits after the 9:30 cheap tube passes start. The long but fast-moving line is worst on Sunday. Also on Sunday, visitors are welcome on the grounds to worship in the Royal Chapel (free, 11:00 service with fine choral music).

Cost: £9

Tour length: Three hours

Getting there: Located in East London (tube: Tower Hill). For speed, take the tube there, for romance take the boat back. Boats run between Tower of London and Westminster Pier near Big Ben (£4.40, round-trip £5.60, 3/hrly from 10:20–21:00 in peak season, until 18:00 in winter, 30-minute cruise).

Information: The free, worthwhile 50-minute Beefeater tour leaves regularly from inside the gate (last one usually at 15:30). Tel. 0171/709-0765.

TOWER OF LONDON TOUR

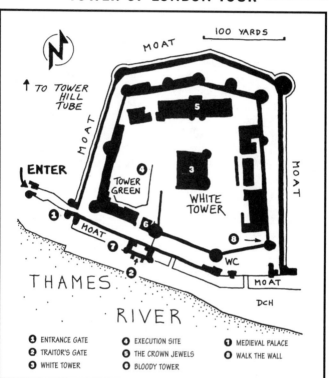

ENTER

WC

DCH

THAMES RIVER

① ENTRANCE GATE	④ EXECUTION SITE	⑦ MEDIEVAL PALACE
② TRAITOR'S GATE	⑤ THE CROWN JEWELS	⑧ WALK THE WALL
③ WHITE TOWER	⑥ BLOODY TOWER	

Photography: Yes, but not of the jewels.
Starring: Crown jewels, Beefeaters, William the Conqueror, and
Henry VIII

1. Entrance Gate

Even an army the size of the ticket line couldn't storm this castle.
After they pulled the drawbridge up and slammed the iron
portcullis down, you'd have to swim the moat (now grass), then
toss a grappling hook onto the wall and climb while the enemy
poured boiling oil on you. Yes, it was difficult to get into the
Tower . . . but almost impossible to get out.
• *The fun, entertaining 50-minute tours by the Yeoman Warders (nicknamed "Beefeaters" for the rations of beef they earned) begin just inside the
entrance gate. The information booth is nearby, and toilets are 100 yards
straight ahead. Otherwise, go 50 yards straight ahead to the . . .*

2. Traitor's Gate

This entrance into the Tower was originally a waterway passage from the Thames. Princess Elizabeth I, who was a prisoner here before she became Queen, was poled through this gate on a barge, as were many other leaders who fell from grace. Nixon wasn't the only one with Water-gate problems. (That's a Beefeater joke, if you're still considering a tour).

• *Pass underneath the "Bloody Tower" into the inner courtyard. The big white tower in the middle is the ...*

3. White Tower

This is the "Tower" that gives this castle complex of 20 towers its name. William the Conqueror built it 900 years ago to put 15 feet of stone between himself and his conquered. Over the centuries the other walls and towers were built around it.

The Tower represents the king's absolute power over his subjects. If you made the wrong move here, you could be feasting on roast boar in the banqueting hall one night, and chained to the walls of the prisons the next. Torture ranged from stretching on the rack, to hanging by the neck until blue, to drawing and quartering with your giblets displayed on the walls as a warning. (Or in the case of Guy Fawkes, who tried to blow up Parliament, all of the above.) Any cries for help were muffled by the thick stone walls—15 feet at the base, a mere 11 feet at the Tower top.

Inside the Tower today, you can see armor and exhibitions recreating medieval life. The rare and lovely Norman chapel (St. John's Chapel, 1080) is simple, plain, and moving.

• *Left of the Tower is the Tower Green, where you'll find a granite-paved square marked "Site of Scaffold."*

4. Execution Site

Here is where enemies of the crown would kneel before the king for the final time, hands tied behind their backs, say a final prayer, lay their heads on a block, and—shlit!—the blade would slice through their necks as their heads tumbled to the ground.

The headless corpses were buried in unmarked graves in the Tower Green or under the floor of the stone church ahead of you. The heads were stuck on a stick and displayed at London Bridge. Passersby did not see heads but spheres of parasites.

Henry VIII axed his exes here—Anne Boleyn, whom he called a witch and an adulteress, and the forgettable Catherine Howard. Next.

Henry even beheaded his friend, Thomas More (a Catholic), because he refused to recognize (Protestant) Henry as head of the Church of England. (Thomas died at the less-prestigious Tower Hill site just outside the walls—near the Tube stop—where most Tower executions took place.)

The most tragic victim was 17-year-old Lady Jane Grey, a simple girl who was manipulated into claiming the crown during the scramble for power after Henry's death. When "Bloody" Mary took control, she forced Jane to kneel at the block. Jane's young husband, locked in the nearby Beauchamp Tower, could vent his grief only by scratching "Jane" into the tower's stone (in the upstairs room).

A Beefeater tired of what he called "Hollywood coverage" of the Tower grabbed my manuscript, read it, and told me that in over 900 years as a fortress, palace, and prison, the place held 8,500 prisoners. But only 120 were executed and of those only six were executed inside the Tower. And, stressing the hospitality of the Tower, he added, "Torture was actually quite rare here."

• *Looking past the White Tower on the left, a line leads to the Crown Jewels. Like a Disney ride, the line is still very long once you get inside. But great videos help the time pass pleasantly. You first pass through a room of wooden chairs and coats of arms—one for every monarch from William the Conqueror to Queen Elizabeth II. Next, a film of Elizabeth's 1953 coronation—a chance to see the jewels in action. You'll also see video close-ups of the jewels. Finally, you pass into a huge vault and reach . . .*

5. The Crown Jewels

In the first display case notice the 12th-century Coronation Spoon for anointing (used in 1953). Most of the original crown jewels were lost during the 1648 Revolution, so this is the most ancient object here. After scepters, robes, trumpets, and wristlets, a moving sidewalk takes you past the most precious of the crown jewels.

• *The crowns are all facing you as you approach them (ride the nearest walkway). You're welcome to circle back and glide by the back side and hang out on the elevated viewing area with the Beefeater guard. Chat with the guard. Ask him what happens if you shoot a photo.*

These are the most important pieces:
• **St. Edward's Crown**, in the first glass case, is placed by the archbishop upon the head of each new monarch in Westminster Abbey on coronation day. It's worn for twenty minutes, then locked away until the next coronation. Although remodeled, this five-pound crown is older than the Tower itself, dating back to 1061, the time of King Edward the Confessor, "the last English king" before William the Conqueror invaded (1066).

• **The Sovereign's Scepter**, in the second case, is encrusted with the world's largest cut diamond, the 530-carat Star of Africa.
• **The Koh-i-Noor diamond**, with 106 carats, glitters on the front of the highest crown in the fourth case.
• **The Imperial Crown**, in the fifth and last case, is the crown worn for coronation festivities, official state functions, and the annual opening of Parliament. Among its 3,733 jewels are Queen Elizabeth I's former earrings (the hanging pearls) and Edward the Confessor's ring (the sapphire on top).

• *Don't leave the complex without seeing the following sights. Enter near the Traitor's Gate for sights #6 and #7 . . .*

6. Bloody Tower

Not all prisoners died at the block. During the War of the Roses, 13-year-old future king Edward and his kid brother were kidnapped by their uncle Richard III and locked in the Bloody Tower, never to be seen again (until two centuries later when two children's bodies were discovered).

Sir Walter Raleigh—poet, explorer, and political radical—was imprisoned here for 13 years. In 1603, the English writer and adventurer was accused of plotting against King James and sentenced to death. The king commuted the sentence to life imprisonment in the Tower. While in prison, Raleigh wrote the first volume of his *History of the World*. See his rather cushy bedroom, study, and walkway (courtesy of the powerful tobacco lobby?). Raleigh promised the king a wealth of gold if he would release him to search for El Dorado. The expedition was a failure. Upon Raleigh's return, the displeased king had him beheaded in 1618.

More recent prisoners in the complex include Rudolf Hess, Hitler's henchman who parachuted into Scotland in 1941 (kept in bell tower). Hess claimed to have dropped in to negotiate a separate peace between Germany and Britain. Hitler denied any such plan.

7. Medieval Palace

The Tower was a royal residence as well as a fortress. These rooms are furnished as they might have been during the reign of Edward I in the 13th century.

• *Enter near where you leave the Medieval Palace to . . .*

8. Walk the Wall

The tower was defended by state-of-the-art walls and fortifications in the 13th century. This walk offers a good look.

DAY TRIPS
IN ENGLAND

Greenwich • Cambridge • Bath

Near London are some great day trip possibilities: Greenwich, Cambridge and Bath (listed from nearest to farthest, and from simplest to most interesting). Greenwich is England's maritime capital, Cambridge its best university town, and Bath an elegant spa town dating from Roman times.

You could fill a book with the many easy and exciting day trips from London (Earl Steinbicker did: *Daytrips in Britain by Rail, Bus or Car from London and Edinburgh*).

Getting Around

By Bus Tour: Several tour companies take London-based travelers out and back every day. Evan Evans' tours leave from behind Victoria Station daily at 9:00, include a full day of sightseeing with £5 to £10 worth of admissions, and leave you in Bath before returning to London (£30 for Stonehenge and Bath; £46 for Salisbury Cathedral, Stonehenge, and Bath; tel. 0181/332-2222). Travelline does a tour of Bath and Stonehenge for £24 (tel. 0181/668-7261, office in Fountain Square directly south of Victoria Station). If you want to stay in Bath, consider using a bus tour as a "free" way to get to Bath (saving you the cost of the £28.50 London–Bath train ticket); just stow your luggage under the bus, and when the tour drops you in Bath, stay there, rather than return to London.

By Train: The British rail system uses London as a hub and normally offers round-trip fares (after 9:30) that cost virtually the same as one-way fares. You can save even more if you purchase Super Advance tickets before 14:00 on the day before your trip.

By Train Tour: Original London Walks offers a variety of day trips using the train for about £10 plus transportation costs (see their walking tour brochure; for recorded schedule, tel. 0171/624-3978, Web site: http:\\london.walks.com).

GREENWICH

The Tudor kings preferred Greenwich to their other palaces. Henry VIII was born here. Later kings commissioned Inigo Jones and Christopher Wren to beautify the place. In spite of Greenwich's architectural and royal treats, this is England's maritime capital, and visitors go for things salty. And now, as the millennium approaches, the home of the Zero Meridian will be more visited than ever.

Wander beyond the touristy Greenwich Church Street and Greenwich High Road to where flower stands spill into the side streets, and antique shops sell brass nautical knickknacks. King William Walk, College Approach, Nelson Road, and Turnpin Lane are all worth a look. A variety of street markets are held every weekend, including the arts & crafts market, an entertaining mini-Covent Garden (between College Approach and Nelson Road). Greenwich will throb with daytrippers on weekends as the Millennium approaches. To avoid crowds, visit on a weekday. The TI is at 46 Greenwich Church Street (tel. 0181/858-6376).

Planning Your Time

Cruise from London's Westminster Pier to Greenwich (see Transportation, below). Upon arrival, visit the two great ships—*Cutty Sark* and *Gipsy Moth IV*—and check out the Millennium Experience Visitors Centre. Then walk the shoreline promenade with a possible lunch or drink in the venerable Trafalgar Tavern before heading up to the National Maritime Museum and Old Royal Observatory. Finally, browse the town before catching the tube or train back to London.

Sights—Greenwich

▲▲**Cutty Sark**—The Scottish-built *Cutty Sark* was the last of the great China tea clippers. Handsomely restored, she was the queen of the seas when first launched in 1869. With 32,000 square feet of sail, she could blow with the wind 300 miles in a day. Below deck you'll see the best collection of merchant ships' figureheads in Britain and exhibits giving a vivid peek into the lives of Victorian sailors back when Britain ruled the waves. Stand at the big wheel and look up at the still rigged main mast towering 150 feet above. During summer afternoons costumed storytellers tell tales of the high seas (£3.50, Monday–Saturday 10:00–18:00, Sunday 12:00–18:00, October–April 10:00–17:00, Sunday 12:00–17:00, tel. 0181/858-3445, Web site: www.cuttysark.org.uk).

▲**Gipsy Moth IV**—Tiny next to the *Cutty Sark*, the 53-foot *Gipsy Moth IV* is the boat Sir Francis Chichester used for the first solo circumnavigation of the world in 1966-67. Climb through to see the clever and fascinating ways the boat was custom-designed for its historic voyage. Upon his return, Queen Elizabeth II knighted Chichester in Greenwich using the sword Elizabeth I had used to knight Francis Drake in 1582 (50p, Easter–October Monday–Saturday 10:00–18:00, Sunday 12:00–18:00).

Millennium Experience Visitors Centre—Throughout 1999, the Millennium Experience Visitors Centre (next to the *Cutty Sark* in Greenwich) will give visitors a sneak preview of the grand festivities planned for the millennium.

The Millennium Experience will take place under a vast dome a mile downriver from Greenwich town. This dome—covering over 20 acres—is the biggest ever built. Throughout 2000, millions will gather here to celebrate British ideas and technology at the birth of the third millennium.

There's plenty of futuristic hoopla as everyone wonders what exactly the Millennium Dome will be filled with (Visitors Centre free, weekdays 11:00–19:00, weekends 10:00–18:00, Web site: www.mx2000.co.uk).

Stroll the Thames to Trafalgar Tavern—From the *Cutty Sark* and *Gipsy Moth*, pass the Pier and wander along the Thames on Five Foot Walk (the width of the path) for grand views in front of the Royal Naval College. Founded by William III as a naval hospital and designed by Wren, the College was split in two because Queen Mary didn't want the view from Queen's House blocked. The riverside view's good, too: with the twin-domed towers of the college (one giving the time, the other, the direction of the wind) framing Queen's House and the Old Royal Observatory crowning the hill beyond.

Continuing downstream, just past the college, you'll see the Trafalgar Tavern. Dickens knew the pub well, even using it as the setting for the wedding breakfast in Our Mutual Friend. Built in 1837 in the Regency style to attract Londoners downriver, the tavern is still popular with Londoners for its fine lunches. And the upstairs Nelson Room is still used for weddings. Its formal moldings and elegant windows with balconies over the Thames are a step back in time (bar meals 10:00–20:00 except Sunday, restaurant meals 12:00–15:00).

In 1999, the Royal Naval College's buildings will no longer be a military training installation. Whether they'll be open to the public is still uncertain. From the Trafalgar Tavern, walk the two long blocks up Park Walk and turn right onto Ha Ha Walk, bordering the park.

▲**Queen's House**—This was the first Palladian-style villa in Britain. Designed in 1616 by Inigo Jones for James I's wife, Anne of Denmark, it's the architectural centerpiece of Greenwich.

Exploring its Great Hall and Royal Apartments offers a sumptuous look at royal life in the 17th century—or lots of stairs if you're suffering from manor house fatigue (combo ticket to Queen's House, Maritime Museum, and Observatory costs £5.50, daily 10:00–17:00, off-season 10:30–15:30, tours every 15 minutes).

▲▲▲**National Maritime Museum**—At the largest and most important maritime museum in the world, visitors can taste both the romance and harshness of life at sea. Experience 20th-century naval warfare on a WWII frigate or get to know Britain's greatest naval hero, Nelson, whose display covers both his public career and scandalous private life (don't miss the uniform coat in which he was fatally shot). The Museum's ambitious Neptune Court development opens in June 1999, greatly increasing the number of galleries to better profile the sweep of Empire and the role of the sea in British history (combo ticket to Queen's House, Maritime Museum, and Observatory costs £5.50, daily 10:00–17:00, tel. 0181/312-6565, Web site: www.nmm.ac.uk).

▲▲**Old Royal Observatory**—On December 31, 1999, the eyes of the world will be focused on Greenwich and its Observatory. All time is measured from Longitude 0 degrees, the Prime Meridian Line—the point from which the new Millennium will actually begin. However, the Observatory's early work had nothing to do with coordinating the world's clocks to GMT, Greenwich Mean Time. The Observatory was founded in 1675 by Charles II to find a way to determine longitude at sea. Today, the Greenwich Time Signal is linked with the BBC (which broadcasts the "pips" worldwide at the top of the hour). Straddle the Prime Meridian and set your wristwatch to the new digital clock showing GMT to a tenth of a second (and whizzing down the seconds to New Year 2000). See how your foot measures up to "the" foot where the public standards of length are cast in bronze. View historic astronomical instruments and watch the Time Ball, visible from the Thames, drop daily at 13:00.

Finally, enjoy the view: the symmetrical royal buildings, the Thames, the square mile "City" of London with its skyscrapers and the dome of St. Paul's, the Docklands with its busy cranes, and the Millennium Dome itself (combo ticket to Queen's House, Maritime Museum, and Observatory costs £5.50, daily 10:00–17:00).

Transportation Connections—Greenwich

Getting to Greenwich is a joy by boat or a snap by tube. You have three good choices: 1) cruise down the Thames from any of central London's piers at Westminster, Charing Cross, or Tower of London (£5.80 from Westminster Pier, round-trip £7, 2/hrly from 10:00–17:00, 50 min, tel. 0171/930-4097); 2) take the tube to

Island Gardens in Zone 2, then walk under the Thames pedestrian tunnel; or 3) catch the train from Charing Cross station.

CAMBRIDGE

Cambridge, 60 miles north of London, is world famous for its prestigious university. Wordsworth, Newton, Tennyson, Darwin, and Prince Charles are a few of its illustrious alumni. This historic town of 100,000 people is more pleasant than its rival, Oxford. Cambridge is the epitome of a university town with busy bikers, stately residence halls, plenty of bookshops, and proud locals who can point out where electrons and DNA were discovered and where the first atom was split.

In medieval Europe, higher education was the domain of the Church and was limited to ecclesiastical schools. Scholars lived in "Halls" on campus. This scholarly community of residential halls, chapels, and lecture halls connected by peaceful garden courtyards survives today in the colleges that make the universities at Cambridge and Oxford. By 1350 Cambridge had eight colleges (Oxford is roughly 100 years older), each with a monastic-type courtyard and lodgings. Today Cambridge has 31 colleges. While a student's life revolves around his or her independent college, the university organizes lectures, presents degrees, and promotes research.

The university dominates—and owns—most of Cambridge. Approximate term schedule is January 15 through March 15, April 15 through June 18, and October 8 through December 8. The colleges are closed to visitors during exams, from mid-April until late June. But the town is never sleepy.

Planning Your Time

Cambridge is worth most of a day, but not an overnight. Catch a train from London's King's Cross station (2/hrly, one-hour trip), and arrive in Cambridge in time for the 11:30 walking tour, an essential part of any visit. Spend the afternoon touring King's College and the Fitzwilliam Museum, and simply enjoying the ambience of this stately old college town.

Orientation (tel. code: 01223)

Cambridge is small but congested. There are two main streets separated from the river by the most interesting colleges. The town center has a TI, a colorful marketplace, and several parking lots. Everything is within a pleasant walk.

Tourist Information: The TI is on the town square (Monday–Saturday 10:00–18:00 or 18:30, summer Sundays 11:00–16:00, closed winter Sundays, tel. 01223/322-640).

Arrival in Cambridge: To get to downtown Cambridge from the train station, take a 20-minute walk, a £3.50 taxi ride, or bus #1 (90p, every eight minutes).

Tours of Cambridge

▲▲**Walking Tour of the Colleges**—A walking tour is the best way to understand Cambridge's mix of "town and gown." Walks give a good rundown on the historic and scenic highlights of the university, as well as some fun local gossip. Walks are run by and leave from the tourist office. July and August tours start at 10:30, 11:30, 13:30, and 14:30; the rest of the year, generally at 11:30 and 13:30. Tours cost £6.25 and include admission to King's College Chapel. Drop by the TI early to reserve a spot, or call to book a spot with your credit card (TI tel. 01223/322-640). Particularly if you're coming from London, try calling to at least confirm that a tour is scheduled and has space available. Private guides are also available.

Bus Tours—Guide Friday hop-on and hop-off bus tours (£7.50, departing every 15 minutes) are informative and cover the outskirts, but walking tours go where buses can't: right into the center.

Sights—Cambridge

▲▲**King's College Chapel**—Built from 1446 to 1515 by Henrys VI through VIII, England's best example of Perpendicular Gothic is the single most impressive building in town. Stand inside, look up, and marvel, as Christopher Wren did, at what was the largest single span of vaulted roof anywhere—2,000 tons of incredible fan vaulting. Wander through the Old Testament via the 25 16th-century stained-glass windows (the most Renaissance stained glass anywhere in one spot—it was taken out for safety during WWII, then painstakingly replaced). Walk to the altar and admire Rubens' masterful Adoration of the Magi (£3, erratic hours depending on school and events, but generally 9:30–16:30). During term you're welcome to enjoy a Cambridge-quality evensong ervice (Tuesday–Saturday at 17:30, Sunday at 15:30).

▲▲**Trinity College**—Half of Cambridge's 63 Nobel Prize winners came from this richest and biggest of the town's colleges, founded in 1546 by Henry VIII. Don't miss the Wren-designed library with its wonderful carving and fascinating original manuscripts (free, Monday–Friday 12:00–14:00; during term also open Saturday 10:30–12:30). Just outside the library entrance Sir Isaac Newton, who spent 30 years at Trinity, clapped his hands and timed the echo to measure the speed of sound as it raced down the side of the cloister and back. In the library you can read Newton's handwritten account of this experiment, alongside the original, handwritten *Winnie-the-Pooh* manuscript.

▲▲**Fitzwilliam Museum**—Britain's best museum of antiquities and art outside of London is the Fitzwilliam. Enjoy its wonderful painting collection (Old Masters, an impressive English section featuring Gainsborough, Reynolds, Hogarth and others, works by all the famous Impressionists), old manuscripts, and Greek, Egyptian, and Mesopotamian collections (free, Tuesday–Saturday 10:00–17:00, Sunday 14:15–17:00, closed Monday, tel. 01223/332-900).

Museum of Classical Archeology—While this museum contains no originals, it offers a unique chance to see accurate copies (from 19th-century casts of the originals) of virtually every famous ancient Greek and Roman statue (over 600 statues, free, Monday–Friday 9:00–17:00, Sidgwick Avenue, tel. 01223/335-153).

▲**Punting on the Cam**—For a little levity and probably more exercise than you really want, try hiring one of the traditional (and inexpensive) flat-bottom punts from any of four places along the river (look for stalls at either bridge) and pole yourself up and down (around and around, more likely) the lazy Cam. Once you get the hang of it, it's a fine way to enjoy the scenic side of Cambridge. After 17:00, it's less crowded and less embarrassing.

Transportation Connections—Cambridge

Cheap same-day train tickets make Cambridge an easy, economical side trip from London. Train info tel. 0345/484-950.

By train from London: King's Cross Station to Cambridge (one way £13.10, cheap day return for £13.20, 2/hrly, 60 min, fast trains depart at :15 and :45 past each hour each way; the budget ticket requires a departure after 9:30 except Saturday and Sunday).

By train from Cambridge to: York (hrly, 2.5-hr, transfer in Petersborough), Birmingham (6/day, 3 hrs), Liverpool (5/day, 5 hrs), Heathrow (hrly buses, 3.5 hrs).

BATH

The best city to visit within easy striking distance of London is Bath—just a 75-minutes train ride away. Two hundred years ago this city of 80,000 was the trend-setting Hollywood of Britain. If ever a city enjoyed looking in the mirror, Bath's the one. It has more "government-listed" or protected historic buildings per capita than any other town in England. The entire city, built of the creamy warm-tone limestone called "Bath stone," beams in its cover-girl complexion. An architectural chorus line, it's a triumph of the Georgian style. Proud locals remind visitors that the town is routinely banned from the "Britain in Bloom" contest to give other towns a chance to win. Bath's narcissism is justified. Even with its mobs of tourists, it's a joy to visit.

BATH

The map contains the following labels:

MUSEUM
TO INDUSTRIAL HERITAGE CENTRE
Brock's Guest House
BENNETT
TO A46 & LONDON
ROYAL CRESCENT
BROCK ST
TO BATHURST GUEST HOUSE
ROYAL AVE
ROYAL Victoria PARK
THE CIRCUS
GAY ST
GEORGE
WALCOT
N
D C H
ELGIN VILLA
Woodville House B&B
JOHN ST
MILSOM
YMCA
LAURA PLACE
UPPER BRISTOL ROAD
LAUNDRY
QUEEN SQUARE
WOOD
QUEEN
WALLS
BRIDGE
PULTENEY BRIDGE
MONMOUTH
UPPER BOR. WALLS
MKT.
ABBEY
PARADE GARDENS
THEATRE ROYAL
WESTGATE
CHEAP
YORK ST.
NORTH PARADE RD.
HOLLY VILLA GUEST HOUSE
PULTENEY ROAD
ROMAN BATHS & Pump Room
ABBEY GREEN
LWR. BOR.
ST. JAMES PARADE
HENRY ST.
SOUTHGATE
GREEN PARK ROAD
RIVER AVON
BUS STATION
NEW KING
MANVERS
DORCHESTER
RAIL STATION
& TOURIST INFO
LOWER BRISTOL RD
GOOD B&B AREA
200 YDS.
to WELLS VIA A-367
WELLS ROAD

Legend:
1. TOURIST INFO
2. MEET TOURS HERE
3. HARINGTON'S OF BATH HOTEL
4. PARADE PARK HOTEL
5. PRATT'S HOTEL
6. LAURA PLACE HOTEL
7. KENNARD HOTEL
8. HENRY GUEST HOUSE
9. COSTUME MUSEUM

TINY ARROWS (→) INDICATE ONE WAY STREETS.

Long before the Romans arrived in the first century, Bath was known for its hot springs. What became the Roman spa town of Aquae Sulis has always been fueled by the healing allure of its 116-degree mineral hot springs. The town's importance carried through Saxon times when it had a huge church on the site of the present-day Abbey and was considered the religious capital of Britain. Its influence peaked in 973 when England's first king, Edgar, was crowned in the Abbey. Bath prospered as a wool town.

Bath then declined until the mid-1600s, when it was just a huddle of huts around the Abbey and a hot springs with 3,000 residents oblivious to the Roman ruins 18 feet below their dirt floors. Then, in 1687, Queen Mary, fighting infertility, bathed here. Within 10 months she gave birth to a son . . . and a new age of popularity for Bath.

The town boomed as a spa resort. Ninety percent of the buildings you'll see today are from the 18th century. Local architect John Wood was inspired by the Italian architect Palladio to build a "new Rome." The town bloomed in the Neoclassical style and streets were lined not with scrawny sidewalks but with wide "parades," upon which the women in their stylishly wide dresses could spread their fashionable tails.

Beau Nash (1673–1762) was Bath's "master of ceremonies." He organized both the daily regimen of the aristocratic visitors and the city—lighting and improving security on the streets, banning swords, and opening the Pump Room. Under his fashionable baton, Bath became a city of balls, gaming, concerts, and the place to see and be seen in England. This most civilized place became even more so with the great Neoclassical building spree that followed.

Planning Your Time

Bath needs two nights even on a quick trip. There's plenty to do and it's a joy to do it. On a one-week trip to London, consider spending two nights in Bath with one entire day for the city. Ideally, use Bath as your jet-lag recovery pillow and do London at the end of your trip.

Consider starting a London vacation this way:

Day 1: Land at Heathrow. Catch the National Express bus to Bath (9/day, 2.5-hr trip).

Day 2: 9:00–Tour the Roman Baths, 10:30–Catch the free city walking tour, 12:30–Picnic on the open deck of a Guide Friday bus tour, 14:30–Free time in the shopping center of old Bath, 16:00–Tour the Costume Museum.

Day 3: Early train into London.

Orientation (tel. code: 01225)

Bath's town square, three blocks in front of the bus and train station, is a bouquet of tourist landmarks including the Abbey, Roman and medieval baths, and royal Pump Room.

Tourist Information: The TI is in the Abbey churchyard (walk two blocks up Manvers Street from the bus or train station and turn left, Monday–Saturday 9:30–18:00, Sunday 10:00–16:00, shorter hours off-season, tel. 01225/477-101). Pick up the 25p Bath map/mini-guide and the free, packed-with-info This Month in Bath, and browse through scads of flyers. There's an American Express outlet in the TI (decent rates, no commission on any checks, open seven days a week).

Arrival in Bath: The Bath train station is a pleasure (small-town charm, an international tickets desk, and a Guide Friday office masquerading as a tourist information service). The bus station is immediately in front of the train station. My recommended B&Bs are all within a 10- or 15-minute walk or a £3.50 taxi ride. For Brock House and the B&Bs on Marlborough Lane, consider using the Guide Friday city bus tour (described below) as transportation

(5/hrly, from Lane 1 of the bus station). Start the tour, jump out, check into your B&B, and hop back on to finish the circle.

Tours of Bath

▲▲**City Bus Tours**—The Guide Friday green-and-cream, open-top tour bus makes a 70-minute figure-eight circuit of Bath's main sights with an exhaustingly informative running commentary. For one £7.50 ticket (buy from driver), tourists can stop and go at will for a whole day. The buses cover the city center and the surrounding hills (14 signposted pick-up points, 5/hrly in summer, hrly in winter, about 9:25–18:00, tel. 01225/464-446). This is great in sunny weather and a feast for photographers. You can munch a sandwich, work on a tan, and sightsee at the same time. Several competing hop-on, hop-off tour bus companies offer basically the same tour but in 45 minutes and without the swing through the countryside for a couple pounds less. Generally, the Guide Friday guides are better.

▲▲▲**Walking Tours**—These two-hour tours, offered free by trained local volunteers who want to share their love of Bath with its many visitors, are a chatty, historical gossip-filled joy, essential for your understanding of this town's amazing Georgian social scene. How else will you learn that the old "chair ho" call for your sedan chair evolved into today's "cheerio" greeting? Tours leave from in front of the Pump Room daily at 10:30 (often at 14:00 and 19:00, May–October). For Ghost Walks and Bizarre Bath Comedy Walks, see Evening Entertainment, below. For a private walking tour from a local gentleman who is an excellent guide, contact Patrick Driscoll (2 hours for £40, tel. 01225/462-010).

Sights—Bath

▲▲▲**Roman and Medieval Baths**—Back in ancient Roman times, high society enjoyed the mineral springs at Bath. From Londinium, Romans traveled so often to Aquae Sulis, as the city was called, to "take a bath" that finally it became known simply as Bath. Today a fine Roman museum surrounds the ancient bath. The museum, with its well-documented displays, is a one-way system leading you past Roman artifacts, mosaics, a temple pediment, and the actual mouth of the spring piled high with Roman pennies. Enjoy some quality time looking into the eyes of Minerva, goddess of the hot springs. The included self-guided tour audio-wand makes the visit easy and plenty informative. In-depth 40-minute tours leave from the end of the museum at the edge of the actual bath for those with a big appetite for Roman history (included, on the hour, a poolside clock is set for the next depar-ture time). You can revisit the museum after the tour. (£6.30, £8.40 combo ticket includes Costume Museum at a good savings, a family combo costs £22, daily 9:00–18:00, in August also 20:00–22:00, slightly shorter hours off-season, tel. 01225/477-000.)

▲**Pump Room**—After a centuries-long cold spell, Bath was reheated when the previously barren Queen Mary bathed here and in due course bore a male heir to the throne (1687). Once Bath was back on the aristocratic map, high society soon turned the place into one big pleasure palace. The Pump Room, an elegant Georgian hall just above the Roman baths, offers the visitor's best chance to raise a pinky in this Chippendale elegance. Drop by to sip coffee or tea to the rhythm of a string trio (tea/coffee and pastry for £4, live music all year 10:30–13:00, summers until 17:00, good place for a traditional high tea—after 14:30). Above the newspaper table and sedan chairs a statue of Beau Nash himself sniffles down at you. Now's your chance to have a famous (but forgettable) "Bath bun" and split (and spit) a 45p drink of the awfully curative water. The Pump Room's toilets are open to the discreet public.

A quarter of a million gallons of mineral water still bubble through the spa daily. And in 2001 a new spa facility will be opened for the public to once again bathe in Bath.

▲**Abbey**—Bath town wasn't much in the Middle Ages. But an important church has stood on this spot since Anglo-Saxon times. In 973, Edgar, the first king of England, was crowned here. Dominating the town center, the present church—the last great medieval church of England—is 500 years old and a fine example of Late Perpendicular Gothic, with breezy fan vaulting and enough stained glass to earn it the nickname "Lantern of the West" (Monday–Saturday 9:00–18:00, Sunday 13:00–18:00, concert and evensong schedule posted on the door, worth the £1.50 donation, handy flier narrates a 19-stop tour). The Abbey's Heritage Vaults, a small but interesting exhibit, tells the story of Christianity in Bath since Roman times (£2, Monday–Saturday 10:00–16:00, closed Sunday). From the Abbey Green square, take a moment to really appreciate the Abbey's architecture.

▲**Pulteney Bridge and Boats**—Bath is inclined to compare its shop-lined bridge to Florence's Ponte Vecchio. That's pushing it. But to best enjoy a sunny Bath kind of day, pay £1 to go into the Parade Gardens below the bridge (free after 20:00). Across the bridge at Pulteney Weir, tour boats run cruises from under the bridge (£3.80, 50 minutes to Bathampton and back, one boat stops there if you'd like to walk back, the other company has a sundeck ideal for picnics).

▲▲**Royal Crescent and The Circus**—If Bath is an architectural cancan, these are the kickers. These first elegant Georgian "condos" by John Wood (the Elder and the Younger) are well-explained in the city walking tours. "Georgian" is British for "Neoclassical," dating from the 1770s. Stroll the Crescent after dark. Pretend you're rich. Pretend you're poor. Notice the "ha ha fence," a drop in the front yard offering an barrier, invisible from the windows, to sheep and peasants.

▲▲**Georgian House**—This museum offers your best look into a period house. It's worth the £3.50 admission to get behind one of those classy exteriors. The volunteers in each room are determined to fill you in on all the fascinating details of Georgian life . . . like how high-class women shaved their eyebrows and pasted on carefully trimmed strips of furry mouse skin in their place (Tuesday–Sunday 10:30–17:00, closed Monday, "no stiletto heels, please," at 1 Royal Crescent, on the corner of Brock Street and the Royal Crescent, tel. 01225/428-126).

▲▲▲**Costume Museum**—One of Europe's great museums, displaying 400 years of fashion—from Anne Boleyn to Twiggy—one frilly decade at a time, is housed in Bath's elegant Assembly Rooms. Follow the included and excellent CD wand self-guided tour. Learn why Yankee Doodle "stuck a feather in his cap and called it macaroni," and much more (£3.80, cheaper on combo ticket with Roman Baths, daily 10:00–17:00, tel. 01225/477-789).

▲▲**Industrial Heritage Centre**—This is the grand title for Mr. Bowler's Business, a turn-of-the-century engineer's shop, brass foundry, and fizzy-drink factory with a Dickensian office. It's just a pile of meaningless old gadgets until a volunteer guide lovingly resurrects Mr. Bowler's creative genius. Take the fascinating 60-minute tour (call ahead to be sure a volunteer guide is available). Or if a tour is in progress when you arrive, join in. (£3.50, plus a few pence for a glass of genuine Victorian lemonade, daily 10:00–17:00, weekends only in winter, two blocks up Russell Street from the Assembly Rooms, tel. 01225/318-348.) There's a Bath stone exhibit downstairs and a café/shop upstairs.

The Building of Bath Museum—This offers a fascinating look behind the scenes at how the Georgian city was actually built. This is just one large room of exhibits but those interested in construction find it worth the £3 (Tuesday–Sunday 10:30–17:00, closed Monday, near the Circus on a street called "The Paragon," tel. 01225/333-895).

Royal Photographic Society—A hit with shutterbugs, this exhibits the earliest cameras, photos, and their development, along with temporary contemporary exhibits (£3, daily 9:30–17:30, on Milsom Street, tel. 01225/462-841).

▲**American Museum**—I know, you need this in Bath like you need a Big Mac. But this museum offers a fascinating look at colonial and early-American lifestyles. Each of 18 completely furnished rooms (from the 1600s to the 1800s) is hosted by an eager guide waiting to fill you in on the candles, maps, bedpans, and various religious sects that make domestic Yankee history surprisingly interesting. One room is a quilter's nirvana (£5, Tuesday–Sunday 14:00–17:00, closed Monday and November–March, at Claverton Manor, tel. 01225/460-503). The museum is outside of town and a headache to reach if you don't have a car (15-minute walk from the Guide Friday stop or a 10-minute walk from bus #18).

Evening Entertainment

This Month in Bath (available at the TI and many B&Bs) lists events and evening entertainment.

Plays—The Theatre Royal, newly restored and one of England's loveliest, offers a busy schedule of London West End–type plays, including many "pre-London" dress rehearsal runs (£10–20, cheap stand-by tickets, tel. 01225/448-844). You can often get late cancellation seats for sold-out performances (drop by around 18:00).

Bizarre Bath Walks—For a walking comedy act—street theater at its best "with absolutely no history or culture"—follow JJ or Noel Britten on their creative and entertaining Bizarre Bath walk. Their 90-minute "tour," which plays off local passersby as well as tour members, is a kick (£3.50, 20:00 nightly April–September; heavy on magic, careful to insult all kinds of minorities and sensitivities, just racy enough but still good family fun; leaves from the Huntsman pub near the Abbey; confirm time and starting place at TI or call 01225/335-124). Ghost Walks are another way to pass the after-dark hours (£3, 20:00, 2 hrs, unreliably Monday–Friday, tel. 01225/463-618). And for the scholarly types, there are almost nightly historical walks (19:00, 2 hrs, ask at TI).

Drinks—For a good spit-and-sawdust pub, drink real ale at the Star Pub (top of Paragon Street, Bass sold by the jug if you don't want to mess with pints). Or, for maximum entertainment, look up two particularly musical local residents, Van Morrison and Peter Gabriel.

Sleeping in Bath

(£1 = about $1.70, tel. code: 01225)

Sleep Code: S = Single, **D** = Double/Twin, **T** = Triple, **Q** = Quad, **b** = bathroom, **t** = toilet only, **s** = shower only, **CC** = Credit Card (**V**isa, **M**asterCard, **A**mex).

Bath is one of England's busiest tourist towns. To get a good B&B, make a telephone reservation in advance. Competition is stiff, and it's worth asking any of these places for a non-weekend, three nights-in-a-row, or off-season deal. Friday and Saturday nights are tightest—especially if you're staying only one night, since B&Bs favor those staying longer. If staying only Saturday night, you're very bad news. There's a laundrette around the corner from Brock's Guest House on the cute pedestrian lane called Margaret's Buildings and a scruffier place on Upper Bristol Road (tel. 01225/429-378).

Sleeping near the Royal Crescent

Brock's Guest House will put bubbles in your Bath experience. Marion Dodd and her husband Geoffrey have redone their Georgian townhouse (built by John Wood in 1765) in a way that would make the famous architect proud. This charming house is perfectly located between the prestigious Royal Crescent and the elegant Circus (Db-£58–68, Tb-£78–82, Qb-£90–95, reserve with a credit-card number far in advance, strictly non-smoking, 32 Brock Street, BA1 2LN, tel. 01225/338-374, fax 01225/334-245, e-mail: marion@brocks.force9.net). If you can't find a sedan chair, Brock's is a 15-minute uphill walk, £3.50 taxi, or short bus ride (to Assembly Rooms and short walk) from the station. Guide Friday buses stop on Brock Street. If you're in a transportation jam, Marion can occasionally arrange a reasonable private car hire.

Woodville House is run by Anne and Tom Toalster. This grandmotherly little house has three charming rooms, one shared shower, and a TV lounge. Breakfast is a help-yourself buffet around a big, family-style table (D-£36, minimum two nights, anyone who smokes at all is not welcome, below the Royal Crescent at 4 Marlborough Lane, BA1 2NQ, tel. & fax 01225/319-335, e-mail: AnneToalster@compuserve.com).

Other recommended B&Bs on Marlborough Lane: **Elgin Villa** is also a fine value (Ds-£36, Db-£40, minimum two nights, kids £10 extra, four rooms, parking, nonsmoking, big continental breakfast in your room, 6 Marlborough Lane, BA1 2NQ, tel. & fax 01225/424-557). Or consider **Athelney Guest House** (D-£38, three rooms, continental breakfast in your room, non-smoking, parking, 5 Marlborough Lane, tel. & fax 01225/312-031, Sue and Colin Davies). **Parkside Guest House** is more upscale, renting five classy Edwardian rooms (Db-£60, non-smoking, 11 Marlborough Lane, tel. & fax 01225/429-444, Erica and Inge Lynall). The **Marlborough House** is a Victorian place renting five rooms (tel. 01225/ 318-175, fax 01225/466-127, run by Americans Laura and Charles). **Armstrong House B&B**, cozy and well run, is closer to town on a busier road but behind double-paned windows (5 rooms, Db-£50, continental breakfast in room, non-smoking, 41 Crescent Gardens, Upper Bristol Road, tel. 01225/442-211, fax 01225/460-665, Tony Conradi).

Sleeping behind the Train Station in a Residential Area

Holly Villa Guest House, with a cheery garden and a cozy TV lounge, an eight-minute walk from the station and center, is enthusiastically and thoughtfully run by Jill McGarrigle (seven rooms, Ds-£40, Db-£48, Tb-£63, prices good with this book, strictly non-smoking, easy parking, 14 Pulteney Gardens, BA2 4HG, tel. 01225/310-331, fax 01225/339-334). From the city center, walk over North Parade Bridge, take the first right, then the second left. It's a block from a Guide Friday bus stop.

Muriel Guy's B&B, another fine value, mixes Georgian elegance with homey warmth and fine city views (Db-£45, non-smoking, 14 Raby Place, tel. 01225/465-120, fax 01225/465-283). It's a 10-minute walk out of town: go over the bridge on North Parade Road, take a left on Pulteney Road, a right up Bathwick Hill, and it's on your left at 14 Raby Place.

Sleeping in the Town Center

Henry Guest House is a clean and vertical little eight-room, family-run place two blocks in front of the train station on a quiet side street (S-£19, D-£38, T-£57, TVs in rooms, lots of narrow stairs, one shower and one bath for all, 6 Henry Street, BA1 1JT, tel. 01225/424-052). This kind of decency at this price, centrally located, is found nowhere else in Bath.

Harington's of Bath Hotel, with 13 newly renovated rooms on a quiet street in the town center, is run by Susan Pow (Db-£86, family room deal, slow-time discounts, non-smoking, lots of stairs, CC:VMA, extremely central at 10 Queen Street, tel. 01225/461-728, fax 01225/444-804).

Parade Park Hotel, with clean rooms and helpful owners, is centrally located (Sb-£45, Db-£55–65, special four-poster Db-£75, Tb-£90, Qb-£105, non-smoking rooms available, 10 North Parade, BA2 4AL, tel. 01225/463-384, fax 01225/442-322, Nita and David Derrick).

Pratt's Hotel is as proper and old English as you'll find in Bath. Its creaks and frays are aristocratic. Its public places make you want to sip a brandy and its 46 rooms are bright and spacious, with all the comforts (Sb-£65, Db-£95, prices promised with this book in 1999, dogs £2.95 but children free, CC:VMA, elevator, two blocks immediately in front of the station on South Parade, BA2 4AB, tel. 01225/460-441, fax 01225/448-807, e-mail: martin@prattshotel.demon.co.uk).

Sleeping near Pulteney Bridge

Kennard Hotel is a comfortable hotel with 14 charming Georgian rooms. Richard Ambler runs this place warmly, with careful attention to detail (S-£45, Db-£85–95 depending upon size, non-smoking, CC:VMA, just over Pulteney Bridge at 11 Henrietta

Street, BA2 6LL, tel. 01225/310-472, fax 01225/460-054, e-mail: kennard@dircon.co.uk).

Laura Place Hotel is another elegant Georgian place (eight rooms, two on the ground floor, Db-£60–90 from small and high up to huge and palatial, 10 percent discount with cash and this book, family suite, non-smoking, easy parking, CC:VMA, 3 Laura Place, Great Pulteney Street, just over Pulteney Bridge, tel. 01225/463-815, fax 01225/310-222, Patricia Bull).

Henrietta Hotel is a very plain place in the same elegant neighborhood with nearly no character (10 rooms, Db-£45–65, cash discount when quiet, CC:VM, 32 Henrietta Street, tel. 01225/447-779, fax 01225/444-150).

Cheap Dorm Beds

The **YMCA**, institutional but friendly and wonderfully central (on a leafy square down a tiny alley off Broad Street), has industrial-strength rooms and scuff-proof halls (S-£14, D-£26, T-£39, Q-£52, beds in big dorms-£11, includes breakfast, surcharge for one night, families offered a day nursery for kids under five, cheap dinners, CC:VM, tel. 01225/460-471, fax 01225/462-065, e-mail: info@ymcabath.u-net.com).

Bath Backpackers Hostel (while likely to close in 1999), bills itself as a totally fun-packed mad place to stay. It's an Aussie-run hostel three blocks up from the station renting bunk beds in 6- to 10-bed co-ed rooms (£12 per bed with continental breakfast, non-smoking, no lockers, internet cafe, 13 Pierrepont Street, tel. 01225/446-787, fax 01225/446-305).

The **Youth Hostel** is in a grand old building outside of town (£10 per bed without breakfast in 2- to 14-bed rooms, bus #18 from the station, tel. 01225/465-674).

Eating in Bath

While not a great pub grub town, Bath is bursting with quaint eateries. There's something for every appetite and budget—just stroll around the center of town. A picnic dinner of take-out fish and chips in the Royal Crescent Park is ideal for aristocratic hoboes.

Eating between the Abbey and the Station

Four fine and popular places share North Parade Passage, a block behind the Abbey: **Tilley's Bistro** serves healthy French, English, and vegetarian meals at great prices with fine atmosphere (three-course meals for £15, nightly 18:30–23:00, smoke-free, North Parade Passage, tel. 01225/484-200). **Sally Lunn's House** is a cutesy, quasi-historic place for expensive doily meals, tea, pink pillows, and lots of lace. It's fine for tea and buns. Customers get a free peek at the basement museum—otherwise 30p (£12 meals, nightly, 4 North Parade Passage, tel. 01225/461-634). Next door, **Demuth's Vegetarian Restaurant** serves good three-course £10 meals (nightly, tel. 01225/446-059). **Crystal Palace Pub**, with hearty meals under rustic timbers or in the sunny courtyard, is a handy standby (meals under £5, daily from 12:00–14:30, 18:00–20:30, closed Sunday; children welcome on the patio, not indoors; 11 Abbey Green, tel. 01225/423-944).

Evans Self-Service Fish Restaurant is the best eat-in or take-out fish-and-chips deal in town (Monday–Wednesday 11:30–18:30, Thursday–Saturday 11:30–20:30, closed Sunday, student discounts, 7 Abbeygate, tel. 01225/463-981). For very cheap meals, try **Spike's Fish and Chips** (open very late) and the neighboring café just behind the bus station.

Eating between the Abbey and the Circus

George Street is lined with cheery eateries (Thai, Italian, wine bars, and so on). Guildhall Market, across from Pulteney Bridge, is fun for browsing and picnic shopping, with a very cheap cafeteria if you'd like to sip tea surrounded by stacks of used books, bananas on the push list, and honest-to-goodness old-time locals.

Eastern Eye has tasty Indian food under the sumptuous domes of an Georgian auction hall (£15 meals, daily 12:00–14:30, 18:00–23:00, 8a Quiet Street, tel. 01225/422-323). The **Green Tree Pub** is a rare pub with good grub and a non-smoking room, on Green Street (lunch only, no children).

Pasta Galore is a bit scruffy but serves decent Italian food (daily 18:00–22:30, good homemade pasta, call to reserve a table—avoid the basement, 31 Barton Street, tel. 01225/463-861). Next door is a cheap and fast Mexican joint.

Devon Savouries serves greasy, delicious take-out pasties, sausage rolls, and vegetable pies (on the main walkway between New Bond Street and Upper Borough Walls). The Waitrose **supermarket**, at the Podium shopping center, is great for groceries (open until 19:00 or 20:00, across from the post office on High Street).

For a classy, intimate setting and "new English" cuisine worth the splurge, dine at **No. 5 Bistro** (main courses with vegetables £12–15, Monday and Tuesday are "bring your own bottle of wine" nights—no corkage charge, don't be shy . . . buy a bottle on your way there from a store, Monday–Saturday 18:30–22:00, closed Sunday, just over Pulteney Bridge at 5 Argyle Street, smart to reserve, tel. 01225/444-499).

The **Bathtub Restaurant**, just around the corner from No. 5 on

Grove Street, is cheaper (£8 meals) and funkier, serving international vegetarian cuisine (nightly 18:00–23:00, tel. 01225/460-593).

Eating near the Circus and Brock's Guest House

Circus Restaurant is intimate and a good value with Mozartian ambience and candlelit prices: £15 for a three-course dinner special including great vegetables and a selection of fine desserts (daily, 34 Brock Street, tel. 01225/318-918, Felix Rosenow).

Woods Restaurant serves modern English cuisine to well-dressed locals in a sprawling candlelit brasserie (£7 lunches, £16 three-course dinners, closed Sunday, 9-13 Alfred Street near Assembly Rooms, tel. 01225/314-812).

On the opposite end of the decency spectrum, the **Chequers Inn** (2 blocks up the hill, 50 Rivers Street) is a smoky dive of a pub with cheap, finger-sticking, disgusting grub and darts.

Transportation Connections—Bath

To: London's Paddington station by train (hrly, 75 min, £28.50 one-way or round-trip) or cheaper by National Express bus (hrly, 3 hrs, £19 round-trip, £18 one-way, ask about £8 day returns). To get from London to Bath, consider using an all-day Stonehenge and Bath organized bus tour from London. For about the same cost as the train ticket, you can see Stonehenge, tour Bath, and leave the tour before it returns to London (they'll let you stow your bag underneath). Evan Evans (£29.50, tel. 0181/332-2222) and Travelline (£24, tel. 0181/668-7261) offer Stonehenge/Bath day trips from London. Train info tel. 0345/484-950.

London's airports: By National Express bus to Heathrow Airport (9/day, at 10:35, 12:35, 13:35, 14:35, 16:35, and so on, 2.5 hrs, £10, tel. 0990-808-080), and Gatwick (8/day, 4.5 hrs, change at Heathrow). Trains are faster but more expensive (hrly, 2.5 hrs, £22.50). Coming from Heathrow, you can also take the tube from the airport to London's Paddington station, then catch the Exeter train to Bath.

DAY TRIP
TO PARIS

13

The most exciting single day trip from London is Paris, just a three-hour trip by Eurostar train. Paris offers sweeping boulevards, sleepy parks, world-class art galleries, chatty crêpe stands, sleek shopping malls, the Eiffel Tower, and people-watching from outdoor cafés. Climb the Notre-Dame and the Eiffel Tower, master the Louvre museum, and cruise the grand Champs-Élysées levard. Many fall in love with Paris, one of the world's most mantic cities. This chapter is excerpted from *Rick Steves France, lgium & the Netherlands 1999* (by Rick Steves and Steve Smith).

Getting to Paris
You can order tickets for the Eurostar train from London to Paris by phone with a credit card in the U.S.A. (800/EUR0STAR) or in Britain at any train station or by phone (0345/303-030; pick up tickets at London's Waterloo station an hour before the Eurostar departure). For more information, see Transportation Connections chapter.

Planning Your Time
Ideally, spend the night in Paris, but if all you have is a day, here's the plan:
7:10–Depart London.
11:30–Arrive in Paris. Take a taxi or the Métro to Notre-Dame.
12:00–Explore Notre-Dame and Sainte-Chapelle.
14:00–Taxi or Métro to the Arc de la Triomphe.
14:30–Walk down Champs-Élysées and through the Tuileries Gardens.
16:00–Tour the Louvre (open until 18:00, closed Tuesday, after 15:00 it's half price and not crowded).
18:00–Taxi or Métro to Trocadero, walk to Eiffel Tower (if you

PARIS OVERVIEW

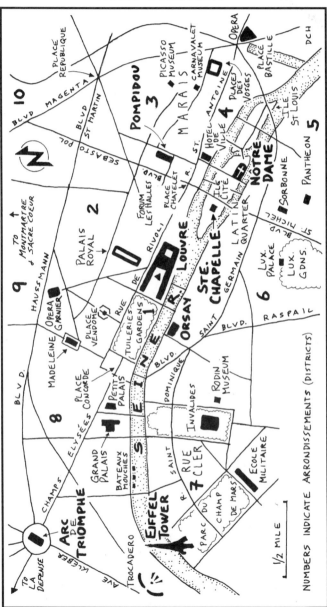

NUMBERS INDICATE ARRONDISSEMENTS (DISTRICTS)

1/2 MILE

ascend, allow plenty of time for delays). One hour before departure, catch a taxi or the Métro back to Paris' Gare du Nord train
station.
20:07 or 21:13–Depart Paris.
22:13 or 23:16–Arrive in London.
Note: For a trip of more than one day, it's worth getting *Rick
Steves' Paris*, which includes extensive museum tours and interesting walks, along with great places to eat and sleep.

Arrival in Paris
(5.5F = about $1)
The Eurostar train from London zips you to Paris' Gare du Nord
train station. Paris has six major train stations, each serving different regions. The Gare du Nord serves London. You'll find a
handy train information booth and a Paris Tourist Office near
track 18. There are also information booths for Eurostar trains
in the center of the arrival area. Change offices, the Métro, and
taxis are easy to find.

Passengers departing for London via the Eurostar must check
in on the second level, opposite track 4. A peaceful waiting area
overlooks the tracks.

Orientation
Paris is split in half by the Seine River. You'll find Paris easier to
negotiate if you know which side of the river you're on, and which
subway stop (abbreviated "Mo") you're closest to. If you're north
of the river (above on any city map), you're on the Right Bank (*rive
droite*). If you're south of it, you're on the Left Bank (*rive gauche*).

Tourist Information
Avoid the Paris TIs—long lines, short information, and a 5F
charge for maps. This chapter and a map (cheap at newsstand or
freebies available at any hotel) are all you need for a short visit. If
you're staying longer than a day, get a *Pariscope* weekly magazine
(or one of its clones, 3F at any newsstand), which lists museum
hours, concerts, plays, movies, nightclubs, and art exhibits.

Getting Around Paris
By Taxi: Two people with only one day should taxi everywhere.
You'll save lots of time and spend only a few bucks per ride.
Parisian cabs are wonderful: comfortable, with hassle-free meters,
and easy to flag down (or ask for a nearby taxi stand).

By Métro: In Paris you're never more than a 10-minute walk
from a Métro station. One ticket takes you anywhere in the system
with unlimited transfers for about $1. These are your essential

Métro words: *direction, correspondance* (transfer), *sortie* (exit), *carnet* (cheap set of 10 tickets), and *Donnez-moi mon porte-monnaie!* (Give me back my wallet!) Thieves thrive in the Métro.

Helpful Hints

On **Monday,** the Orsay Museum, Rodin Museum, and Versailles are closed. The Louvre is more crowded because of this. On **Tuesday,** the Louvre is closed. Versailles and the Orsay Museum can be jammed.

Paris Museum Pass: Serious sightseers save time (less time in lines) and money by getting this pass. Sold at museums, major Métro stations, and tourist information offices, it pays for itself in two admissions and gets you into nearly all the sights (major exceptions: Eiffel Tower and Disneyland Paris). The pass also allows you to skip to the front of lines at sights—saving hours of waiting in the summer (one day-80F, three consecutive days-160F, five consecutive days-240F).

Sights—Paris

Start your visit where the city did—on the Île de la Cité (the island of the city)—facing the Notre-Dame.

▲▲**Notre-Dame Cathedral**—The 700-year-old cathedral is packed with history and tourists. Study its sculpture (Notre-Dame's forte) and windows, eavesdrop on guides, and walk all around the outside of the church dedicated to "Our Lady" (Notre-Dame). The facade is the worth a close look. Mary is center stage—cradling Jesus, surrounded by the halo of the rose window. Adam is on the left, and Eve is on the right. Below Mary and above the arches is a row of 28 statues known as the Kings of Judah. During the French Revolution, these Biblical kings were mistaken for the hated French kings. The citizens stormed the church, crying, "Off with their heads." All were decapitated but have since been recapitated. (Free, daily 8:00–18:45; treasury-15F, daily 9:30–17:30; free English tours usually offered Wednesday and Thursday at noon and Saturdays at 14:30. Métro: Cité.) Climb to the top for a great gargoyle's-eye view of the city; you get 400 steps for only 30F (entrance on outside, north tower open 9:30–17:30, closed at lunch and earlier off-season). Clean 2.70F toilets in front of the church near Charlemagne's statue.

If you're hungry near Notre-Dame, the only grocery store on the Île de la Cité is tucked away at 16 rue Chanoinesse, one block north of the church (9:00–13:30, 16:00–20:30, closed Sunday). Nearby Île St. Louis has inexpensive *créperies* and grocery stores open daily on its main drag. Plan a picnic for the quiet bench-filled park immediately behind the church (public WC). Two blocks west of Notre-Dame is the . . .

▲▲▲**Sainte-Chapelle**—The triumph of Gothic church architecture is a cathedral of glass like no other. It was speedily built from 1242–1248 for St. Louis IX (France's only canonized king) to house the supposed Crown of Thorns. Its architectural harmony is due to the fact that it was completed under the direction of one architect in only six years—unheard of in Gothic times. (Notre-Dame took more than 200 years to build.) Climb the spiral staircase to the *Chapelle Haute* and "let there be light." There are 15 huge stained-glass windows (two-thirds of it 13th-century original), with more than 1,100 different scenes, mostly from the Bible (32F, daily 9:30–18:30, off-season 10:00–16:30, concerts nearly nightly in summer, call 01 48 01 91 35 for concert information, Métro: Cité).

▲▲▲**Arc de Triomphe**—Napoleon had the magnificent Arc de Triomphe commissioned to commemorate his victory at the Battle of Austerlitz. There's no triumphal arch bigger (50 meters high, 40 meters wide). And, with 12 converging boulevards, there's no traffic circle more thrilling to experience—either behind the wheel or on foot (take the underpass). An elevator or a spiral staircase leads to a cute museum about the arch and a grand view from the top, even after dark (35F, Tuesday–Saturday 9:00–23:00, Sunday and Monday 9:30–18:00, tel. 01 43 80 31 31, Métro: Étoile).

▲▲**Champs-Élysées and the Place de la Concorde**—This famous boulevard, carrying the city's greatest concentration of traffic, leads to the place de la Concorde, the city's largest square. This was the place where the guillotine took the lives of thousands—including King Louis XVI. Back then it was called the place de la Revolution.

Catherine de Medici wanted a place to drive her carriage, so she started draining the swamp that would become the Champs-Élysées. Napoleon put on the final touches, and it's been the place to be seen ever since. The Tour de France bicycle race ends here, as do all parades (French or foe) of any significance. While the boulevard has become a bit hamburgerized, a walk here is a must. Take the Métro to the Arc de Triomphe (Métro: Étoile) and saunter down the Champs-Élysées. (Métro stops are located every three blocks along the boulevard.)

▲▲▲**Louvre**—This is Europe's oldest, biggest, greatest, and possibly most crowded museum. It's packed with masterpieces from ancient Greece, Rome, medieval jewels, Michelangelo statues, and paintings by the greatest artists from the Renaissance to the Romantic movement of the mid-1800s. A security check with metal detectors creates a line in front of the pyramid; if you enter directly from the Métro stop, you'll get in quicker, though there is no grander entry than through the pyramid.

Pick up the free *Louvre Handbook in English* at the information desk under the pyramid as you enter. Don't try to cover the museum thoroughly. The 90-minute English-language tours, which leave six times daily except Sunday, boil this overwhelming museum down to size (33F, tour tel. 01 40 20 52 09, Web site: www.louvre.fr). Clever new 30F digital audio tours (after ticket booths, at top of stairs) give you a receiver and a directory of about 130 masterpieces, allowing you to dial a (rather dull) commentary on included works as you stumble upon them. Rick Steves' and Gene Openshaw's museum guidebook, *Rick Steves' Mona Winks* (buy in U.S.A.), includes a self-guided tour of the Louvre.

If you can't get a guide, start in the Denon wing and visit these highlights, in this order: Michelangelo's *Slaves*, Ancient Greek and Roman (Parthenon frieze, *Vénus de Milo*, Pompeii mosaics, Etruscan sarcophagi, Roman portrait busts, Nike of Samothrace); Apollo Gallery (jewels); French and Italian paintings in the Grande Galerie (a quarter-mile long and worth the hike); the *Mona Lisa* and her Italian Renaissance roommates; the nearby Neoclassical collection *(Coronation of Napoleon)*; and the Romantic collection, with works by Delacroix *(Liberty at the Barricades—*see your 100F note) and Géricault *(Raft of the Medusa)*.

Cost: Admission 45F until 15:00, 26F after 15:00 and all day Sunday, free on the first Sunday of the month and if you're under 18.

Hours: Open Wednesday–Monday from 9:00–18:00; the Richelieu wing open Monday until 21:45, all wings open Wednesdays until 21:45, closed Tuesday. Tel. 01 40 20 53 17 or 01 40 20 51 51 for recorded information.

Getting to the Louvre: Get off at the Palais-Royal/Musée du Louvre Métro stop (not the Louvre Rivoli stop, which is farther away). Exiting the Métro, follow *Musée du Louvre* signs and head for the inverted pyramid, where you'll uncover a handy TI, glittering boutiques, a dizzying assortment of good-value eateries (up the escalator), and the underground entry to the Louvre.

▲▲▲**Eiffel Tower**—Crowded and expensive but worth the trouble. The Tower is 1,000 feet tall (six inches taller in hot weather), covers 2.5 acres and requires 50 tons of paint. Its 7,000 tons of metal are spread out so well at the base that it's no heavier per square inch than a linebacker on tiptoes.

Built a hundred years after the French Revolution (and in the midst of an Industrial one), the Tower served no function but to impress. To a generation hooked on technology, the Tower was the marvel of the age, a symbol of progress and of human ingenuity.

There are three observation platforms, at 200, 400 and 900 feet; the higher you go the more you pay. Each requires a separate elevator (and a line), so plan on at least 90 minutes if you want to

EIFFEL TOWER TO INVALIDES

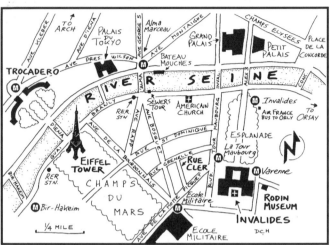

go to the top and back. The view from the 400-foot-high second level is plenty. It costs 20F to go to the first level, 40F to the second, and 57F to go all the way for the 1,000-foot view (summers daily 9:00–24:00, off-season 9:30–23:00, tel. 01 44 11 23 23, Métro: Trocadero). Go early (arrive by 9:30) or late in the day (after 18:00) to avoid most crowds; weekends are worst. *Pilier Nord* (the north pillar) has the biggest elevator and, therefore, the fastest moving line.

More Sights—Paris
▲▲▲**Orsay Museum**—This is Paris' 19th-century art museum (actually, art from 1848–1914), including Europe's greatest collection of Impressionist works. The museum is housed in a former train station (Gare d'Orsay) across the river and 10 minutes downstream from the Louvre (the Métro stop "Solferino" is three blocks south of the Orsay).

Start on the ground floor. The "pretty" conservative establishment art is on the right. Then cross left into the brutally truthful and, at that time, very shocking art of the realist rebels and Manet. Then ride the escalators at the far end (detouring at the top for a grand museum view) to the series of Impressionist rooms (Monet, Renoir, Dégas, et al). Don't miss the Grand Ballroom (room 52, *Arts et Decors de la IIIème République*) and Art Nouveau on the mezzanine level.

Cost: 39F, 27F for the young and old, under 18 free, tickets good all day. The booth near the entrance gives free floor plans in English. English-language tours usually run daily except Sunday at 11:30, cost 38F, take 90 minutes, and are also available on audiotape. City museum passes are sold in the basement; if there's a long line you can skip it by buying one there, but you can't skip the metal detector line into the museum. Tel. 01 40 49 48 48.

Hours: Tuesday, Wednesday, Friday, Saturday 10:00–18:00, Thursday 10:00–21:45, Sunday 9:00–18:00, closed Monday. From June 20 to September 20, the museum opens at 9:00. Last entrance is 45 minutes before closing. Galleries start closing 30 minutes early. The Orsay is very crowded on Tuesday, when the Louvre is closed.

▲▲**Napoleon's Tomb and the Army Museum**—The emperor lies majestically dead inside several coffins under a grand dome—a goose-bumping pilgrimage for historians. Napoleon is surrounded by the tombs of other French war heroes and Europe's greatest military museum in the Hôtel des Invalides. Follow signs to the crypt, where you'll find Roman Empire–style reliefs listing the accomplishments of Napoleon's administration. The restored dome glitters with 26 pounds of gold (37F, daily 10:00–18:00, closes off-season at 17:00, tel. 01 44 42 37 67, Métro: La Tour Maubourg or Varennes).

▲▲**Rodin Museum**—This user-friendly museum is filled with passionate works by the greatest sculptor since Michelangelo. See *The Kiss, The Thinker, The Gates of Hell*, and many more. Don't miss the room full of work by Rodin's student and mistress, Camille Claudel. (28F, 18F on Sunday, 5F for gardens only, which may be Paris' best deal as many works are well-displayed in the beautiful gardens; Tuesday–Sunday 9:30–17:45, closed Monday, closes off-season at 17:00, 77 rue de Varennes, tel. 01 44 18 61 10, Metro: Varennes, near Napoleon's Tomb.) Good self-serve cafeteria and idyllic picnic spots in family-friendly back garden.

▲**Latin Quarter**—The left bank neighborhood just opposite the Notre-Dame is the Latin Quarter. This was a center of Roman Paris. But its touristic fame relates to the Latin Quarter's intriguing artsy, bohemian character. This was perhaps Europe's leading university district in the Middle Ages—home, since the 13th century, to the prestigious Sorbonne University. Back then, Latin was the language of higher education. And, since students here came from all over Europe, Latin served as their linguistic common denominator. Locals referred to the quarter by its language: Latin. In modern times this was the center of Paris' cafe culture. The neighborhood's main boulevards (St. Michel and St. Germain) are lined with cafés—once the haunts of great poets and philosophers, but now the hangout of tired tourists. While still youthful and artsy, the area has become a tourist ghetto filled with cheap North African eateries.

▲▲**Sacré-Coeur and Montmartre**—This Byzantine-looking church, while only 130 years old, is impressive. It was built as a "praise the Lord anyway" gesture, after the French were humiliated by the Germans in a brief war in 1871. The church is open daily until 23:00. One block from the church, the square called the place du Tertre was the haunt of Toulouse-Lautrec and the original bohemians. Today it's mobbed by tourists and unoriginal bohemians, but still fun. Either use the Anvers Métro stop (plus one Métro ticket for the funicular to avoid stairs) or the closer but less scenic Abbesses stop. A taxi to the top of the hill saves time and sweat.

Sights—Near Paris

▲▲▲**Palace of Versailles**—Every king's dream, Versailles was the residence of the French king and the cultural heartbeat of Europe for about 100 years—until the Revolution of 1789 ended the notion that God deputized some people to rule for Him on Earth. Louis XIV spent half a year's income of Europe's richest country turning his dad's hunting lodge into a palace fit for a divine monarch. Louis XV and Louis XVI spent much of the 18th century gilding Louis XIV's lily. In 1837, about 50 years after the royal family was evicted, King Louis Philippe opened the palace as a museum. Europe's next-best palaces are Versailles wannabes.

Information: You'll find TIs across from the Versailles' R.G. train station (tel. 01 39 50 36 22), two information desks on the approach to the palace, and at the palace (entrance C). Their free "Versailles Orientation Guide" explains your sightseeing options.

Ticket Options: The main palace self-guided one-way palace romp, including the Hall of Mirrors, costs 45F (35F after 15:30, on Sunday, or for those under 26). To supplement this with a private tour through the other sections, you'll need to pay the 45F base price then add 25F for a one-hour guided tour, 37F for a 90-minute guided tour, or 25F for a self-guided Walkman-cassette tour.

Hours: Tuesday–Sunday 9:00–18:30, October–April 9:00–17:30, last entry 30 minutes before closing, closed Monday. The palace is most crowded on Tuesday, Sunday, and from 10:00–15:00. To minimize crowds and get a reduced entry ticket, arrive after 15:30. Tour the gardens after the palace closes. The palace is great late. Information tel. 01 30 84 76 18 or 01 30 84 74 00.

Getting to Versailles: Versailles, 12 miles from downtown Paris, is a quick and easy ride on the RER train (not covered by a standard Paris Métro ticket). Take the Métro to an RER-C station (Gare d'Austerlitz, St. Michel, Orsay, Invalides, Pont de l'Alma, or Champs de Mars/Tour Eiffel), follow the RER signs, and buy a round-trip ticket to Versailles (26F). Look at the schedule for

VERSAILLES

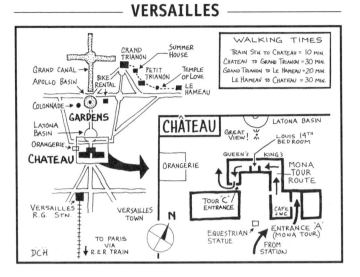

trains, usually named VICK, going to Versailles R.G., the Rive
Gauche station (4/hrly, 30 min; confirm that your train stops at
Versailles R.G. rather than Versailles C.H., farther from the
palace). Leaving the station, turn right, then left on the major
boulevard to reach the palace (10-minute walk).

▲▲**Disneyland Paris**—Europe's Disneyland is basically a modern
remake of California's, with most of the same rides and smiles.
The main difference is that Mickey Mouse speaks French (and you
can buy wine with your lunch). My kids went ducky. Locals love it.
It's worth a day if Paris is handier than Florida or California.
Crowds are a problem. If possible, avoid Saturday, Sunday,
Wednesday, school holidays, and July and August. The park can
get very crowded. When 60,000 have entered, they close the gates
(tel. 01 64 74 30 00 for the latest). After dinner, crowds are gone,
and you'll walk right on to rides that had a 45-minute wait three
hours earlier. Food is fun but expensive. To eat reasonably, smug-
gle in a picnic. Disney brochures are in every Paris hotel.

   Cost: 200F for adults, 155F for kids 3–11, 25F less in spring
and fall.

   Hours: Daily 9:00–23:00 late June–early September and Saturday and Sunday off-season, shoulder-season weekdays
9:00–19:00, off-season 10:00–18:00.

   Getting to Disneyland Paris: The RER train drops you right
in the park (40F each way; from downtown Paris to Marne-la-Vallee

in 30 minutes). The last train back into Paris leaves shortly after midnight. Disneyland Paris is actually a stop on the London Eurostar route.

Sleeping in Paris (5.5F = about $1)
Sleep Code: S = Single, **D** = Double/Twin, **T** = Triple, **Q** = Quad, **b** = bathroom, **t** = toilet only, **s** = shower only, **CC** = Credit Card (**V**isa, **M**asterCard, **A**mex), * = French hotel rating system (0–4 stars).

If you're calling Paris from the U.S.A., dial 011-33 (or from Britain dial 00-33), then the local number without the initial zero.

Sleeping in the Rue Cler Neighborhood
(7th district, Métro: École Militaire, zip code: 75007)
Rue Cler, a village-like pedestrian street, is safe, tidy, and makes me feel like I must have been a poodle in a previous life. How such coziness lodged itself between the high-powered government/business district and the expensive Eiffel Tower and Invalides areas, I'll never know. Living here ranks with the top museums as one of the city's great experiences.

The street called rue Cler is the glue that holds this pleasant neighborhood together. On rue Cler you can eat and browse your way through a street full of tart shops, cheeseries, and colorful outdoor produce stalls.

Hôtel Leveque** has been entirely renovated. With a helpful staff and a singing maid, it's still cozy. It's a fine value with the best location on the block, comfortable rooms, cable TV, hair dryers, safes, an ice machine, and tasteful decor throughout (Sb-270F, Db-380–450F, Tb-550F, breakfast-30F but free for readers of this book, CC:VMA, 29 rue Cler, tel. 01 47 05 49 15, fax 01 45 50 49 36, Web site: http://interresa.ca/hotel/leveque/fr, e-mail: hotellev@club-internet.fr). Laurence at the front desk speaks English.

Hôtel du Champs de Mars**, with charming pastel rooms, is an even cosier rue Cler option. The hotel has a Provence-style small-town feel from top to bottom. Rooms are comfortable and a very good value. Single rooms can work as tiny doubles (Db-390–420F, Tb-505F, CC:VMA, cable TV, hair dryers, etc., 30 yards off rue Cler at 7 rue du Champs de Mars, tel. 01 45 51 52 30, fax 01 45 51 64 36, Web site: www: adx.fr/hotel-du-champ-de-mars, e-mail: stg@club-internet.fr).

Hôtel Relais Bosquet*** is bright, spacious, and a bit upscale with sharp, comfortable rooms (Db-550–900F, most at 750F, CC:VMA, 19 rue du Champs de Mars, tel. 01 47 05 25 45, fax 01 45 55 08 24, e-mail: Webmaster@relais-bosquet.com).

The similar **Hotel Beaugency***** offers similar comfort for less (Db-720F, includes a buffet breakfast, 21 rue Duvivier, tel. 01 47 05 01 63, fax 01 45 51 04 96).

Hôtel de l'Alma*** is a tight and tidy place with 32 delightful look-alike rooms all with TV and minibar (Sb-400F, Db-450F, breakfast included, no triples but a kid's bed can be moved in for free, popular with Mexican and Russian groups, CC:VMA, 32 rue de l'Exposition, tel. 01 47 05 45 70, fax 01 45 51 84 47).

Hôtel La Tour Maubourg*** is particularly romantic. It lies alone five minutes east of the rue Cler, just off the Esplanade des Invalides, and feels like a slightly faded, elegant manor house with spacious Old World rooms. It overlooks a cheery green within sight of Napoleon's tomb (Sb-550–650F, Db-690–850F, suites for up to four 900–1,400F, prices include breakfast with fresh-squeezed juice, prices reduced from mid-July–mid-August, CC:VM, immediately at the La Tour Maubourg Métro stop, 150 rue de Grenelle, tel. 01 47 05 16 16, fax 01 47 05 16 14, e-mail: victor@worldnet.fr).

Transportation Connections—Paris

To London: The sleek Eurostar train makes the 190-mile trip in three hours, with 12 departures daily in each direction, costing $109 each way for a second-class Leisure Ticket (cheaper for rail-pass holders). For Eurostar details, call 800/EUROSTAR in the U.S.A., go to www.eurostar.com, or visit any major train station in Europe. *Note that time zone is one hour earlier than the Continent's. Times listed on tickets are local times.*

To Other Destinations: Paris is Europe's transportation hub. The city has six central rail stations, each serving different regions. You'll find trains (day and night) to most any French or European destination. For train schedule information, call 08 36 35 35 35 (3F/minute).

SLEEPING IN LONDON

London is expensive. For £50 ($80), you'll get a sleepable double with breakfast in a safe, clean, tiny, dreary place where the landlords are absent and service is minimal. (Hang up your towel to dry and reuse.) For £60 ($95) you'll get a basic, clean, reasonably cheery double in a usually cramped, cracked-plaster building. My London splurges, at £100–140 ($170–240), are spacious, thoughtfully appointed places you'd be happy to entertain or make love in. Hearty English (as opposed to skimpy continental) breakfasts are included unless otherwise noted, and TVs are nearly standard in rooms.

Reserve your London room with a phone call or e-mail as soon as you can commit to a date. Many places will hold a room with no deposit if you promise to arrive by midday. Others want your credit-card number as security. Most have expensive cancellation policies. If you must send a deposit, ask if you can send a signed $100 traveler's check. (Leave the "pay to" line blank and include a note explaining that you'll be happy to pay cash upon arrival, so they can avoid bank charges, if they'll just hold your check until you arrive.)

Sleep Code
S = Single, **D** = Double/Twin, **T** = Triple,
Q = Quad, **b** = bathroom, **t** = toilet only, **s** = shower only,
CC = Credit Card (**V**isa, **M**asterCard, **A**mex). Unless otherwise noted, prices include a big English breakfast and all taxes.
Exchange rate: £1=about $1.70. **Tel. code:** 0171.

Sleeping in Victoria Station Neighborhood, Belgravia

The streets behind Victoria Station teem with budget B&Bs. It's a safe, surprisingly tidy and decent area without a hint of the trashy

VICTORIA STATION

1. TUBE, TOURIST INFO, TAXI & CITY BUSES
2. CITY BUS TOURS
3. WOODVILLE
4. LIME TREE
5. CHERRY COURT
6. LIMEGROVE
7. ELIZ. HOTEL
8. ELIZ. HOUSE
9. TOPHAM'S BELGRAVIA
10. STARLIGHT EXPRESS

touristy glitz of the streets in front of the station. This neighborhood is proud to be part of Belgravia. Even with Margaret Thatcher living around the corner (you'll see the policeman standing outside 73 Chester Square), this is a classy and peaceful place to call home in London. Decent eateries abound (see Eating). The cheaper listings are relatively dumpy. Don't expect £80 cheeriness in a £50 room. Those traveling on a shoestring off-season save a few pounds by arriving late without a reservation and checking around. Competition is fierce and prices are often soft, especially for multi-night stays. Particularly for Warwick Way hotels (and in the summer when you'll want the window open at night), request a quiet back room. All are within a five-minute walk of the Victoria tube, bus, and train stations. There's an £8-per-day garage and a nearby launderette (self-serve or full-serve, 3 Westmoreland Terrace, tel. 0171/821-8692).

In **Woodville House**, the quarters are dollhouse tight, showers are down the hall, and several rooms are noisy on the street (doubles are on the quiet backside, twins and singles on the street), but this well-run, well-worn place is a good value with lots of travel tips, and endless tea, coffee, and friendly chat (especially about the local rich and famous) from Rachel Joplin (S-£39, D-£58, bunky family deals—£75-100—for three, four, or five in a room; CC:VM, easy credit-card reservations, 107 Ebury Street, SW1W 9QU, tel. 0171/730-1048, fax 0171/730-2574).

Lime Tree Hotel is enthusiastically run by David and Marilyn Davies. The thoughtfully decorated public areas and rooms are spacious for this area and guests can relax in the peaceful garden off the fun-loving breakfast room. (Sb-£70, Db-£90–100, Tb-£120, family room-£140, David will deal in slow times and is creative at helping travelers in a bind, CC:VMA, 135 Ebury Street, SW1W 9RA, tel. 0171/730-8191, fax 0171/730-7865). Each room comes with a TV, phone, hair dryer, safe, and teapot.

Cherry Court Hotel, run by the friendly Patel family, offers cramped rooms, tiny bathrooms, and a worthless shrink-wrapped breakfast at youth hostel prices. It's on a quiet street very close to the station (S-£28, Sb-£35, Db-£45, Tb-£65, CC:VMA, no twins—only double beds, pleasant garden, 23 Hugh Street, SW1V 1QJ, tel. 0171/828-2840, fax 0171/828-0393, e-mail: cherryc@globalnet.co.uk).

Cedar Guest House, across the street, is a minimal place with eight rooms at youth-hostel prices. It's run by a Polish organization to help Poles afford London, but all are welcome (D-£38, T-£54, 30 Hugh Street, SW1V 1RP, tel. 0171/828-2625).

Limegrove Hotel, run by harried Joyce, is a little smoky but its nine rooms are a fine value with a full English breakfast in the room (S-£26, small D-£36, D-£38, Db-£45, T-£45, Tb-£60, cheaper off-season or for stays of six days or more, 101 Warwick Way, SW1V 4HT, tel. 0171/828-0458). Back rooms are quieter.

Elizabeth House (not related to the Elizabeth Hotel) feels institutional and a bit bland—as you might expect from a former YMCA—but the rooms are clean and bright and the price is right (S-£30, D-£50, Db-£60, T-£75, Q-£85, CC:VMA, 118 Warwick Way, SW1 4JB, tel. 0171/630-0741, fax 0171/630-0740).

Tophams Belgravia Hotel packs the formality and service of a top-class hotel into a tight and tangled building beautifully situated on a quiet corner two blocks from Victoria station. Carefully attired rooms come with all the comforts, and carefully attired maids serve breakfast with none of the chat at funkier places (S-£85, Sb-£110, Db-£120–140, Tb-£155, CC:VMA, 28 Ebury Street, SW1W 0LU, tel. 0171/730 8147, fax 0171/823 5966, Web site: www.tophams .com, e-mail: tophams_belgravia.compuserve.com).

Lesser values near Victoria Station for travelers wanting more comforts: **Quality Hotel Eccleston** is big and modern (Db-£87-100, 82 Eccleston Square, SW1V 1PS, tel. 0171/834-8042, fax 0171/630-8942, e-mail: admin@gb614.u-net.com). Smaller, warmer, and farther from Victoria Station is **Windermere Hotel** (S-£59, Sb-£70, D-£70, Db-£85–100, CC:VMA, 142 Warwick Way, London SW1V 4JE, tel. 0171/834-5163, fax 0171/630-8831, e-mail: 100773.1171@compuserve.com).

Elizabeth Hotel, once a budget bargain, is currently undergoing renovation into a four-star hotel. Its prices will be sky-high, though it will still have a great location and traditional feel, a large elegant lobby with an elevator, airy and pleasant rooms, and free access to the private park the hotel overlooks (call for prices and re-opening info, 37 Eccleston Square, SW1V 1PB, tel. 0171/828-6812, fax 0171/828-6814).

Big, Cheap, Modern Hotels

The Travel Inn chain runs three hotels in London, each offering 200 plus cookie-cutter rooms with all the necessary comforts. With long soulless halls and cheesy restaurants and bars, you won't want to savor the ambience, but you can't beat the price for a no-nonsense hotel room (Db-£55 for two adults and up to two children, breakfast extra, book long in advance, no-show rooms are released at 16:00, elevator, some smoke-free and easy-access rooms, CC:VMA, tel. 01582/414-341, fax 01582/400-024 for all). Choose from **London Euston** near the British Library and Euston Station (141 Euston Road, NW1 2AU London) and the much more central **London County Hall**, just across Westminster Bridge from Big Ben, built into the old County Hall building (Belvedere Road, SE1 7PB London). A third Travel Inn, **London Putney Bridge**, is farther away at London's Putney Bridge (tube: Putney Bridge).

"South Kensington," She Said, Loosening His Cummerbund

To live on a quiet street so classy it doesn't allow hotel signs, surrounded by trendy shops and colorful restaurants, call "South Ken" your London home. Shoppers like being a short walk from Harrods and the designer shops of King's Road and Chelsea. Budget ethnic eateries line Old Brompton Road (each hotel has restaurant scrapbooks or wall charts). But this ultimate fairy-tale London home-away-from-home comes with a price. When I splurge, I splurge here. Sumner Place is 200 yards from the South Kensington tube station (on Circle Line, two stops from Victoria Station, direct Heathrow connection). At top of the stairs of South Ken tube stop, exit left, cross doubled street,

go right two blocks down Old Brompton Road, left onto
Sumner Place).

Aster House Hotel has classy rooms, each with a TV, telephone, and fridge. Enjoy breakfast in the whisper-elegant Orangerie,
a Victorian greenhouse and lounge in the tidy back garden
(Sb-£60–80, third floor Db-£110, Db-£120, deluxe four-poster Db
with both bath and shower-£135, CC:VM, entirely non-smoking,
3 Sumner Place, SW7 3EE, tel. 0171/581-5888, fax 0171/584-4925,
e-mail: asterhouse@btinternet.com, run by manager Simon Tan).

Five Sumner Place Hotel is informal but professional, "highly
commended" and recently voted "the best small hotel in London."
You'll talk softly but not feel like you have to dress up as you wander under the chandeliers out to the breakfast room, a Victorian-
style conservatory/greenhouse. In this 150-year-old building, each
room is tastefully decorated with traditional period furnishings
(Sb-£88, Db-£130–141, third bed is £24 extra, elevator, CC:VMA,
easy CC reservations, non-smoking, 5 Sumner Place, South
Kensington, SW7 3EE, tel. 0171/584-7586, fax 0171/823-9962,
e-mail: no.5@dial.pipex.com).

Nearby are lesser values for classier travelers: **16 Sumner
Place** has over-the-top formality and class (Db-£155–185,
CC:VMA, no breakfast room, 16 Sumner Place, London SW7
3EG, tel. 0171/589-5232, fax 0171/584-8615, USA tel. 800/592-
5387). **Kensington Juries Hotel** is big and stately (Sb/Db/
Tb-£99–145 depending upon "availability," breakfast extra, piano
lounge, elevator, Queen's Gate, South Kensington, SW7 5LR,
tel. 0171/589-6300, fax 0171/581-1492). **The Claverley**, just a
couple of blocks from Harrods, is on a quiet street similar to
Sumner Place. The rooms are warmly furnished with elegant drap-
ery and all the comforts (S-£70, Sb-£75–115, Db-£110–140,
sofabed Tb-£160–215, CC:VMA, some balconies, 13-14 Beaufort
Gardens, SW3 1PS, tube: Knightsbridge, tel. 0171/589-8541,
fax 0171/584-3410, USA tel. 800/747-0398).

Sleeping in Notting Hill Gate Neighborhood

Residential Notting Hill Gate has quick and easy bus or tube access to downtown, it's on the A2 Airbus line from Heathrow (second and third stops from airport, after Kensington Hilton), and,
for London, is very "homely." Notting Hill Gate has a self-serve
launderette, an artsy theater, a late-hours supermarket, and lots of
fun budget eateries (see Eating). All recommended accommodations are near the Holland Park or Notting Hill Gate tube stations.
(Notting Hill Gate is in the central zone and on the Circle Line,
handier and 40p cheaper from anywhere in the center than the
Holland Park station.)

NOTTING HILL GATE

❶ WESTLAND HOTEL
❷ VICARAGE PRIVATE HOTEL & ABBEY HOUSE HOTEL
❸ RAVNA GORA HOTEL
❹ NORWEGIAN YWCA
❺ MAGGIE JONES RESTAURANT
❻ CHURCHILL ARMS PUB
❶ LADBROKE ARMS PUB
❷ GEALE'S FISH & CHIPS
❸ MODHUBON INDIAN REST.

Westland Hotel is comfortable, convenient, and hotelesque with a fine lounge and friendly family-run feel. The spacious 1970s-style rooms come with a phone, video-player, hair dryer, and coffee-maker (Sb-£80, Db-£95, cavernous deluxe Db-£110, sprawling Tb-£120, gargantuan Qb-£135, elevator, free garage, CC:VMA, reserve with credit card, midway between Notting Hill Gate and Queensway tube stations, 154 Bayswater Road, W2 4HP, tel. 0171/229-9191, fax 0171/727-1054). A block away, their **Westland Annex** offers plainer, quieter, cheaper rooms (Sb-£66, Db-£82, family deals also, same front desk and breakfast room as hotel).

Vicarage Private Hotel, understandably popular, is family-run and elegantly British in a quiet, classy neighborhood. It has 19 rooms furnished with taste and quality, lots of stairs, a TV lounge, and facilities on each floor. Mandy, Richard, and Tere maintain a homey and caring atmosphere. Reserve long in advance with a one-night deposit. There's no better room for the price (S-£40, D-£63, T-£80, Q-£88, a six-minute walk from the Notting Hill Gate and High Street Kensington tube stations, near Kensington Palace at 10 Vicarage Gate, Kensington, W8 4AG, tel. 0171/229-4030, fax 0171/792-5989, Web site: www.londonvicaragehotel.com).

Abbey House Hotel, next door, is similar but has no lounge and is a bit less cozy (S-£40, D-£65, T-£78, Q-£90, Quint-£100, 11 Vicarage Gate, Kensington, W8 4AG, tel. 0171/727-2594).

Hotel Ravna Gora was formerly the mansion of 18th-century architect Henry Holland. Now it's a large Slavic-run B&B—eccentric and well-worn, but handy for the price. Wry Manda and jocular Rijko offer a royal pre-Tito TV room and a good English breakfast. It has plain, tired rooms, musty shower stalls, a creaky spiral staircase, easy parking, and a Balkan ambience. With the right approach, a stay here is a fun memory. With the wrong approach, it's a big mistake (S-£30, D-£50, Db-£60, T-£60, Tb-£80, Q-£80, Qb-£88, CC:VM, 50 yards from Holland Park tube station, facing but set back from a busy road, 29 Holland Park Avenue, W11 3RW, tel. 0171/727-7725, fax 0171/221-4282).

Norwegian YWCA (Norsk K.F.U.K.) is for women under 30 only (and men with Norwegian passports). It's an incredible value. Located on a quiet, stately street, it offers smoke-free rooms, a study, TV room, piano lounge, and an open-face Norwegian ambience. All rooms (except singles) have private showers. They have mostly quads, so those willing to share with strangers are most likely to get a place (July–August: Ss-£27, bed in shared double-£25, shared triple-£21 apiece, shared quad-£18 apiece, with breakfast. September–June: same prices but with dinner included, CC:VM, 52 Holland Park, W11 3R5, tel. & fax 0171/727-9897). With each visit I wonder which is easier—getting a sex change or a Norwegian passport?

Sleeping in Other Neighborhoods

Near British Library: Methodist International House is a youthful Christian residence filled mostly with Asian and African students. It's great if you want a truly worldwide dorm experience at a price that will bolster your faith. The smoke-free rooms are studious, with a desk and reading lamp. The atmosphere is friendly, safe, clean, and controlled, with a silent study room, reading lounge, TV lounge, game room, and laundry facilities (S-£26, D-£46, a bed in a shared T-£21, includes breakfast and a cafeteria dinner, 81-103 Euston Street, W1 2EZ, tube: King's Cross, reserve long in advance, tel. 0171/380-0001, fax 0171/387-5300). Rooms are most likely available during school breaks, including summer. The included evening "tea" (that means supper) is great for meeting other residents.

Bloomsbury, near the British Museum: The **Cambria House,** a fine value, is run by the Salvation Army (a plus when it comes to cheap big-city hotels.) This smoke-free old building with a narrow maze of halls is all newly painted and super clean, if institutional. The rooms are large and perfectly good. You'll find ample showers and toilets on each floor, a TV lounge, and a warm welcome (S-£27, D-£43, Db-£53, T-£64, CC:VM, north of Russell Square, 37 Hunter Street, WC1N 1BJ, tel. 0171/837-1654, fax 0171/837-1229).

Downtown near Baker Street: For a homey alternative in the center, consider renting comfortable well-appointed rooms in this B&B (Db-£80, Tb-£120, strictly smoke-free, on 22 York Street between Baker Street and Oxford Street, tel. 0171/224-3990, fax 0171/224-1990, run by Liz and Michael).

Near St. Paul's: The City of London Youth Hostel is clean, modern, friendly, and well-run. You'll pay about £23 for a bed in two- to five-bed rooms, £25 in a single (CC:VM, cheap meals, 36 Carter Lane, EC4V 5AD, tube: St. Paul's, tel. 0171/236-4965, fax 0171/236-7681).

Near Sloane Square: Hotel Oakley is like a rundown B&B in a fine neighborhood (S-£32, D-£42, Db-£56, CC:VMA, 73 Oakley Street, just off King's Road, 10-minute walk from Sloane Square tube stop, tel. 0171/352-5599).

South of London: Mary Ward's Guest House is sleepable but very simple. On a quiet street in a well-worn neighborhood south of Victoria near Clapham Common, this beats the hostel. Friendly Mary Ward (Edith Bunker's English aunt) has been renting her five super-cheap rooms to budget travelers for 25 years (S-£12.50, D-£25 with English breakfast, 98 Hambalt Road, Clapham Common, London SW4 9EJ, tel. 0181/673-1077). It's 15 minutes by tube to Clapham Common, then a short bus ride or a 12-minute walk—exit left down Clapham South Road, left on Elms, right on Abbeville Road, left on Hambalt. Rooms in Mary's son's house are an equally good value.

Sleeping in Hampstead, The Small Town Alternative

If you must "do" London but wish it were a small town, make Hampstead your home-base-on-the-hill. Just 15 to 30 minutes north of the center by tube (to Hampstead on the sometimes tardy Northern Line), and you're in the former resort of wealthy Londoners—drawn by spas in the 1700s and the brilliant views of London from the popular Hampstead Heath, an 800-acre park.

Hampstead today glows with Georgian village elegance—narrow cobblestone lanes, (now electrified) gas lamps, and blue plaques noting where Keats, Freud, and other famous locals lived—even McDonald's has a mock-Tudor facade.

The tube station marks the center of the town. From there, busy High Street cuts downhill though the center, taking you into a cheery business district with side streets flickering with gaslit charm. The B&B is a brisk 10-minute walk downhill from the tube stop. The hotel is a three-minute walk uphill.

Make a point to explore the back lanes where you can pop into churches and peek into windows—drapes left open so their elegant interiors can be envied.

Hampstead Village Guesthouse is run in laissez-faire style by Anne Marie van der Meer, who rents nine rooms and raised her family in this Victorian house. The homey rooms, most named after her children, lack locks but come with a phone, mini-fridge, TV, and even a hot water bottle (S-£32, D-£55, Db-£65, breakfast-£6, CC:VMA only for reservation deposit, payment in cash, non-smoking, extremely quiet, book well in advance, walk 10 minutes from tube stop downhill on High Street, left on Pilgrims Lane to 2 Kemplay Road, Hampstead, London NW3 1SY, tel. 0171/435-8679, fax 0171/794-0254, e-mail: hvguesthouse@dial.pipex.com).

La Gaffe Hotel is a sweet Italian-run hotel and restaurant right on Heath Street. Rooms are small and well-worn but floral, comfy, and quiet (Sb-£55, Db-£80–115, includes breakfast, TV, phones, non-smoking, walk uphill from the tube station three minutes to 107 Heath Street, Hampstead, London NW3 6SS, 0171/435 8965, fax 1071/794-7592, e-mail: la-gaffe@msn.com).

Sleeping near Gatwick Airport

The peaceful **Crutchfield Farm B&B** offers three comfortable rooms in a 600-year-old renovated farmhouse. Gillian Blok includes a ride to the airport (Sb-£45, Db-£65, Tb-£75, Qb-£85, two miles from Gatwick airport—£5 by taxi, 30 minutes by train from London, at Hookwood, Surrey RH6 0HT, tel. 01293/863-110, fax 01293/863-233). **Barn Cottage**, a converted 17th-century barn in a large garden, has quiet rooms 10 minutes from Gatwick (S-£28, D-£45, Leigh/Reigate/Surrey RH2 8RF, tel. 01306/611-347, warmly run by Pat and Mike Comer). **Lynwood Guest House** (10 minutes by train to Gatwick, 30 minutes by train from London) offers a cozy alternative to big-city lodging in Redhill, a normal workaday English town. It's just a five-minute walk from the train station, but the gracious owner Shanta may pick you up if she's got the car. Ask for a quiet room off the street (Ss-£28, Ds-£42, Db-£45, Tb-£58, Qb-£65, cheaper off-season, 50 London Road, Redhill, Surrey RH1 1LN, tel. 01737/766-894, fax 0171/778-253).

EATING IN LONDON

If you want to dine (as opposed to eat), check out the extensive listings in *Time Out* (or the train schedule for Paris). The thought of a £25 meal in Britain generally ruins my appetite, so my London dining is limited mostly to unremarkable, but inexpensive, alternatives. I've listed places by neighborhood—handy to your sightseeing or hotel.

Your £5 budget choices are pub grub, a café, fish and chips, pizza, ethnic, or picnic. Pub grub is the most atmospheric budget option. Many of London's 7,000 pubs serve fresh, tasty buffets under ancient timbers, with hearty lunches and dinners priced around £5. Ethnic restaurants from all over the world more than make up for England's lackluster cuisine. Eating Indian is "going local" in London. It's also going cheap (cheaper if you take out). Chinese and Italian places are not quite the same value. Most large museums (and many churches) have reasonable and handy cafeterias. Of course, picnicking is the fastest and cheapest way to go. Good grocery stores and sandwich shops, fine park benches, and polite pigeons abound in Britain's most expensive city.

Eating near Trafalgar Square

For a tasty meal on a monk's budget in an ancient crypt sitting on somebody's tomb, descend into the **St. Martin-in-the-Fields Café in the Crypt** (Monday–Saturday 10:00–20:00, Sunday 12:00–20:30, £5–7 cafeteria plates, cheaper sandwich bar, profits go to the church; underneath St. Martin-in-the-Fields on Trafalgar Square, tel. 0171/839-4342). Down Whitehall (toward Big Ben), a block from Trafalgar Square, you'll find the touristy but atmospheric **Clarence Pub** (decent grub) and several cheaper cafeterias and pizza joints. For a classy lunch, treat your palate to the pricier **Brasserie** (open daily, on first floor of Sainsbury Wing of the National Gallery). **Simpson's in the Strand** serves a stuffy, aristocratic old-time carvery dinner (where the chef slices your favorite red meat from a fancy trolley at your table) in their elegant smoky old dining room (£20, daily 12:00–15:00, 17:30–23:00, tel. 0171/836-9112).

Chandos Bar's Opera Room is amazingly apart from the tacky crush of tourism around Trafalgar Square. Look for the pub opposite the National Portrait Gallery (corner of William Street and St. Martin's Lane) and climb the stairs to the Opera Room. They serve pub lunches and dinners, and £5 cheese-and-salad cold plate deals all day long (tel. 0171/836-1401). This is my favorite rendezvous point around Trafalgar. Smoky, but a wonderfully London scene.

Gordon's Wine Bar is the place to go for a local crowd and atmosphere. A simple steep staircase leads into a cellar filled with candle light, dusty old wine bottles, faded British memorabilia, and local nine-to-fivers (hot meals only for lunch, fine cheese-and-salad buffet all day until 21:00—one plate of each feeds two for £7). While it's crowded, you can normally corral two chairs and grab the corner of a table (weekdays 11:00–23:00, Saturday 17:00–23:00, closed Sunday, two blocks from Trafalgar Square, bottom of Villiars Street at #47, between the Embankment and Charing Cross tube stations, tel. 0171/930-1408).

Eating near Piccadilly

Hungry and broke in the theater district? Head for Panton Street (just off Haymarket, two blocks southeast of Picadilly Circus) for a line of decent eateries. **Stockpot** is a mushy-peas-kind-of-place, famous and rightly popular for its edible, cheap meals (Monday–Saturday 8:00–23:00, Sunday 8:00–22:00, 40 Panton Street). The **West End Kitchen** (across the street at #5, same hours and menu, fine seating downstairs) is a direct competitor and just as good. The original Stockpot, a few blocks away, has better atmosphere (daily, noon–23:00, a block north of Shaftesbury near Cambridge Circus at 18 Old Compton Street).

The palatial **Criterion Brasserie**, serving a two-course menu for £15 under gilded tiles and chandeliers (12:00–14:30, 18:00–18:30 only) is right on Piccadilly Circus but a world away from the punk junk (tel. 0171/930-0488). The **Wren Café** at St. James Church is exclusively vegetarian, wonderfully green, and in a pleasant garden next to one of Wren's best churches—peek inside (Monday–Saturday 9:00–17:00, Sunday 10:00–16:00, two minutes southwest of Piccadilly Circus, at 192 Piccadilly Street, tel. 0171/437-9419).

Near Covent Garden, the area around Neal Yard is busy with

fun eateries. One of the best is **Food for Thought** (serving until 20:15, closed Sunday, very good £4 vegetarian meals, smoke-free, two blocks north of tube: Covent Garden, 31 Neal Street, tel. 0171/836-0239).

The "Food Is Fun" Dinner Crawl: From Covent Garden to Soho

London has a trendy, generation X scene which most Beefeater-seekers miss entirely. For a multicultural moveable feast and a chance to sample some of London's most popular eateries, consider sampling these. Start around 18:00 to avoid lines, get in on early specials, and find waiters happy to let you split a meal. Prices, while reasonable by London standards, add up. Servings are large enough to share. All are open nightly.

Suggested nibbler's dinner crawl for two: arrive before 18:00 at Belgo and split the early-bird dinner special: a kilo of mussels, fries, and dark Belgian beer; at Soho Spice Indian, split the "Tandoori selections"; at Yo! Sushi, have beer or sake and a few dishes; slurp your last course at Wagamama; for dessert, people-watch at Leicester Square where the serf's always up.

Belgo Centraal is a space station world overrun with Trappist monks serving hearty Belgian specialties. The classy restaurant section requires reservations but just grabbing a bench in the boisterous beerhall is much more fun. Belgians eat as well as the French and as hearty as the Germans. Specialties include mussels, great fries, and a stunning array of dark, blond, and fruity Belgian beers. Belgo actually makes things Belgian trendy—a formidable feat (£12 meals, Monday–Friday 17:00–18:30, "beat the clock" meal specials cost only the time . . . £5.00 to £6.30 and you get mussels, fries, and beer, no meal-splitting after 18:30, £5 lunch special daily, one block north of Covent Garden tube station at intersection of Neal and Shelton Streets, 50 Earlham Street, tel. 0171/813-2233).

Soho Spice Indian is where modern Britain meets Indian tradition—fine Indian cuisine in a trendy jewel-tone ambience (£14 "Tandoori selections" meal is the best "variety" dish and big enough for two, non-smoking section, five blocks due north of Piccadilly Circus at 124 Wardour Street, tel. 0171/434-0808).

Yo! Sushi is a futuristic Japanese food extravaganza experience. With thumping rock, Japanese cable TV, a 60-meter-long conveyor belt sushi bar (the world's longest), automated sushi machines, and a robotic drink trolley, just sipping a sake on a bar stool here is a trip. For £1, you get unlimited tea (on request), water (from spigot at bar, with or without gas), or miso soup. Grab dishes as they rattle by (priced by color of dish; see chart) and a drink off the robot (daily 12:00–24:00, 2 blocks south of Oxford

Street, where Lexington Street becomes Poland Street, 52 Poland Street, tel. 0171/287-0443).

Wagamama Noodle Bar is a mod, watch-it-boiled, pan-Asian slurp-athon. As you enter, check out the kitchen and listen to the roar of the basement where a youthful crowd shares benches and waiters take orders with walkie-talkies. Everything's organic—stand against the wall to feel the energy of all this "positive eating" (daily 12:00–23:00, crowded after 20:00, just past the porno and prostitition core of Soho but entirely smoke-free, 10A Lexington Street, tel. 0171/292-0990).

Soho Soho French Bistro-Rotisserie is a chance to go French in a Matisse-esque setting. The ground floor is a trendy wine bar. Upstairs is an oasis of peace serving £17, three-course French "pre-theater specials"—order from 18:00 to 19:30 (near Cambridge Circus, two blocks east of Charing Cross Road at 11 Frith Street, tel. 0171/494-3491).

Andrew Edmunds Restaurant is a tiny, candle-lit place where you'll want to hide your camera and guidebook and act as local as possible. The continental and traditional cooking is worth the splurge (three courses for £20, 46 Lexington Street, Soho, reservations are smart, tel. 0171/437-5708).

Eating near Recommended Victoria Station Accommodations

Here are places a couple of blocks southwest of Victoria Station where I've enjoyed eating: **Jenny Lo's Tea House** is a simple, for-the-joy-of-good-food kind of place serving up £5 Cantonese meals to locals in the know (Monday–Saturday 12:00–15:00, 18:00–22:00, 14 Eccleston Street, tel. 0171/259-0399). For pub grub with good local atmosphere, consider the **Plumbers Arms** (filling £5 hot meals and cheaper sandwiches, closed Saturday and Sunday nights, indoor/outdoor seating, 14 Lower Belgrave Street, tel. 0171/730-4067; ask about the murdered nanny . . . and the distraught wife who ran into the plumber's arms). Next door, the small but classy **La Campagnola** is Belgravia's favorite budget Italian restaurant (£10 meals, closed Sunday, reservations wise on Thursday and Friday, 10 Lower Belgrave Street, tel. 0171/730-2057). Across the street, the **Maestro Bar** is the closest thing to an English tapas bar I've seen with salads, sandwiches, and 10 bar stools (very cheap).

The **Ebury Wine Bar** offers a French, smoky ambience and pricey but delicious meals (£15, daily 12:00–15:00, 18:00–22:30, 139 Ebury Street, at intersection with Elizabeth Street, near the bus station, tel. 0171/730-5447). Several cheap places are around the corner on Elizabeth Street (#23 for take-out or eat-in fish and chips).

The **Duke of Wellington** pub is good, if smoky, for dinner (£5 meals, 12:00–15:00 and 18:00–21:30, closed Sunday evening, 63 Eaton Terrace). **Peter's Restaurant** is the cabbie's hangout for cheap food, smoke, and chatter (end of Ebury, at intersection with Pimlico). Nearby, the **Flamenco** has decent, if pricey, Spanish tapas (54 Pimlico).

For picnics, the nearest supermarket is **J. Sainsbury**, a five-minute walk from Victoria Station (Monday–Saturday 7:30–20:00, Sunday 10:00–16:00, on Victoria Street, just after intersection with Palace Street). The late-hours **Whistle Stop** grocery at the station has decent sandwiches and a fine salad bar. The **Marche** is an easy cafeteria a couple of blocks north of Victoria Station at Bressenden Place.

Eating near Recommended Notting Hill Gate B&Bs

Best classy English meal in London: The rustic and very English **Maggie Jon**es serves my favorite £20 London dinner. You'll get solid English cuisine with huge plates of vegetables by candle light (daily 18:30–23:00, CC:VMA, 6 Old Court Place, just east of Kensington Church Street, near High Street Kensington tube stop, reservations recommended, tel. 0171/937-6462). If you eat well once in London, eat here (and do it quick, before it burns down).

Good pub grub: The **Churchill Arms** pub is a local hangout with good beer and old English ambience in front and hearty £5 Thai plates in an enclosed patio in the back (Monday–Saturday 11:00–23:00, 119 Kensington Church Street, tel. 0171/727-4242). The **Windsor Castle Pub** is a great, smoky, and happy scene specializing in traditional sausages and oysters (114 Campden Hill, tel. 0171/243-9551). The smoky **Ladbroke Arms Pub** serves country-style meals that are one step above pub grub in quality and price (daily 12:00–14:30, 19:00–22:00, great indoor/outdoor ambience, 54 Ladbroke Road, behind Holland Park tube station, tel. 0171/727-6648).

Top fish and chips: The almost-too-popular **Geale's** has long been considered one of London's best fish-and-chips joints (£8 meals, Tuesday–Saturday 12:00–15:00, 18:00–23:00, 2 Farmer Street, just off Notting Hill Gate behind the Gate Cinema, tel. 0171/727-7969). Get there early for a place to sit (they take no reservations) and the best selection of fish.

Miscellaneous NHG eateries: Costas has eat-in or take-out fish and chips (£5 meals, Tuesday–Saturday 12:00–14:30, 17:30–10:30, near Coronet Theatre at 18 Hillgate Street). Next door, **Hillgate Pub** has good food and famous hot saltbeef sandwiches (daily 11:00–23:00, indoor/outdoor seating, tel. 0171/ 727-8543).

The **Modhubon** Indian restaurant is not too spicy, "vedy vedy nice," and has cheap lunch specials (Sunday–Friday 12:00–15:00 and 18:00–24:00, Saturday 12:00–24:00, 29 Pembridge Road, tel. 0171/727-3399). Next door is a cheap Chinese take-out (daily 17:30–24:00, 19 Pembridge Road) and the tiny **Prost Restaurant and Schnapps Bar** which busily keeps yuppie vegetarians as well as carnivores happy (£10 meals, Monday–Friday 17:30–23:00, weekends 10:30–23:00, 35 Pembridge Road, tel. 0171/727-9620). **Cafe Diana** is a healthy little sandwich shop decorated with photos of Princess Diana (5 Wellington Terrace, on Bayswater Road, opposite Kensington Palace Garden Gates).

For a picnic dinner, shop at the **Europe Superstore** (Monday–Saturday 8:30–23:00, Sunday 12:00–18:00, 50 yards west of Notting Hill tube station on Notting Hill Gate).

Just a short tube ride away, you'll find Old Brompton Road and Thurloe Street (each starting at the South Kensington tube station), lined with popular eateries. Case out the several places along Thurloe Street. At the end you'll see **Daquise**, a smoke-free, authentic-feeling Polish place, ideal if you're in the mood for kielbasa and kraut. It's fast, cheap, faded, family-run, and a part of the neighborhood (daily until 23:30, 20 Thurloe Street, tel. 0171/589-6117).

Eating near Recommended Accommodations in Hampstead

Even if you aren't staying in Hampstead, consider a visit. Hampstead has a small-town feel with easy tube access to London (15 to 30 minutes away; tube stop: Hampstead, on the Northern Line). Enjoy the gaslit elegance and cobblestone lanes of this former resort. The Freemason's Arms pub (best for dinner) is a 10-minute walk downhill from the tube stop; the other pubs and restaurants are within five minutes of the tube station. Everything's near the park.

Freemason's Arms is the place for classy pub grub. If the lighting doesn't make your partner look delicious, the Czech lager will. Set on the edge of the heath with a spacious interior and sprawling beer garden for summer outdoor seating, the Freemason's Arms serves great English food every day (£7 meals, skittles downstairs three nights a week—private but peeking permitted; down High Street, left on Downshire Hill Road to #32, tel. 0171/433-6811).

Down High Street from the tube stop you'll find Hampstead swinging at **The House on Rosslyn Hill** (international cuisine, modern brasserie, young, trendy, popular with locals; meals start at £10, 34 Rosslyn Hill, tel. 0171/435-8037).

French Hampstead cooks a block below the tube station. For a quick bite, **Maison Blanc** not only has the best croissants in town, but also makes great savories like roquefort and walnut *fougasse* (foccacia pockets) or *tarte provençale* (tomato, zucchini, and gruyère mini-quiche); all this plus lovely strong French coffee for £2–3, on Hampstead High Street. **Café des Arts** serves French food in a rustic candlelit English setting (nightly until 23:00, 82 Hampstead High Street). Next door there's even a little *crêpe* cart in search of Paris.

There's a handy grocery store next to the tube station. But for real village atmosphere, shop at the Hampstead Foodhall on Fitzjohn Avenue. There's nowhere better than Hampstead Heath (a 10-minute hike away) for a dinner picnic with a view.

For a laid-back crowd and a good fireplace to enjoy with your beer, visit the **Holly Bush Pub** (no meals but toasted sandwiches, hidden on a quiet lane uphill from tube). For a livelier spit-and-sawdust pub, toss your darts with the locals at **The Flask** (on Flask walk, two blocks below the tube station).

LONDON WITH CHILDREN

This city of 9 million is actually kid-friendly. With plenty of sights—all of them accessible to those who speak English—your children can leave London wanting to return. While you can take your child to play at a London funplex, you can visit a funplex at home. The key to a successful family trip to London is making everyone happy, including the parents. My family-tested recommendations have this objective in mind.

Consider these tips:

• Take advantage of the local newsstand guides in London for children's activities. Look for *Kids Out*. *Time Out* and the others also have handy kids' calenders.

• Ask at London TIs about kids' events. Call Kidsline (weekdays 9:00–18:00; or when school is in session, weekdays 16:00–18:00, tel. 0171/222-8070). The London Tourist Board's Children's Information line, with recorded information 24 hours daily, is a pricey toll call (tel. 0839-123-404-436).

• Eat dinner early (around 18:00) and you'll miss the romantic crowd. Skip the famous places. Look instead for relaxed cafés, pubs (yes, kids are welcome), or even fast-food restaurants where kids can move around without bothering others. Picnic lunches and dinners work well.

• Public WCs can be hard to find: try department stores, museums, and restaurants, particularly fast-food restaurants.

• Follow this book's crowd-beating tips to a tee. With kids, standing in a long line for a museum (that they probably don't even want to see) adds insult to injury.

• The best toy selection is at Hamleys, the biggest toy store in Britain (Monday–Saturday 10:00–20:00, Sunday 12:00–18:00, 118 Regent Street, tube: Oxford Circus).

TOP KIDS' SIGHTS

In East London

Tower of London—The crown jewels are awesome, and the Beefeater tour plays off kids in a memorable and fun way (£9, cheaper for kids, Monday–Saturday 9:00–18:00, Sunday 10:00–18:00, last entry at 17:00, tube: Tower Hill, tel. 0171/709-0765).

Museum of London—This is every London grade-school teacher's best friend. A very kid-friendly presentation takes you from the Romans to the Blitz. Parents will learn something, too. (£4.30, free after 16:30, Monday–Saturday 10:00–18:00, Sunday 12:00–18:00, tube: Barbican or St. Paul's, tel. 0171/600-3699.)

In Central London

Covent Garden—This fire-eater, Punch-and-Judy delight rivals any "Fisherman's Wharf" scene in the U.S.A. for simply people-watching and candy-licking away an afternoon. Try the Cabaret Mechanical Theater, on the lower level of the Market, for kid-pleasing gadgets.

St. Martin-in-the-Fields—This church, on Trafalgar Square, has a brass rubbing center that's fun for kids who'd like a souvenir to show for their efforts. The affordable Café in the Crypt has just the right spooky ambience.

National Gallery—Start your visit in the Micro Gallery computer room. Your child can list his or her interests (cats, naval battles, and so on) and print out a tailor-made tour map (free, Monday–Saturday 10:00–18:00, Wednesday until 20:00, Sunday 12:00–18:00, on Trafalgar Square, tube: Charing Cross or Leicester Square, tel. 0171/839-3321.)

Horse Guards—Horse fans enjoy the Horse Guards' colorful dismounting ceremony daily at 16:00 (on Whitehall, between Trafalgar Square and #10 Downing Street, tube: Westminster). The inspection, less interesting for kids, is at 11:00 Monday–Saturday (at 10:00 on Sunday). It's all canceled if it rains.

Piccadilly Circus—This titillating district has lots of "Planet Hollywood"-type amusements kids will find enjoyably distracting (such as Segaworld, Rock Circus, and Guinness Hall of World Records). Be very careful of fast-fingered riff-raff.

In West London

Natural History Museum—This wonderful world of dinosaurs, volcanoes, meteors, and creepy-crawlies offers plenty of creative interactive displays (£6, family-£16, free after 16:30 and after 17:00 on weekends, Monday–Saturday 10:00–18:00, Sunday 11:00–18:00, a long tunnel leads directly from the South Kensington tube station to the museum, tel. 0171/938-9123, Web site: www.nhm.ac.uk).

In North London

Madame Tussaud's Waxworks—This is popular with kids in spite of the terrible lines. Gory stuff, pop and movie stars, everyone's favorite royals, etc. (£10, children £6.60, under five free, daily from 9:30, last admission at 17:30, Marylebone Road, tube: Baker Street, tel. 0171/935-6861; combined ticket for Tussaud's and Planetarium is £12 for adults, £8 for kids). Buy your ticket at the TI—no more than 24 hours in advance—to save a little money and get in with no wait.

London Zoo—This venerable zoo, with over 8,000 animals, is one of the best in the world (£8.50, cheaper for kids, under four free, family-£26, daily March–October 10:00–17:30, November–April 10:00–16:00, in Regent's Park, tube: Camden Town, then bus 274, tel. 0171/722-3333).

In South London

Museum of the Moving Image—This painless education in the history of movies and TV is a hit for the whole family. The docents dress and talk as if they're from the 1900s. Kids like the make-a-movie activities, and parents reminisce about subjects (movies, TV shows, and commercials) that kids actually find interesting (£6.25, daily 10:00–18:00, last ticket sold at 17:00, from Embankment tube stop, walk across Thames pedestrian bridge and turn left; it's under the Waterloo bridge, tel. 0171/928-3535).

FUN TRANSPORTATION

Thames Cruise—Young sailors delight in boat cruises. Westminster Pier (near Big Ben) offers the most action, with boats to the Tower of London (£4.40, round-trip £5.60, 3/hrly from 10:20–21:00 in peak season, until 18:00 in winter, 30 min), Greenwich (£5.80, round-trip £7, 2/hrly from 10:00–17:00, 50 min), and Kew Gardens (£6, round-trip £10, 7/day, 90 min).

Original London Sightseeing Bus Tour—This two-hour double-decker bus tour, which drives by all the biggies, is fun for kids and stressless for parents. You can stay on the bus the entire time, or "hop on and hop off" at any of the 26 stops and catch a later bus (runs about every 10 minutes in summer, every 20 minutes in winter). For information on times, prices, and pick-up points, as well as how to get a special price with this book, see the Tours listing at the end of the Orientation chapter.

DAY TRIP

Legoland Windsor—If you have a Lego Maniac in the family and won't be in Denmark, consider a quick side trip out to Legoland Windsor (£16, £13 for kids, under three free, daily mid-March–

October 10:00–18:00, until 20:00 in summer, catch train from Paddington station to Windsor Central, tel. 0990-040-404).

AVOID . . .

The **London Dungeon**'s understandable popularity with teenagers makes it one of London's most visited sights. I enjoy gore and torture as much as the next boy, but I do not like this sight and as a parent would not waste the time or money on it with my child.

SHOPPING
IN LONDON

Consider five ways to shop in London:

1) If all you need are souvenirs, a surgical strike at any souvenir shop will do.

2) Large department stores offer relatively painless one-stop shopping. Consider the down-to-earth Marks & Spencer (weekdays 9:00–20:00, Saturday 9:00–21:00, Sunday 12:00–18:00, 173 Oxford Street, tube: Oxford Circus; another at 458 Oxford Street, tube: Bond Street or Marble Arch).

3) Connect small shops with a pleasant walk (see Oxford to Piccadilly Walk, below).

4) For flea market fun, try one of the many street markets.

5) Gawkers or serious bidders can attend auctions.

Most stores are open Monday–Saturday from roughly 10:00–18:00, with a late night (until 19:00 or 20:00) on Wednesday or Thursday, depending on the neighborhood. On Sunday, when most stores are closed, shoppers hit the street markets.

Fancy Department Stores in East London

Harrods—Filled with wonderful displays, Harrods is London's most famous and touristed department store. Big yet classy, Harrods has everything from elephants to toothbrushes. The food halls are sights to savor, with cafeterias (10:00–18:00, until 19:00 on Wednesday, Thursday, and Friday, closed Sunday, on Brompton Road, tube: Knightsbridge, tel. 0171/730-1234). Many readers report that Harrods is now over-priced (its £1 toilets are the most expensive in Europe), snooty, and teeming with American and Japanese tourists.

Harvey Nichols—Princess Diana's favorite, this is the department store *du jour* (Monday–Friday 10:00–19:00, Wednesday until 20:00, Saturday 10:00–18:00, Sunday 12:00–18:00, near Harrods, 109 Knightsbridge, tube: Knightsbridge).

Window shopping—For royal window-shopping, cruise nearby King's Road in Chelsea (tube: Sloane Square). Stores are open in this neighborhood until 19:00 or 20:00 on Wednesday.

Oxford to Piccadilly Walk

For this walk from Oxford Circus to Piccadilly Street, allow ¾ of a mile (and only you know how much money and time). If you're primarily a window shopper and you'd like to stop for high tea (15:00–17:15), take this walk after lunch. Skip this walk on a Sunday, when most stores are closed.

Starting from the Oxford Circus tube stop, Regent Street leads past a fun array of diverse places to shop, all on the lefthand (or east) side of the street. You'll find: **Laura Ashley; Liberty**, a big, stately, local favorite department store (Monday–Saturday 10:00–18:30, closed Sunday, 214 Regent Street); **Hamleys**, the biggest toy store in Britain (Monday–Saturday 10:00–20:00, Sunday 12:00–18:00, 118 Regent Street); **Warner Brothers Studio** Store (at #178); **Beatles Shop** (a block behind Warner Brothers, 8 Kingly Street, tel. 0171/434-0464); **Waterford Wedgewood**; **British Air Travel Shops**, with accessories, guidebooks, travel agents, travelers' clinic, shots, WC, and theater ticket agency (Monday–Friday 9:30–18:00, Saturday 10:00–16:00); **Disney Store** (at #144); **Garrard the Crown Jewelers** (at #112; notice the three royal seals indicating that this shop is a favorite of the Queen, her mom, and Prince Charles); **The Scotch House** (knits, sweaters, woolens); and Piccadilly Circus.

From Piccadilly Circus, turn right and wander down Piccadilly Street. You'll pass Christopher Wren's **St. James Church**, with its tiny flea market and healthy café, and **Fortnum & Mason**, an extremely classy department store. Consider a traditional tea in its **St. James Restaurant**, on the fourth floor (£13.50, Monday–Saturday 15:00–17:15, closed Sunday, 181 Piccadilly, tel. 0171/734-8040). As you relax in plush seats under the elegant tea room's chandeliers, you'll get the standard three-tiered silver tea tray: finger sandwiches on the bottom, fresh scones with jam and clotted cream on the first floor and decadent pastries and "tartlets" on the top floor, with unlimited tea.

Just past Fortnum & Mason is the **French Travel Center**, across the street is the delightful **Burlington Arcade**, and a block farther down is the original **Ritz Hotel**, where the tea is much fancier.

Street Markets

Antique buffs, people-watchers, and folks who brake for garage sales love London's street markets. There's some good early morning market activity somewhere any day of the week. The best are Portobello Road and Camden Market. The tourist office has a complete, up-to-date list. If you like to haggle, there are no holds barred in London's street markets. Warning: Markets attract two kinds of people—tourists and pickpockets.

Portobello Road Market—This flea market hops the most on Saturday but it's open daily. Antiques are featured on Saturday and clothing on Friday through Sunday. Hours are roughly Monday–Wednesday 9:00–17:00, Thursday 9:00–13:00 (but organic food market is open until 18:00), Friday–Saturday 7:00–18:00, and Sunday 9:00–16:00 (quietest on Sunday when mainly just clothing is sold; tube: Notting Hill Gate, near recommended B&Bs).

Camden Market—This huge, trendy arts and crafts festival is held Saturday and Sunday from 10:00–17:00 (tube: Camden Town).

Brick Lane Market—You'll see it all, from frozen food and scrap metal to CDs and furniture (Sunday 6:00–13:00, tube: Liverpool Street).

Brixton Market—The food, clothing, hair-braiding, and records throb with an Afro-Caribbean beat (Monday–Saturday 8:30–17:30, closes at 13:00 on Wednesday, tube: Brixton).

Petticoat Lane Market—Expect budget clothing, shoes, and crowds (Sunday 9:00–14:00, tube: Liverpool Street).

Spitalfields Market—This is best on Sunday and Friday when a lively organic food market (with eateries) joins the crafts and antique market (Monday–Friday 11:00–15:00, Sunday 9:00–16:00, closed Saturday, tube: Liverpool Street).

Greenwich Market—You'll find homemade crafts, bric-a-brac, antiques, and clothing (Saturday and Sunday 9:00–17:00; Saturday also has a produce market, Sunday offers more crafts and fleas). To get to Greenwich, choose among three alternatives: catch a boat from London (from Westminster Pier, Charing Cross, or Tower of London), take the tube (to Island Gardens in Zone 2, then walk through pedestrian Thames tunnel), or catch the train from Charing Cross station. See the Day Trips chapter for information on Greenwich's sights.

Famous Auctions

London's famous auctioneers welcome the curious public. For schedules, call **Sotheby's** (Monday–Friday 9:00–16:30, 34 New Bond Street, tube: Oxford Circus, tel. 0171/493-8080) or **Christie's** (Monday and Wednesday–Friday 9:30–16:30, Tuesday 14:00–17:00, 8 King Street, tube: Green Park, tel. 0171/839-9060).

ENTERTAINMENT

London bubbles with top-notch entertainment seven days a week. Everything's listed in the monthly *Time Out* magazines, available at newsstands. Choose from classical, jazz, rock, and far-out music, Gilbert and Sullivan, dance, comedy, Bahai meetings, poetry readings, spectator sports, film, and theater.

Music

For easy, cheap or free concerts in historic churches, check the TI's listings for lunch concerts (especially Wren's St. Bride's Church, tel. 0171/353-1301, and St. Martin-in-the-Fields, most weekdays at 13:05, tel. 0171/930-1862). St. Martin-in-the-Fields also hosts fine evening concerts by candlelight (Thursday, Friday, Saturday, 19:30, £6–15, tel. 0171/930-0089).

Even music-loving agnostics could enjoy an evensong, a religious service in song. At St. Paul's, evensong is held at 17:00 on weekdays. At Westminster Abbey, it's sung weekdays at 17:00 (but not on Wednesday), Saturday and Sunday at 15:00, and an organ recital is held Sunday at 17:45.

For a fun classical event (June–September only), attend a "Prom Concert." This is an annual music festival with almost nightly concerts in the Royal Albert Hall at give-a-peasant-some-culture prices (£3 standing-room spots sold at the door, tel. 0171/589-8212).

Walks

Guided walks are offered several times a day. Original London Walks is the most established company (for recorded schedule, tel. 0171/624-3978, Web site: http:\\london.walks.com). Daytime walks are varied: ancient London, museum tours, Legal London, Dickens, Beatles, Jewish Quarter, Christopher Wren, and so on). In the evening, expect a more limited choice of ghosts, Jack the

Ripper, pubs, or an occasional literary theme. Get the latest schedules from a London TI, fliers at hotels, or *Time Out*. Simply show up at the listed time and place, pay £5, and enjoy a two-hour tour.

Cruises

During the summer, boats sail as late as 21:00 between Westminster Pier (near Big Ben) and the Tower of London (£4.40, round-trip £5.60, 3/hrly from 10:20–21:00 in peak season, until 18:00 in winter, 30-minute cruise, tel. 0171/930-9033). Day-time cruises leave Westminster Pier for Greenwich (£5.80, round-trip £7, 2/hrly from 10:00–17:00, 50 min, tel. 0171/930-4097) and Kew Gardens (£6, round-trip £10, 7/day, 90 min, tel. 0171/930-2062).

Theater

London's theater rivals Broadway's in quality and beats it in price. Choose from the Royal Shakespeare Company, top musicals, comedy, thrillers, sex farces, and more. Performances are nightly except Sunday, usually with one matinee a week. Matinees (Wednesday, Thursday, or Saturday) are cheaper and rarely sold out. Tickets range from about £8 to £35.

Most theaters, marked on tourist maps, are in the Piccadilly–Trafalgar area. Box offices, hotels, and TIs have a handy "Theater Guide" brochure listing what's playing.

To book a seat, simply call the theater box office directly, ask about seats and dates available, and buy one with your credit card. You can call from the U.S.A. as easily as from England (photocopy your hometown library's London newspaper theater section or visit the Web site: www.officiallondontheatre.co.uk). Pick up your ticket 15 minutes before the show.

Ticket agencies are scalpers with an address. Booking through an agency (at most TIs or scattered throughout London) is quick and easy, but prices are inflated by a standard 25 percent fee. If buying from an agency, look at the ticket carefully (your price should be no more than 30 percent over the printed face value; the 17 percent VAT tax is already included in the face value) and understand where you're sitting according to the floorplan (if your view is restricted it will say on ticket). Agencies are worthwhile only if a show you've got to see is sold out at the box office. They scarf up hot tickets, planning to make a killing after the show is sold out. U.S.A. booking agencies get their tickets from another agency, adding even more to your expense by involving yet another middleman. Many tickets sold on the streets are forgeries. With cheap international phone calls and credit cards, there's no reason not to book direct.

Theater lingo: stalls (ground floor), dress circle (first balony), upper circle (second balcony), balcony (sky-high third balcony).

Cheap theater tricks: Most theaters offer cheap returned tickets, standing room, matinee, and senior or student stand-by deals. These "concessions" are indicated with a "conc" or "s" in the listings. Picking up a late return can get you a great seat at a cheap-seat price. Standing room can be very cheap. If a show is "sold out," there's usually a way to get a seat. Call the theater box office and ask how. The famous (but overrated) "half-price booth" in Leicester (pronounced "Lester") Square sells cheap tickets to shows on the push list the day of the show only (Monday–Saturday 14:30–18:30). I buy the second-cheapest tickets directly from the theater box office. Many theaters are so small that there's hardly a bad seat. After the lights go down, "scooting up" is less than a capital offense. Shakespeare did it.

Royal Shakespeare Company—If you'll ever enjoy Shakespeare, it'll be in Britain. The RSC splits its season between the Royal Shakespeare Theatre in Stratford (tel. 01789/295-623) and the Barbican Centre in London (daily 9:00–20:00, credit-card booking, tel. 0171/638-8891, or for recorded information, tel. 0171/628-9760). To get a schedule, either request it by phone (tel. 0171/638-8891) or write to the Royal Shakespeare Theatre, Stratford-upon-Avon, CV37 6BB Warwickshire. Tickets range in price from £7 (preview) to £40. The best way to book is direct, by telephone and credit card. You can pick up your ticket at the door (Barbican Centre, Silk Street, tube: Barbican). Stand-by tickets for £6 are sold to students and seniors at 9:00 the day of the show.

Shakespeare at the New Globe Theater—To see Shakespeare in an exact replica of the theater for which he wrote his plays, attend a play at the Globe. This thatch-roofed, open-air round theater does the plays as Shakespeare intended (with no amplification). From May through September, curtain times are usually at 14:00 and 19:30, Sundays at 16:00 only, with no plays on Monday. You'll pay £5 to stand and £10–20 to sit (on a backless bench). The £5 "groundling" tickets (while the only ones open to rain) are most fun. You're a crude peasant. You can walk around, munch a picnic dinner, lean your elbows on the the stage, and even interact with the actors. I've never enjoyed Shakespeare as much as here, performed as it was meant to be in the "wooden O." The theater is on the south bank directly across the Thames over Southwark Bridge from St. Paul's (tube: Mansion House, tel. 0171/902-1500 to book a ticket with your credit card). Plays are long. Many groundlings leave before the end. If you like, hang out an hour before the finish and beg or buy a ticket off someone leaving early (groundlings are allowed to come and go). The Globe is far from public transport but the courtesy phone in the lobby gets a mini-cab in minutes. Confirm the cost, but they seem to be much cheaper than the official black cabs (£5 or £6 to Victoria Station).

TRANSPORTATION
CONNECTIONS

19

london

Flying into London's Heathrow Airport

Heathrow Airport is user-friendly. Read signs, ask questions. For Heathrow's airport, flight, and transfers information, call 0181/759-4321.

Terminal 3: Most flights from the U.S.A. land at Terminal 3, where you'll find: exchange bureaus (24 hours daily, okay rates, £3 fees), an airport terminal information desk (pick up a map and ask questions, but for the official Tourist Information office, see below), car rental agencies, a £3-a-day baggage check desk, and a TI.

Heathrow's TI gives you all the help that London's Victoria Station does, with none of the crowds (daily 8:30–18:00, a five-minute walk from Terminal 3, TI next to tube station, follow signs to the "underground"). If you're riding the Airbus into London, have your partner stay with the bags at the terminal. At the TI, get a free simple map and brochures, and if you're taking the tube (subway) into London, buy a Travel Card day pass (see below).

Terminal 4: British Air's trans-Atlantic flights land at Terminal 4, which has the same services as Terminal 3, but lacks a TI office. The American Express desk, with better rates than the banks, is in the underground at Terminal 4.

Transportation to London from Heathrow Airport

By Tube (subway): For £3.20, the tube takes you 14 miles to Victoria Station in 45 minutes (6/hrly, one change). Even better, buy a £4.30 Travel Card that covers your trip into London and all your tube travel for the day (starting at 9:30).

By Airbus: All my recommended hotel neighborhoods are on one of the two airbus lines (serving each terminal, £6, 2/hrly, 5:00–20:00, buy ticket on bus, tel. 0181/400-6655). If you take A1, South Kensington is the third stop, and Victoria Station is the last stop. On A2, the second and third stops cover Notting Hill Gate. The tube works fine, but with baggage I prefer the airbus—no connections underground and a lovely view from the top of the double-decker bus. Ask the driver to remind you when to get off. If you're going to the airport, exact pick-up times are clearly posted at each bus stop.

By Taxi: Taxis from the airport cost about £35. For four traveling together this can be a deal. Hotels can often line up a cab back to the airport for £28.

By Heathrow Express Train: This new train service zips air travelers between Heathrow and London's Paddington Station (£5, 4/hrly from 5:10–22:40, 30 min, tel. 0845/600-1515). Unfortunately, Paddington is far from the recommended B&Bs.

Buses from Heathrow to Destinations beyond London

The National Express Central Bus Station offers direct bus connections to **Cambridge** (hrly, 3.5 hrs, £16), **Cheltenham** (6/day, 2 hrs, £19), **York** (3/day, 6 hrs, £32), **Gatwick** (2/hrly, 1 hr), and **Bath** (9/day, starting at 8:35, 10:35 and so on, 2.5 hrs, £19, direct, tel. 0990-808-080). Or try the slick 2.5-hour Heathrow–Bath bus/train connection via Reading. Buy the £26 ticket at the desk in the terminal (credit cards accepted), then catch the twice-hourly shuttle bus to Reading (RED-ding) to hop on the express train to Bath.

Flying into London's Gatwick Airport

More and more flights, especially charters, land at Gatwick Airport, halfway between London and the southern coast. Trains—clearly the best way into London from here—shuttle conveniently between Gatwick and London's Victoria Station (4/hrly, 30 min, £9).

Trains and Buses

London, Britain's major transportation hub, has a different train station for each region. The train station you arrive at (or leave from) depends on where you came from (or where you're going). King's Cross covers northeast England and Scotland (tel. 0171/278-2477). Paddington covers west and southwest England and South Wales (tel. 0171/262-6767). For the others, call 0171/928-5100. Also see Britrail map on page 193.

National Express's excellent bus service is considerably cheaper than trains. (For a busy signal, call 0990-808-080, or visit www.nationalexpress.co.uk or the bus station a block southwest of Victoria Station.)

To Bath: Trains leave London's Paddington Station every hour (at a quarter after) for the £28.50, 75-minute ride to Bath. As an alternative, consider taking a guided bus tour from London to

Stonehenge and Bath, and simply leaving the tour in Bath. Both Evan Evans (tel. 0181/332-2222) and Travelline (tel. 0181/668-7261) offer Stonehenge/Bath day trips from London.

To points north: Trains run hourly from London's King's Cross Station stopping in York (2 hrs), Durham (3 hrs), and Edinburgh (5 hrs).

To Dublin, Ireland: The boat/rail journey takes 10 hours, all day or all night (£40-60). Consider a 70-minute British Midland flight instead (see below).

Flights

British Midland, the local discount airline, offers some flights cheaper than train connections. For around £120 you can fly round-trip to Dublin (as little as £70 return for a stay over Saturday), Paris, Amsterdam, or Frankfurt. For the latest, call 0345/554-554, or in the U.S.A., 800/788-0555.

Crossing the English Channel

By Eurostar Train: The fastest and most convenient way to get from Big Ben to the Eiffel Tower is now by rail. Eurostar is the speedy passenger train which zips you (and up to 800 others in 18 sleek cars) from downtown London to downtown Paris (12/day, 3 hrs) or Brussels (6/day, 3 hrs), faster and easier than flying. The train goes 100 mph in England and 160 mph on the Continent. The actual tunnel crossing is a 20-minute black, silent, 100 mph non-event. Your ears won't even pop. You can change at Lille to catch a TGV directly to Paris' De Gaulle airport or Disneyland Paris. Yes!

Channel fares (essentially the same to Paris or Brussels) are reasonable but complicated. For the latest fares, call 800/EUROSTAR in the U.S.A. (or go to www.eurostar.com). The "Leisure Ticket" is cheap ($109 second class, $179 first class, 50 percent refundable up to two days before departure). "Full Fare" first class costs $219 including a meal (a dinner departure nets you more grub than breakfast); second class (or "standard") costs $149 (fully refundable even after departure).

Discounts are available for travelers holding railpasses that include France, Belgium, or Britain (about $50 off "Full Fare"), youths under 26 ($70 off second-class "Full Fare"), and children under 12 (half the fare of your ticket). Cheaper seats can sell out. You can book your ticket from the U.S.A. When you're ready to commit to a date and time, book an "instant reservation" through your travel agent. Prices do not include Fed Ex delivery. *Note: Britain's time zone is one hour earlier than the Continent's. Times listed on tickets are local times.*

If you buy your Eurostar ticket in London, here are some sample fares for standard (second-class) travel from London to Paris or Brussels: Those with a railpass pay £45 one-way, any day. Without a railpass, a same-day round-trip on a Saturday or Sunday costs £79. A Leisure Ticket, if you stay at least three nights or over a Saturday night, is £119 round-trip. Excursion fares (purchased seven days in advance for travel on Tuesday, Wednesday or Thursday, with a round-trip over a Saturday) are cheaper: round-trip for £109, and one-way for £79.

Sample first class and business class fares from London to Paris or Brussels: A regular first-class round-trip costs £319, one-way £179. A regular business-class round-trip is £220, one-way £120. A first-class Leisure Ticket, if you stay at least three nights or over a Saturday night, costs £199 round-trip. is £119 round-trip. Excursion fares (purchased seven days in advance for travel on Tuesday, Wednesday or Thursday, with a round-trip over a Saturday) are cheaper: round-trip for £109, and one-way for £79.

Sample first class and business class fares from London to Paris or Brussels: A regular first-class round-trip costs £319, one-way £179. A regular business-class round-trip is £220, one-way £120. A first-class Leisure Ticket, if you stay at least three nights or over a Saturday night, costs £199 round-trip.

In Europe, get your Eurostar ticket at any major train station (in any country) or at any travel agency that handles train tickets (expect a booking fee). In Britain, you can order your tickets over the phone with a credit card by calling 0345/303-030; pick up your tickets at London's Waterloo station an hour before the Eurostar departure.

By Bus and Boat, or Train and Boat: The old-fashioned way of crossing the Channel is very competitive and cheaper than Eurostar; it's also twice as romantic, complicated, and time-consuming. You'll get better prices arranging your trip in London than you would in the U.S.A. Taking the bus is cheapest, and round-trips are a bargain. By bus to Paris or Amsterdam from Victoria Coach Station: £33 one-way, £49 round-trip, 10 hrs, day or overnight, on Eurolines (tel. 0990-143-219) or CitySprint (tel. 0990-240-241). By train and ship: £42 one-way overnight, £59 by day, 7 hrs.

By Plane: Typical fares are £90 regular, £40 student stand-by. Call in London for the latest fares. Consider British Midland (see Flights, above) for its cheap round-trip fares.

APPENDIX
LONDON

What's So Great About Britain?

Regardless of the revolution we had 200 years ago, many American travelers feel that they "go home" to Britain. This most popular tourist destination has a strange influence and power over us.

As long as Britain has been important, London has been its capital. With London at the helm, Britain was created by force and held together by force. The city and the country are a product of the 19th century—the Victorian Age—when the British Empire was at its peak. Generally, the nice and bad stories are not true and the boring ones are. To best understand the many fascinating guides you'll encounter in your London travels, get a handle on the sweeping story of this land.

Britain is small—about the size of Uganda (or Idaho)—600 miles long and 300 miles at its widest. Its highest mountain is 4,400 feet, a foothill by our standards. The population is a quarter of the U.S.A.'s. Politically and economically, Great Britain is closing out the 20th century only a weak shadow of the days when it boasted, "The sun never sets on the British Empire."

At one time Britain owned one-fifth of the world and accounted for more than half of the planet's industrial output. Today the Empire is down to token and troublesome scraps such as the Falklands and Northern Ireland. Great Britain's industrial production is now about 5 percent of the world's total, and Italy has a higher per-capita income.

Still, Britain is a world leader. Her heritage, her culture, and her people cannot be measured in traditional units of power.

The United Kingdom is a union of four countries: England, Wales, Scotland, and Northern Ireland. Cynics call it an English Empire ruled by London, and there is some tension between the dominant Anglo-Saxon English (46 million) and their Celtic brothers and sisters (10 million). In the Dark Ages, the Angles moved into this region from Europe, pushing the Celtic inhabitants to the undesirable fringe of the islands. The Angles settled in Angle-land (England), while the Celts made do in Wales, Scotland, and Ireland.

Just like the United States' congress is dominated by Democrats and Republicans, two parties dominate Britain's parliament: Labor and Conservatives. (Ronald Reagan would fit the Conservative Party and Bill Clinton the Labor Party like political gloves.) Today Britain's Labor party, currently in charge, is shoring up a social service system undercut by years of Conservative rule (Thatcher, Major). While in charge, the Conservatives, who consider themselves proponents of Victorian values (community, family, hard work, thrift, and trickle-down economics), took a Reaganesque approach to Britain's serious problems.

This led to a huge Labor victory and the election of Tony Blair as prime minister. He's the most popular PM in memory and his party rules parliament with a vast majority. Blair's Labor party is "New Labor." Akin to Clinton's "New" Democrats, it's fiscally conservative but with a keen sense for the needs of the people. The Conservative Party's fears of old-fashioned big-spending Liberalism have proven unfounded. The economy is booming with very low inflation, unemployment, and interest rates. Social programs such as health, education, and the minimum wage are being bolstered but in ways more measured than Conservatives predicted. Britain's liberal parliament is also more open to integration with Europe. It looks like Britain is in for a long period of Labor rule.

London Timeline

A.D. 43   Romans invade Britain and establish a small port on the Thames River near today's London Bridge. They call it Londinium.

200   City walls are built. Their shadow survives, arcing out from the Thames in today's street plan.

450   As Rome falls, the Roman Emperor sends a letter to Britain saying, "You're on your own." Angles and Saxons overrun England and set up their kingdoms.

1050   Saxons unite England and their King Edward builds his palace and a church in what becomes the city of Westminster. The church becomes Westminster Abbey and the palace becomes the Houses of Parliament.

1066   Normans, led by William the Conqueror, invade from France. William becomes King of England (and builds the Tower of London).

1500   Henry VIII is king and London is a city of over 50,000.

1600   This is the age of Queen Elizabeth and Shakespeare.

1650   London is now a world capital with 500,000 people. England is torn by Civil War. Cromwell and Parliament oppose the divine power of the king and nobility. King Charles I is beheaded.

1660   The monarchy is restored as Charles II is crowned.

1665   Thousands die as the Great Plague ravages London.

1666   Thousands more lose homes as 80 percent of medieval London burns down.

1670s   London is rebuilt. Christopher Wren ornaments the city with 50 churches, including St. Paul's.

1800s   The sun never sets on the British Empire as London becomes the world's biggest city with over a million people.

1847   British Museum opens.

1914–18   London bombed during WWI.

1939–40   London survives blitz bombing.

1944–45   London survives blitz bombing.

1953   Queen Elizabeth crowned.

1981   Prince Charles and Lady Diana are married in St. Paul's Cathedral.

1990s   Royal scandals, death of Princess Diana, Channel Tunnel opens.

London's History Is Britain's History

When Julius Caesar landed on the misty and mysterious isle of Britain in 55 B.C., England entered the history books. The primitive Celtic tribes he conquered were themselves invaders who had earlier conquered the even more mysterious people who built Stonehenge. The Romans built towns and roads and established their capital at "Londinium." The Celtic natives, consisting of Gaels, Picts, and Scots, were not subdued so easily in Scotland and Wales. The Romans built Hadrian's Wall near the Scottish border to consolidate their rule in the troublesome north. Even today, the Celtic language and influence are strongest in these far reaches of Britain.

As Rome fell, so fell Roman Britain, a victim of invaders and internal troubles. Barbarian tribes from Germany and Denmark, called Angles and Saxons, swept through the southern part of the island, establishing Angle-land. These were the days of the real King Arthur, possibly a Christianized Roman general fighting valiantly, but in vain, against invading barbarians. The island was plunged into 500 years of Dark Ages—wars, plagues, and poverty—lit only by the dim candle of a few learned Christian monks and missionaries trying to convert the barbarians. The sightseer sees little from this Saxon period.

Modern England began with yet another invasion. William the Conqueror and his Norman troops crossed the English Channel from France in 1066. William crowned himself king in Westminster Abbey (where all subsequent coronations would take place) and began building the Tower of London. French-speaking Norman kings ruled the country for two centuries. Then followed two centuries of civil wars, with various noble families vying for the crown. In one of the most bitter feuds, the York and Lancaster families fought the War of the Roses, so-called because of the white and red flowers the combatants chose as their symbols. Battles, intrigues, kings, nobles, and ladies imprisoned and executed in the Tower—it's a wonder the country survived its rulers.

England was finally united by the "third-party" Tudor family. Henry VIII, a Tudor, was England's Renaissance king. He was handsome, athletic, highly sexed, a poet, a scholar, and a musician. He was also arrogant, cruel, gluttonous, and paranoid. He went through six wives in 40 years, divorcing, imprisoning, or beheading them when they no longer suited his needs.

Henry also "divorced" England from the Catholic Church, establishing the Protestant Church of England (the Anglican Church) and setting in motion years of religious squabbles. He also "dissolved" the monasteries (around 1540), leaving just the shells of many formerly glorious abbeys dotting the countryside and pocketing their land and wealth for the crown.

Henry's daughter, Queen Elizabeth I, who reigned for 45 years, made England a great trading and naval power (defeating the Spanish Armada) and presided over the Elizabethan era of great writers (such as Shakespeare) and scientists (Francis Bacon).

The long-standing quarrel between England's "divine right" kings and nobles in Parliament finally erupted into a civil war (1643). Parliament forces under the Protestant Puritan farmer Oliver Cromwell defeated—and beheaded—King Charles I. This civil war left its mark on much of what you'll see in England. Eventually, Parliament invited Charles' son to take the throne. This "restoration of the monarchy" was accompanied by a great colonial expansion and the rebuilding of London (including Christopher Wren's St. Paul's Cathedral), which had been devastated by the Great Fire of 1666.

Britain grew as a naval superpower, colonizing and trading with all parts of the globe. Her naval superiority ("Britannia rules the waves") was secured by Admiral Nelson's victory over Napoleon's fleet at the Battle of Trafalgar in 1805, while Lord Wellington stomped Napoleon on land at Waterloo. Nelson and Wellington—both buried in London's St. Paul's—are memorialized by many arches, columns, and squares throughout England.

Economically, Britain led the world into the industrial age with her mills, factories, coal mines, and trains. By the time of Queen Victoria's reign (1837–1901), Britain was at the zenith of power with a colonial empire that covered one-fifth of the world.

The 20th century has not been kind to Britain. Two world wars devastated the population. The Nazi blitzkrieg reduced much of London to rubble. The colonial empire has dwindled to almost nothing, and Britain is no longer an economic super-power. The "Irish Troubles" are constant as the Catholic inhabitants of British-ruled Northern Ireland fight for the inde-pendence their southern neighbors won decades ago. The war over the Falkland Islands in 1982 showed how little of the British Empire is left, but also how determined the British are to hang on to what remains.

But the tradition (if not the substance) of greatness continues, presided over by Queen Elizabeth II, her husband Prince Philip, and Prince Charles. With economic problems, the turmoil of Charles and the late Princess Diana, the Fergie fiasco, and a relent-less popular press, the royal family is having a tough time. But the queen has stayed above it all and most British people still jump at an opportunity to see royalty. With the death of Princess Diana and the historic outpouring of grief, it's clear that the concept of royalty is alive and well as Britain enters the third millenium.

Britain's Royal Families

802–1066	Saxon and Danish kings
1066–1154	Norman invasion, Norman kings (William the Conqueror)
1154–1399	Plantagenet
1399–1461	Lancaster
1462–1485	York
1485–1603	Tudor (Henry VIII, Elizabeth I)
1603–1649	Stuart (with civil war and beheading of Charles I)
1649–1659	Commonwealth, Cromwell, no royal head of state
1660–1714	Stuart restoration of monarchy
1714–1901	Hanover (four Georges, Victoria)
1901–1910	Edward VII
1910–present	Windsor (George V, Edward VII, George VI, Elizabeth II)

British TV

British television is so good—and so British—that it deserves a mention as a sightseeing treat. After a long day of museum-going, watch the telly over a pot of tea in your room.

England has five channels. BBC-1 and BBC-2 are government regulated, commercial-free, and traditionally highbrow. Channels

3, 4 and 5 are private, a little more Yankee, and they have commercials—but those commercials are clever and sophisticated and provide a fun look at England. Broadcasting is funded by an £80-per-year-per-household tax. Hmmm, 35 cents per day to escape commercials and public television pledge drives.

Britian is about to leap into the digital age ahead of the rest of the TV-watching world. In 1999 a new TV age will dawn in Britain. Ultimately every house will enjoy literally hundreds of high-definition channels with no need for cable or satellites.

Whereas California "accents" fill our airwaves 24 hours a day, homogenizing the way our country speaks, England protects and promotes its regional accents by its choice of TV and radio announcers. Commercial-free British TV is looser than it used to be, but still careful about what it airs and when.

American shows (such as *Frazier* and *ER*) are very popular. Be sure to tune your TV to a few typical English shows, including the top-notch BBC evening news and a dose of English situation and political comedy fun. Quiz shows are taken very seriously here. Michael Parkinson is the Johnny Carson of Britain for late night talk. For a tear-filled slice-of-life taste of British soap dealing in all the controversial issues, see the popular *Brookside*, *Coronation Street*, or *Eastenders*.

Benny Hill comedy has become politically incorrect but is rumored to be coming back. And if you like Monty Python–type comedy, you've come to the right place.

Let's Talk Telephones

Here's a brief primer on making direct phone calls. For information on Britain only, see the Introduction: Telephones.

Dialing Direct

Calling Between Countries: Dial the international access code (of the country you're calling from), the country code (of the country you're calling), the area code (if it starts with zero, drop the zero), and the local number.

Calling Long Distance Within a Country: First dial the area code (including its zero), then the local number.

Europe's Exceptions: France, Italy, Spain, Norway, and Denmark have dispensed with area codes entirely. To make an international call to these countries, dial the international access code (011 for America, 00 for most other countries), the country code (see chart below), and then the local number in its entirety (okay, so there's one exception; for France, drop the initial zero of the local number). To make long-distance calls within any of these countries, simply dial the local number.

International Access Codes

When dialing direct, first dial the international access code of the country you're calling from. Most European countries use "00" as their international access code. Exceptions follow:

Estonia: 800	Russia: 810	U.S.A./Canada: 011
Finland: 990	Spain: 07	
Lithuania: 810	Sweden: 009	

Country Codes

After you've dialed the international access code, dial the code of the country you're calling.

Austria: 43	Germany: 49	Portugal: 351
Belgium: 32	Greece: 30	Russia: 7
Britain: 44	Ireland: 353	Spain: 34
Czech Republic: 420	Italy: 39	Sweden: 46
Denmark: 45	Latvia: 371	Switzerland: 41
Estonia: 372	Lithuania: 370	U.S.A./Canada: 1
Finland: 358	Netherlands: 31	
France: 33	Norway: 47	

Telephone Directory

Understand the various prefixes: Any prefix starting with 01 is a normal long distance call. 0891 numbers are telephone sex-type expensive. Prefixes 0345 and 0845 are local calls nationwide. And 0800 numbers are entirely toll-free. If you have questions about a prefix, call 100 for free help.

Useful Numbers in Britain

Emergency Services (police or ambulance): 999
Operator Services: 100
Directory Assistance: 192 (free from phone booth, otherwise expensive)
International Information: 153 (80p); Assistance: 155
U.S. Embassy: 0171/499-9000

Emergencies and Medical Problems

Ambulance: 999
Hospital With 24-Hour Service: Royal Free Hospital, Pond Street, tube: Belsize Park, tel. 0171/794-0500.
Non-emergency Medical Services: Great Chapel Street Medical Centre, 13 Great Chapel Street, tube: Tottenham Court Road, tel. 0171/437-9360.
Dental Emergencies: Referral service, Monday–Friday 8:45–13:00, 14:00–15:30, tel. 0171/955-2186.

Train Information

Train info for anywhere within Britain: 0345/484-950.
Eurostar (Chunnel Info): 0345/303-030
Train and Boats to Europe Info: 0990-848-848

London's Airports and Airlines

Heathrow

• General Information: 0181/759-4321 (flights, transfers, airline phone numbers)
• Air Canada: 0181/745-6584
• American: 0345/789-789
• British Air: 0345/222-111, 0181/759-5511
• British Midlands: 0345/554-554, 01332/854-000
• SAS: 0171/734-4020, 0181/750-7675
• United Airlines: 0800-888-555, 0845/844-4777

Gatwick

General Information: 01293/535-353 for all airlines—except British Airways at 0990-444-000.

Climate Chart

The chart below gives average daytime temperatures and average number of days with more than a trickle of rain.

	J	F	M	A	M	J	J	A	S	O	N	D
London												
	43°	44°	**50°**	56°	**62°**	69°	**71°**	71°	**66°**	58°	**51°**	45°
	15	13	**11**	12	**11**	11	**12**	11	**13**	14	**15**	15
S. Wales												
	45°	45°	**50°**	56°	**61°**	68°	**69°**	69°	**65°**	58°	**51°**	46°
	18	14	**13**	13	**13**	13	**14**	15	**16**	16	**17**	18
York												
	43°	44°	**49°**	55°	**60°**	67°	**70°**	70°	**65°**	57°	**49°**	45°
	17	15	**13**	13	**13**	14	**15**	14	**14**	15	**17**	17
Edinburgh												
	42°	43°	**46°**	51°	**56°**	62°	**65°**	64°	**60°**	54°	**48°**	44°
	17	15	**15**	14	**14**	15	**17**	16	**16**	17	**17**	18
Dublin												
	40°	41°	**44°**	47°	**52°**	57°	**60°**	59°	**56°**	50°	**45°**	42°
	13	10	**10**	11	**10**	11	**13**	12	**12**	11	**12**	14

THE BEST OF GREAT BRITAIN IN 22 DAYS

Day 1: Arrive in London

Day 2: London

Day 3: London

Day 4: Stonehenge, Bath

Day 5: Bath

Day 6: Glastonbury, Wells

Day 7: South Wales, Folk Museum

Day 8: Cotswold villages, Blenheim

Day 9: Stratford, Warwick Castle, Coventry

Day 10: Industrial Revolution Museum

Day 11: North Wales, Snowdonia, Caenarfon Castle, Medieval Banquet

Day 12: Blackpool

Day 13: Lake District

Day 14: Lake District

Day 15: Scottish West Coast

Day 16: Highlands, Loch Ness

Day 17: Edinburgh

Day 18: Edinburgh

Day 19: Hadrian's Wall, Durham Cathedral, Beamish Folk Museum

Day 20: Moors, York

Day 21: York

Day 22: Cambridge, back to London

For all the specifics, see *Rick Steves' Great Britain & Ireland 1999.*

BRITRAIL ROUTES

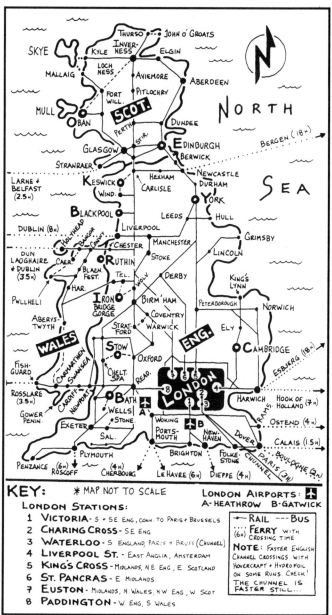

KEY: ✳ MAP NOT TO SCALE

LONDON AIRPORTS: ✈
A - HEATHROW   B - GATWICK

LONDON STATIONS:

1. **VICTORIA** - S & S.E. ENG., CONN. TO PARIS & BRUSSELS
2. **CHARING CROSS** - S.E. ENG
3. **WATERLOO** - S. ENGLAND, PARIS & BRUSS. (CHUNNEL)
4. **LIVERPOOL ST.** - EAST ANGLIA, AMSTERDAM
5. **KING'S CROSS** - MIDLANDS, N.E. ENG., E. SCOTLAND
6. **ST. PANCRAS** - E. MIDLANDS
7. **EUSTON** - MIDLANDS, N WALES, N W ENG, W SCOT
8. **PADDINGTON** - W ENG, S WALES

←→ RAIL   - - - BUS
⋮⋮ (6H) **FERRY** WITH CROSSING TIME

NOTE: FASTER ENGLISH
CHANNEL CROSSINGS WITH
HOVERCRAFT & HYDROFOIL
ON SOME RUNS. CHECK!
THE CHUNNEL IS
FASTER STILL...

Numbers and Stumblers
•Europeans write a few of their numbers differently than we do.
1 = 1 , 4 = 4 , 7 = 7 . Learn the difference or miss your train.
•In Europe, dates appear as day/month/year, so Christmas is
25-12-99.
•Commas are decimal points and decimals commas. A dollar and a
half is 1,50 and there are 5.280 feet in a mile.
•When pointing, use your whole hand, palm downward.
•When counting with fingers, start with your thumb. If you hold
up your first finger to request one item, you'll probably get two.
•What we Americans call the second floor of a building is the first
floor in Europe.
•Europeans keep the left "lane" open for passing on escalators and
moving sidewalks. Keep to the right.
•And please . . . don't call your waist pack a "fanny pack."

Weights and Measures (approximate)
1 British pint = 1.2 U.S. pints
1 imperial gallon = 1.2 U.S. gallons or about 5 liters
1 stone = 14 lbs. (a 175-lb. person weighs 12 stone)
28 degrees Centigrade = 82 degrees Fahrenheit
Shoe sizes = about .5 to 1.5 sizes smaller than in U.S.

British-Yankee Vocabulary

advert advertisement

afters dessert

anti-clockwise counter-clockwise

aubergine eggplant

Balloons Belgians

banger sausage

bangers and mash sausage and mashed potatoes

bank holiday legal holiday

bap hamburger-type bun

ben Scottish for mountain

billion ten of our billions (a million million)

biro ballpoint pen

biscuit cookie

black pudding sausage made from dried blood

bloke man, guy

bobby policeman ("copper" is more common)

Bob's your uncle there you go (with a shoulder shrug), naturally

bomb success

bonnet car hood

boot car trunk

BR British Rail

braces suspenders

bridle way path for walkers, bikers, and horse riders

BTA British Tourist Authority

bubble and squeak cold meat fried with cabbage and potatoes

bum bottom or "backside"

candy floss cotton candy

car boot sale temporary flea market with car trunk displays

caravan trailer

cat's eyes reflectors on the road

cheap and nasty cheap and bad quality (pay monkeys, get peanuts)

cheeky (or saucy) smart alecky

cheerio goodbye

cheers thanks (also, a toast)

chemist pharmacist

chips french fries

chock-a-block jam-packed

cider alcoholic apple cider

clearway road where you can't stop

coach long-distance bus

concession discounted admission

courgette zucchini

courier tour escort or guide

crisps potato chips

cuppa cup of tea

dear expensive

digestives round graham crackers

dinner lunch or dinner

diversion detour

draughts checkers

drawing pin thumbtack

dual carriageway divided highway (four lanes)

face flannel wash cloth

fag cigarette

fagged exhausted

faggot meatball

fanny vagina

fell mountain, hill, or high plain

first floor second floor

flat apartment

football soccer

force waterfall (lake district)

fortnight two weeks

Frogs French people

Full Monty The whole sha-bang. Everything.

gallery balcony

gallon 1.2 American gallons

gangway aisle

gaol jail (same pronunciation)

garden yard

give way yield

glen narrow valley

goods wagon freight truck

grammar school high school

half eight 8:30 (not 7:30)

heath open land without trees

holiday vacation

homely likeable or cozy

hoover vacuum cleaner

hundredweight 112 pounds

ice lolly popsicle

ironmonger hardware store

jelly jello

Joe Bloggs John Doe

jumble sale, rummage sale

jumper sweater

keep your pecker up be brave

kiosk booth

kipper smoked herring

knackered exhausted

knickers ladies' panties

knocking shop brothel

knock up wake up or visit

let rent

loo toilet or bathroom

lorry truck

mac macintosh coat, raincoat

mate buddy, friend

mean stingy

mews courtyard stables, often used as cottages

minced meat hamburger meat

nappy diaper

natter talk and talk
neat a straight drink
nosh food or eat
nought zero
off license liquor store or a place selling take-away liquor
take away to go
pasty crusted savory (usually meat) pie
pavement sidewalk
petrol gas
pissed (rude), paralytic, bevvied, sloshed, wellied, popped up, ratted, "pissed as a newt" drunk
pillar box postbox
pitch playing field
plaster Band-Aid
poppers (or press studs) snaps
pram baby carriage
public convenience public toilets
put a sock in it shut up
queue line
queue jump crowd in line
queue up line up
quid pound (money, worth about $1.60)
randy horny
redundant, made fired or laid off
return ticket round-trip
ring up call (telephone)
rubber eraser
sanitary towel sanitary napkin/pad
sausage roll sausage wrapped in a flaky pastry
Scotch egg hard-boiled egg wrapped in sausage meat
self-catering accommodation with kitchen facilities, rented by the week

sellotape scotch tape
serviette napkin
single ticket one-way ticket
smalls underwear
snogging kissing and cuddling
solicitor lawyer
stone 14 lbs. (weight)
subway underground pedestrian passageway
suss out figure out
swede rutabaga
sweet dessert
sweets candy
ta thank you
taxi rank taxi stand
tea towel dish towel
telly TV
theater live stage
tick a check mark
tight as a fish's bum cheapskate (water-tight)
tipper lorry dump truck
tin can
to let for rent
top hole first rate
topping excellent
top up refill a drink
torch flashlight
towpath path along a river or canal
tube subway
twee quaint, cute
underground subway
VAT value added tax
verge grassy edge of road
wellingtons, wellies rubber boots
wee urinate
whacked exhausted
witter on gab and gab
yob hooligan
zebra crossing crosswalk
zed the letter "z"

Road Scholar Feedback for London

We're all in the same travelers' school of hard knocks. Your feedback helps us improve this guidebook for future travelers. Please fill this out (attach more info or any tips/favorite discoveries if you like) and send it to us. As thanks for your help, we'll send you our quarterly travel newsletter free for one year. Thanks! Rick

Of the recommended accommodations/restaurants used, which was:

Best _____

    Why? _____

Worst _____

    Why? _____

Of the sights/experiences/destinations recommended by this book, which was:

Most overrated _____

    Why? _____

Most underrated _____

    Why? _____

Best ways to improve this book:

_____

I'd like a free newsletter subscription:

___ Yes   ___ No   ___ Already on list

Name

_____

Address

_____

City, State, Zip

_____

E-mail Address

Please send to: ETBD, Box 2009, Edmonds, WA 98020

Jubilee 2000—Let's Celebrate the Millennium by Forgiving Third World Debt

Let's ring in the millennium by convincing our government to forgive the debt owed to us by the world's poorest countries. Imagine spending over half your income on interest payments alone. You and I are creditors and poor countries owe us more than they can pay.

Jubilee 2000 is a worldwide movement of concerned people and groups—religious and secular—working to cancel the international debts of the poorest countries by the year 2000.

Debt ruins people: In the poorest countries, money needed for health care, education, and other vital services is diverted to interest payments.

Mozambique, with a per capita income of $90 and life expectancy of 40, spends over half its national income on interest. This poverty brings social unrest, civil war, and often costly humanitarian intervention by the U.S.A. To chase export dollars, desperate countries ruin their environment. As deserts grow and rain forests shrink, the world suffers. Of course, the real suffering is among local people born long after some dictator borrowed (and squandered) that money. As interest is paid, entire populations go hungry.

Who owes what and why? Mozambique is one of 41 countries defined by the World Bank as "Heavily Indebted Poor Countries." In total, they owe $200 billion. Because these debts are unlikely to be paid, their market value is only a tenth of the face value (about $20 billion). The U.S.A.'s share is under $2 billion.

How can debt be canceled? This debt is owed mostly to the U.S.A., Japan, Germany, Britain, and France either directly or through the World Bank. We can forgive the debt owed directly to us and pay the market value (usually 10 percent) of the debts owed to the World Bank. We have the resources. (Norway, another wealthy creditor nation, just unilaterally forgave its Third World debt.) All America needs is the political will . . . people power.

While many of these poor nations are now democratic, corruption is still a concern. A key to Jubilee 2000 is making certain that debt relief reduces poverty in a way that benefits ordinary people: women, farmers, children, and so on.

Let's celebrate the new millennium by giving poor countries a break. For the sake of peace, fragile young democracies, the environment, and countless real people, forgiving this debt is the right thing for us in the rich world to do.

Tell Washington, DC.: If our government knows this is what we want, it can happen. Learn more, write letters, lobby legislators, or even start a local Jubilee 2000 campaign. For details, contact Jubilee 2000 (tel. 202/783-3566, www.j2000usa.org). For information on lobbying Congress on J2000, contact Bread for the World (tel. 800/82-BREAD, www.bread.org).

Faxing Your Hotel Reservation

Most hotel managers know basic "hotel English." Faxing is the preferred method for reserving a room. It's more accurate and cheaper than telephoning and much faster than writing a letter. Use this handy form for your fax. Photocopy and fax away.

One-Page Fax

To: _____ @ _____

hotel   fax

From: _____ @ _____

name   fax

Today's date: ____ / ____ / ____

day   month   year

Dear Hotel _____,

Please make this reservation for me:

Name: _____

Total # of people: _____   # of rooms: _____   # of nights: _____

Arriving: ____ / ____ / ____   My time of arrival (24-hr clock): _____

day   month   year   (I will telephone if I will be late)

Departing: ____ / ____ / ____

day   month   year

Room(s):   Single___   Double___   Twin___   Triple___   Quad___

With: Toilet___   Shower___   Bath___   Sink only___

Special needs: View___   Quiet___   Cheapest Room___

Credit card: Visa___   MasterCard___   American Express___

Card #: _____

Expiration Date:_____

Name on card: _____

You may charge me for the first night as a deposit. Please fax or mail me confirmation of my reservation, along with the type of room reserved, the price, and whether the price includes breakfast. Thank you.

_____
Signature

_____
Name

_____
Address

_____
City   **State**   **Zip Code**   **Country**

_____
E-mail Address

INDEX